Kahn

Louis I. Kahn
David B. Brownlee
David G. De Long

Introduction by
Vincent Scully

Principal photography by
Grant Mudford

Thames & Hudson

First published in the United Kingdom in 1997 by
Thames & Hudson Ltd.
181A High Holborn, London WC1V 7QX

Reprinted in 2000

© 1997 The Museum of Contemporary Art,
Los Angeles
250 Grand Avenue, Los Angeles, CA 90012

British Library Cataloguing-in-Publication Data

A catalogue record for this book is available from the
British Library

ISBN: 0-500-28025-8

Printed in Italy

Contents

Preface

Julia Moore Converse
Director
Architectural Archives of
the University of Pennsylvania
May 1997

Architect, philosopher, artist, and teacher, Louis I. Kahn inspired students through his work and teaching, drawing followers to Philadelphia from all over the world. In the last twenty-five years of his life, he redefined architecture for his generation. Now, nearly a quarter of a century after his death, a new generation turns once again to the work of this master for its lessons. The 1997 edition of *Louis I. Kahn: In the Realm of Architecture* has been undertaken in order to make this publication available to as wide an audience as possible. Work on the original book began in 1983 when David B. Brownlee and David G. De Long, professors at the University of Pennsylvania, initiated an intense period of scholarly exploration into the resources of the Louis I. Kahn Collection, a vast archive that had only recently been made accessible to scholars at Penn's Architectural Archives. Brownlee and De Long directed a series of graduate seminars that reviewed all documents in the archives—a five-year process that involved more than fifty researchers. This unprecedented investigation produced a fully documented list of Kahn's buildings and projects as well as a complete description of the sequence of design phases in Kahn's works both of which corrected previously published sources.

At the same time Richard Koshalek, Director of the Museum of Contemporary Art, Los Angeles, and Sherri Geldin, Associate Director of MOCA (now Director of the Wexner Center for the Arts in Columbus, Ohio) were considering a comprehensive retrospective exhibition of Kahn's work. After initial conversations with Brownlee, De Long, and myself as curator of the Kahn Collection, and with funding from the Ford Motor Company, MOCA organized an outstanding team that included Koshalek and Geldin, authors and exhibition curators Brownlee and De Long, architect and exhibition designer Arata Isozaki, long-time Kahn associate

Marshall Meyers, and myself. Peter S. Reed, Perkins Post-Doctoral Fellow at Penn (now Associate Curator of Architecture and Design at the Museum of Modern Art), served as research director for the Kahn retrospective project.

Louis I. Kahn: In the Realm of Architecture was produced in a large format in 1991 as a collaborative publication by Rizzoli International Publications and MOCA. The exhibition of the same title opened at the Philadelphia Museum of Art in October 1991 and traveled to seven museums on three continents before closing at the Wexner Center for the Arts in February 1994. The book and exhibition together stimulated a greatly invigorated interest in Kahn's work and generated hundreds of articles and reviews both in the popular and the scholarly press.

The book investigates major themes in Kahn's work, exploring his philosophy of architecture across the span of his life and career. Presented are not only Kahn's best-known masterpieces such as the Salk Institute in La Jolla, California (1959–65) and the Kimbell Art Museum in Fort Worth, Texas (1966–72), but also many significant buildings that had been relatively unknown, such as early work in public housing, private residential works, unbuilt institutional commissions, and Philadelphia city plans. Grant Mudford's spectacular photography brings many of Kahn's buildings into the public eye for the very first time. We are delighted that the publication of this volume in a new compact format will further disseminate Kahn's work and make it accessible to readers worldwide.

We are enormously grateful to Richard Koshalek and Sherri Geldin for their early leadership and their unfaltering commitment to the Kahn retrospective project. During the course of the project, many readers and scholars, as well as members of the Kahn family and former Kahn associates and clients, offered invaluable guidance and support. We continue to be grateful to all who contributed to the original publication, with special thanks to Denise Scott Brown, Balkrishna Doshi, William Jordy, Sue Ann Kahn, Michael Meister, Harriet Pattison, Vincent Scully, Anne Griswold Tyng, Carles Vallhonrat, Robert Venturi, Massimo Vignelli, Henry Wilcots, Richard Saul Wurman, and especially to David Morton, Senior Editor at Rizzoli International Publications, and the late Esther Israeli Kahn, whose spirit inspired all our work.

We also wish to acknowledge the very significant contributions of a number of scholars whose texts could not be included in the current publication but whose research added immeasurably to the knowledge and understanding of Kahn's work: Daniel S. Friedman, Kathleen James, Peter Kohane, Michael J. Lewis, Patricia Cummings Loud, Alex Soojung-Kim Pang with Preston Thayer, Peter S. Reed, Susan G. Solomon, Michelle Taillon Taylor, Elise Vider, Marc Philippe Vincent, Robin B. Williams, and Carla Yanni.

This new edition has evolved through the initiative of Alexandra Mairs, Editor, and Charles Miers, Publisher, at Universe Publishing and Russell Ferguson, Editor at MOCA. Abigail Sturges has once again exhibited her particular design genius. Special thanks are due the staff of the Architectural Archives, most especially research assistants Kazi Khaleed Ashraf, Allison Kelsey, Shilpa Mehta, and Glenn Sanchez, and collection manager William Whitaker.

As always, we wish to acknowledge the Pennsylvania Historical and Museum Commission (Timothy Buchanan, Chairman, and Brent G. Glass, Executive Director), for the crucial role it has played in assuring the preservation of the Kahn Collection as a public resource open to all who wish to learn from the life and work of this great master.

Introduction

Vincent Scully

Kahn was a supremely great architect. That fact is becoming more apparent with every passing year. His work has a presence, an aura, unmatched by that of any other architect of the present day. Far beyond the works even of Frank Lloyd Wright, Mies van der Rohe, and Le Corbusier, it is brooding, remote, mysterious. Wright's buildings richly resolve the play of wonderful rhythms; those of Mies reduce space and matter to ultimate essentials, while Le Corbusier's do something of everything, embodying the twentieth-century human gesture most of all, at first light and urbane, at the end heavy, primitive, violent. Kahn's buildings, the very distillation of the twentieth century's later years, are primitive too, but they are wholly devoid of gesture, as if beyond that, or of a different breed. Their violence is latent, potential, precisely because they do not gesture or seem to strike any attitude at all. They are above all *built*. Their elements—always elemental, heavy—are assembled in solemn, load-bearing masses. Their joints are serious affairs, like the knees of *kouroi*, but have the articulation of beings not in human form. Their body is Platonic, abstractly geometric in the essential shapes of circle, square, and triangle translated into matter, as if literally frozen into mute musical chords. They shape spaces heavy with light like the first light ever loosed on the world, daggers of light, blossoms of light, suns and moons. They are silent. We feel their silence as a potent thing; some sound, a roll of drums, an organ peal, resonates in them just beyond the range of our hearing. They thrum with silence, as with the presence of God.

We try to think what other works of modern art have this curious high seriousness in the same degree: this determined link to the Ideal, this wholly specific physicality. Perhaps only some Russian novels come to mind, the works of Tolstoy most of all, perhaps those of Dostoyevski. I am reminded of the remark of a Russian student in Leningrad in 1965. It was at an exhibition of American architecture. Kahn and I were present. I ran a little seminar for especially interested students. Robert Venturi's house for Vanna Venturi came under discussion. One student, mindful perhaps of the Soviet Union's massive needs in housing and so on, asked, "Who needs it?" But another student instantly replied, "Everybody needs everything." And I thought, there it is, the real stuff, the generous, excessive Russian soul. We tend to forget that Kahn was Russian, after all. Those blue Tartar eyes didn't come from nowhere. Here we have to thank David Brownlee and David De Long for finding a photograph of Kahn's father in his uniform. Poor, Jewish, Estonian, only a paymaster, and noncommissioned, he nevertheless comes across as an Imperial Russian officer to the life, a veritable Vronski, played by Fredric March. He looks much like his son, jaunty and proud, while Lou Kahn himself, at his graduation from the University of Pennsylvania, glares ferociously at the camera like the young Gorky or the student Tolstoy. And like them Kahn wanted "everything," wanted to make everything true, right, deep, ideal, and whole if he could. I suppose he wanted all that more passionately than any other architect of our era has ever done. That is surely why, despite their obvious deficiencies in many fundamental aspects of architecture—contextuality, to name a contemporary interest, for one— Kahn's works convince us that their own intrinsic being is enough. They are thus the single wholly satisfactory achievement of the late modernist aim in architecture: to reinvent reality, to make all new.

They are more than that, though. They begin something. They effectively bring the International Style to a close and open the way to a much solider modernism, one in which the revival of the vernacular and classical traditions of architecture, and the corollary mass movement for historic preservation, would eventually come to play a central role. Kahn's greatest early associate, Robert Venturi, was to initiate these revivals of the urban tradition and to direct architecture toward a gentle contextuality unsympathetic to Kahn. Aldo Rossi in Italy was to move in a similar direction, creating a haunting poetry of urban types out of a vision of Italian vernacular and classical traditions not so different from that Kahn revealed in his pastels of Italian squares in 1950–51 and in some of his greatest buildings thereafter. Indeed, Kahn changed architecture for the better in every way, to some considerable degree changed the built environment as a whole and, beyond his knowledge or intention, made us value the fabric of the traditional city once more.

It is worth asking how this came about for Kahn. Here we should be as specific as Kahn himself. It came about because, after a lifetime of worrying about such things, Kahn discovered late in life how to transform the ruins of ancient Rome into modern buildings. This relationship, improbable enough on the face of it, is copiously demonstrated by the scores of photographs of Roman ruins that can be directly paired with views of almost all of Kahn's buildings from the Salk Institute onward. Before this Kahn had already spent some years trying to find his way back to history. Cut off from his modern-classical education at Pennsylvania, and thus from history, by the rise of the iconoclastic International Style in the 1930s, Kahn was ready to look sympathetically at history once again at least from the time he began to teach at Yale in 1947. In 1950–51 he was reintroduced to Rome during his term as a fellow at the American Academy, where he studied Roman archaeological sites on his own and in the company of the great classicist Frank E. Brown, and traveled in Greece and Egypt as well. Soon he was making use of the Pyramids at Gizeh and of the Temple of Ammon at Karnak in various ways that I have discussed elsewhere.[1] It was only after he had adopted his early watercolors of

San Gimignano for the towers of the Richards Medical Research Building, with attendant problems having to do largely with the reception of light, that the more purely Roman forms began to appear. They did so in a manner that suggests conversations with Robert Venturi, who had also spent a year in Rome, and most strikingly at the Salk Institute, especially in the project for the community center. "Ruins wrapped around buildings," Kahn called the resultant glass-free, keyhole arched, thermal-windowed Roman forms.

Coincidentally enough, those ruins, open to the air, proved exactly suited to the climate and the simple brick technology of the subcontinent of India. They shaped Ahmedabad and Dhaka, where the crypto-portici can be compared with the Thermopolium at Ostia, while the main rooms at Ahmedabad closely echo the brick and concrete basilica of Hadrian's market, and the National Assembly Building at Dhaka combines the Temple of Jupiter above Ostia's forum with forms derived from plans of English castles and, as Brownlee and De Long suggest, with heaven knows what else. Most of all, Kahn's "brick order" at Ahmedabad and Dhaka derives from Roman brick and concrete construction heavily filtered through Piranesi's etchings of braced brick circles,[2] while a similar configuration in the portico of the outpatients' clinic at Dhaka closely resembles Ledoux's drawing of the architect's all-seeing eye.[3] Here the main historical point emerges clearly: Kahn was a Romantic Classic architect, exactly as Piranesi and Ledoux had been. Like Piranesi he desired sublime effects (I have already tried to describe them), and like Ledoux he wanted them embodied in perfect, hard, geometric forms. Like those architects, and their many colleagues at the dawn of the modern age, Kahn wanted to begin architecture anew by concentrating upon the ruins of the ancient world and starting afresh from them. This is, I think, precisely why Kahn was indeed able to

reinvigorate architecture toward the end of the late phase of the International Style. He was beginning modern architecture again as it had begun in the eighteenth century: with heavy, solid forms derived from structure rather than from the pictorial composition through which modern architects of the twentieth century had later attempted to rival the freedom of abstract painting. So Kahn's work, despite his travel sketches, is itself never pictorial. It is primitively architectural, thus pre-pictorial. That is why Kahn was, like Cézanne in painting, a true primitive in the way he had chosen, always saying that he liked "beginnings" and that a "good question was better than the best answer." It is no wonder that his buildings are full of ancient power. And, though he opened the way to the full classical revival of the present, he persistently refused to use classical details himself, confining himself always, in his own kind of modernist way, to the abstraction of the stripped ruin. Just so, in the last great years of his career, he would hardly use glass. This is true at Exeter, where he simply jammed the glass he did not need in India into the frame of a ruin and would not permit the four walls to join together as a completed building. At the Kimbell he employed only Romanoid arches, directly reflecting a specific set of ruins, and that was all, inside and out. Neither scheme could have been more purely Romantic-Classic.

This renders Kahn's achievement at the Yale Center for British Art all the more surprising. Because there, in his last building, Kahn made what amounted to a great step forward in time and in the development of modern architecture itself. He stepped, in fact, from the eighteenth-century Romantic Classicism of Piranesi and Ledoux to the nineteenth-century Realism of Labrouste. When, in the Bibliothèque Sainte-Geneviève, of 1843–50, Labrouste asked himself how the ruins of Greece and Rome could be truly rationalized into modern buildings on modern streets, he worked out a system of base, block, column frame, and infilling panels of solid and glass which became the classic modern solution to the problem of the urban building all the way on through Richardson and Sullivan to Mies van der Rohe and the present time. It is this system that Kahn adopted at Yale and in which, for the first time and with miraculous reflection, glass came to life in his design.

He therefore seems to have been at the beginning of some new integration in his work when he died. What he would have made of his followers, who have themselves remade the profession of architecture and begun to heal the wounds that the modern age has inflicted on our cities, is perhaps not hard to tell. He would not have liked any of their work very much. He was always the lone hero, after all, pursuing a lonely quest. And while it is true that the journey to Canaan was largely initiated by him, he never completed it himself, shaping his own kingdom outside the promised land.

This catalogue represents the first extensive scholarship devoted to Louis I. Kahn's life and work since his drawings and office files became readily available for study. One is grateful to David Brownlee and David De Long, and to their students, for the good use to which they have put this material and for their painstaking documentation of all of Kahn's most important buildings and projects.

Chapter 1

Adventures of Unexplored Places

Defining a Philosophy, 1901–51

1

1. Plan of an army post, Class A project, Beaux-Arts Institute of Design, Spring 1924.

L ouis I. Kahn lived for fifty years and worked as an architect for more than a quarter century before fame found him. His first five decades do not, however, contradict what he did later; neither do they explain it. He was, during that time, a successful architect within the boundaries imposed by youth, the Great Depression, and the Second World War. He learned, he built, he taught, and he devoted himself to the central preoccupations of his generation in architecture: the search for a modern language and the challenge of housing a needy society. He succeeded. But in later life he reformulated those concerns, subsuming them within a new understanding of the nature of architecture, and in doing so he established more rigorous criteria for success. And by those standards he succeeded again.

An Architect in the Making

Louis Kahn was born in 1901 on the Baltic fringe of imperial Russia, on the island of Ösel (now Saaremaa) in Estonia. His father, Leopold, was an Estonian, and his mother, Bertha Mendelsohn, was from Riga, Latvia, where she had met her husband while he was on leave from the paymaster corps of the Russian army. After his military discharge, they settled on Saaremaa. Both were Jews, raised in the multilingual culture that flourished in the cosmopolitan borderland between Russian- and German-speaking Europe. They were poor, and in 1904 Leopold Kahn emigrated to America. He found work in Philadelphia, and in 1906 Bertha brought Louis, then five years old, and his younger sister and brother, Sarah and Oscar, to join him.

Philadelphia was then in the final decades of its peak industrial era. Preeminent in the manufacturing of clothing, the city had welcomed a vast population of new immigrants to work in its factories. The Kahns settled in the Northern Liberties, a poor immigrant district that lay on the edge of Center City, moving often during their first years in the country.[1] Leopold possessed substantial talents as a designer and glass painter, but he found little skilled employment, and a back injury caused him to give up the work he could find as a laborer. Although he kept a shop for a while, the family was supported principally by Bertha's work, making samples of knitted woolen clothing for local manufacturers. In a poor and sometimes disorderly household, Bertha Kahn preserved some of the cultural trappings of their European background. While this included German and Yiddish language, music, and literature, the family did not keep up the observances of their faith.

Louis had scarred his face in infancy when the bright colors of a coal fire attracted his too-close attention, and soon after arriving in Philadelphia he was stricken with scarlet fever. This raised the pitch of his voice and kept him from entering school on schedule. The combination of these blemishes and his late start made him shy around other students, but he soon found favor with his teachers because of his aptitude in drawing, and Philadelphia's old-fashioned but benevolent art community offered abundant encouragement.

While in grammar school, Kahn began to take courses in drawing, painting, and sculpture, walking several blocks across Philadelphia's gridded plan to the Public Industrial Art School, where talented students from the regular schools were given supplemental training. There he was befriended by the director, J. Liberty Tadd (1854–1917), an important educational theorist who emphasized large-scale drawing on blackboards and hands-on engagement with the media of sculpture.[2] When Kahn was admitted to the flagship of Philadelphia's school system, the selective Central High School, he continued his art with free Saturday classes at the Graphic Sketch Club, later renamed the Samuel S. Fleisher Art Memorial in honor of its great patron. His drawings won a series of citywide prizes. At the same time, he displayed an instinctive talent for music, piggybacking piano lessons on those paid for by a neighbor for her daughter, and so impressing one acquaintance that he was given an old piano. The large instrument filled much of the available space at home, and he often claimed that he had had to sleep on the piano because it displaced his bed.[3] Kahn was offered a music scholarship, but, on Tadd's advice, he turned it down to concentrate on the visual arts. He did make use of his musical talent, however, helping to support his family by playing the organ at movie theaters while a teenager.

In his senior year at Central High School (1919–20), Kahn took a course on architectural history taught by William F. Gray. It combined lectures and drawing assignments, with which Kahn sometimes helped his less talented classmates. The new subject fascinated him—"architecture struck me between the eye and the eyeball," he once told an interviewer—and he decided to give up his plans to study painting at the Pennsylvania Academy of the Fine Arts after graduation.[4] Instead, he would go to the University of Pennsylvania for training in architecture. Philadelphia had treated the young immigrant generously, and he always remembered its early kindness. "The city," he liked to say, "is a place where a small boy, as he walks through it, may see something that will tell him what he wants to do his whole life."[5]

Kahn's life in architecture began at the University of Pennsylvania, which then had the strongest architectural program in the country, one infused with the confident rigor of the École des Beaux-Arts of Paris. Like many American institutions, the university had imported a French-trained architect to head the design program, and in Paul Philippe Cret (1876–1945) they were unusually fortunate in their choice. Cret loved his adopted city and country, and they returned his affection. As a teacher he was reserved, but he and his staff (many of whom, by Kahn's time, were Cret's former students) did not fail to convey the seriousness of architecture and its central cultural position. The methods of the École, where Cret had been schooled on the rational, progressive side under the guidance of his atelier patron, Jean-Louis Pascal, and the professor of theory, Julien Guadet, were explained as something like a scientific system. Despite his unshaken belief in the primacy of classicism, to Cret architecture was not a matter of historical styles but a problem-solving art in which the creative architect translated the demands of the client's program into substance. New kinds of programs necessarily produced new architecture, and Cret taught that modern democracy would consequently achieve its own architectural expression. Without affectation he could proclaim to a gathering of Philadelphia architects in 1923, "Our architecture is modern and cannot be anything else."[6]

Kahn spent four years at the University of Pennsylvania, earning his bachelor's degree in architecture. His first-year studio critic was John Harbeson (1888–1986), a former Cret student and then a senior member of Cret's office. Harbeson was the author of *The Study of Architectural Design* (New York, 1926), an elegant guide to the Beaux-Arts teaching system as it had been reconstituted in America by the national Beaux-Arts Institute of Design, created by former students of the École. The institute set the programs for a ladder of competitions open to students in architecture schools and independent ateliers, leading to the Paris Prize and the chance to study at the fountainhead, the École itself. Many of Harbeson's illustrations were chosen from among the prize-winning work of Penn students, who in Kahn's time outpaced those from all other schools in their share of national awards.[7]

Kahn did well in this environment.[8] He excelled in the watercolor and freehand drawing required of architecture students and in courses devoted to the history of architecture, painting, and sculpture. His marks in the design studio were not as high, but in his senior year, with Cret as his critic, he won two second medals in Class A projects set by the Beaux-Arts Institute of Design (and several mentions as well) and advanced to the second preliminary stage of the Paris Prize competition, finishing sixth and thereby just missing a place in the finals.[9]

Under the influence of his teachers, Kahn in his student work showed a preference for the austere vocabulary of what is sometimes called "stripped classicism," occasionally decorated with a species of free ornament akin to the Art Deco with which Paul Cret himself dabbled in the twenties and thirties. But it was planning, not the decoration of elevations, that stood at the center of Beaux-Arts teaching. In this, Kahn's schooling did not contradict the contemporary thinking of those Europeans who were formulating the philosophy of modern architecture. Proclamations like Le Corbusier's "The plan is the generator" would not have seemed alien. Indeed, at a meeting of Philadelphia's T-Square Club in 1927, Cret gave a generally favorable review of Le Corbusier's *Towards a New Architecture*, which had just been translated into English.[10]

Kahn's own planning in his student years steered away from the unremitting axial symmetry that was and is still often incorrectly judged to be the hallmark of the Beaux-Arts method. Indeed, Beaux-Arts design depended on the regular breaking and disguising of axes in order to preserve the freshness of their organizing effect, and Harbeson devoted an encouraging chapter in *The Study of Architectural Design* to asymmetrical plans. Kahn's last premiated student work, an army post he designed in the spring of his senior year, displayed his verve for just that type of organization *(fig. 1)*. Around one end of a great parade ground he deployed the barracks for three battalions, but the other end of the composition was defined by an administration building (notably blocking the main entrance axis into the post) and two very unequal buildings for the post hospital and its operational headquarters. Dynamic balance rather than symmetry was evidently Kahn's objective, although it was imperfectly attained. This experience with nonaxial planning provided the foundation on which he would build his experiments with modernist composition in the thirties and forties, while the concern for planning in general would persist throughout his career.

When questioned by historians and critics, Kahn never failed to acknowledge the lessons he had learned from Cret and the Beaux-Arts at Penn. Even near the end of his life, when his architecture had moved from the Beaux-Arts, traversed the International Style, and reconstituted itself as a vocabulary of its own, Kahn would trace the roots of this mature style back to his schooling. His emphasis on what he had come to call "form," the inherent essence that an architect had to discern in an architectural program before it was contaminated by practical considerations, was related to the Beaux-Arts emphasis on the preliminary, instinctive *esquisse*. As he said:

> For beginning design problems Beaux-Arts training typically presented the student with a written program without comment from the instructor. He would study the problem, be given a period of a few hours in a cubicle (*en loge*) during which he would make a quick sketch *[esquisse]* of his solution without consultation. This sketch was filed as the basis for the elaboration of the problem which followed. Final drawings could not violate the essence of the initial *esquisse*. . . . This particular aspect of Beaux-Arts training was probably the most controversial because there was no exchange between the advocates of the programme and those who interpreted it, the architect. So the

sketch depended on our intuitive powers. But the intuitive power is probably our most accurate sense. The sketch depended on our intuitive sense of appropriateness. I teach appropriateness. I don't teach anything else.[11]

Kahn also attributed the germ of his highly developed notion of a hierarchy between "served" and "servant" spaces, the latter often inserted in hollowed structural systems, to the *poché* or "pocketing" of spaces within masonry that was typical of the Beaux-Arts. And he claimed that his fascination with lighting as the maker of architectural environment had begun with the lessons about shade and shadow that Beaux-Arts rendering had taught him.[12]

Upon graduation in June 1924 *(fig. 2)*, Kahn found a place in the office of the City Architect of Philadelphia, John Molitor (1872–1928), who had trained briefly in Paris and had made good connections in the city's architectural and political establishments. Kahn worked for a year as a draftsman, detailing drawings, and he was then seconded as chief of design to a special office set up by Molitor to design the major buildings for the Sesquicentennial International Exposition, which opened in Philadelphia in June 1926. In comparison to other international fairs, Philadelphia's celebration of the 150th anniversary of the Declaration of Independence was modest, and its public success was diminished by a dismal, rainy summer, but for a young architect it must have been exhilarating to design and build six huge buildings, constructed of wood and stucco over steel skeletons and totaling more than 1.5 million square feet. It was all done in less than a year.[13]

Although Molitor had two assistant architects assigned to the project, William S. Covell (1872–1956) and John Horace Frank (1873–1957), Kahn always claimed to have led the design work. It was surely he who made the dramatic drawings with which the buildings were introduced to the public in the fall of

2

3

2. *Left to right: Hyman Cunin, Louis Kahn, and Norman Rice on the steps of Hayden Hall, University of Pennsylvania, on graduation day, June 1924.*
3. *Palace of Liberal Arts, Sesquicentennial Exposition, Philadelphia, Pa., 1925-26. Perspective of portico, Fall 1925.*

1925, just in time to reassure the organizing committee, which had begun to worry about the ability of Molitor's office to carry off the huge undertaking *(fig. 3)*.[14] Kahn's perspectives were full of chiaroscuro pyrotechnics, rendered with the slashing diagonal line that was to energize his drawings for the rest of his life. The buildings themselves were great sheds covered with pastel-tinted stucco (Molitor hoped that the fair would be called the "Rainbow City," just as the Columbian Exposition of 1893 had been dubbed the "White City"), and they afforded the young designer some chance to realize work on the scale of the visionary projects of the eighteenth-century architects Étienne-Louis Boullée and Claude-Nicolas Ledoux, with which he had probably become acquainted in college. As in some of his student work, the detailing, limited as it was, applied the waves and zigzags of Art Deco over a body of simplified modern classicism. The Exposition des Arts Décoratifs in Paris the previous summer (whence Art Deco took its name) had brought these motifs to the attention of many young architects.

Almost as soon as it had begun, the sesquicentennial was over, the site cleared and returned to a park, and Kahn was back in the ordinary routine of the City Architect's office, working chiefly on firehouses and playground buildings. After a few more months there he moved to the office of William H. Lee (1884–1971), then designing a number of buildings for Temple University. Kahn lived with his parents during this time, and after a year with Lee he had saved enough money for a long European trip of the kind that architects with his training were expected to make. He landed in Plymouth, England, on May 3, 1928, spent two weeks sketching in England—working in a dry, elegant illustrator's style—before moving on across the Low Countries and northern Germany.[15] He reached Denmark on June 29 and, after ten days, passed quickly through Sweden,

Finland, and Estonia on his way to Riga, Latvia, where he had some relatives. It was also the jumping-off point for a visit to his birthplace on Saaremaa. He spent nearly a month of long Baltic summer evenings in those dimly remembered places, sleeping on the floor in his maternal grandmother's one-room house.[16] In mid-August Kahn left for Berlin, where he inspected the new housing projects (*Siedlungen*).[17] This was probably his first taste of the modern movement. After nearly two weeks in Germany, he headed south, pausing for most of September in Austria and Hungary, where he started drawing again, intrigued by the Danube landscape. Its energetic forms were new to the city-bred architect.

On October 4, 1928, Kahn entered Italy, the traditional mecca for Beaux-Arts architects, where he was to spend five winter months.[18] Here he traveled slowly, drawing and making watercolors in Milan, Florence, San Gimignano, Assisi, and Rome, and he apparently spent a very long time sketching vernacular architecture on the Sorrento peninsula—in Positano, Amalfi, Ravello, and on the island of Capri. He visited the archaic Greek temples at Paestum, but no sketches have been found from there, nor any sketches of Roman antiquities. In Italy he encountered old friends from school and made new ones, notably the architects Louis Skidmore and Edward Durell Stone, with whom he traveled for a while.

It was in Europe that Kahn developed a new drawing style, based in part on a familiarity with contemporary currents in American art. For landscape, he began to rely on a sweeping hand that would lay out strong contours as it moved from side to side across the paper. When rendered in watercolor, the effect could be close to that achieved by American Scene painters or, if he reined in the chromatic range and applied the paint in flat panels, to the work of Charles Demuth

and Georgia O'Keeffe *(fig. 4)*. For architecture, Kahn adopted a similarly broad handling of media, painting planes of color or using a carpenter's pencil whose wide, chisel-shaped lead laid organizing strata across the face of medieval and early Renaissance buildings *(fig. 5)*. Full of the lively energy of nature and the tectonic strength of architecture, his Italian drawings bespoke confidence and independence. As he explained in an article about drawing published soon after his return, "I try in all my sketching not to be entirely subservient to my subject, but I have respect for it, and regard it as something tangible—alive—from which to extract my feelings. I have learned to regard it as no physical impossibility to move mountains and trees, or change cupolas and towers to suit my taste."[19]

Early in March, Kahn followed spring northward to Paris, where he spent about a month visiting with his Penn classmate Norman Rice (see *fig. 2*), whom he had known since they had taken courses together at the Industrial Art School as ten-year-olds. Kahn had also recruited him to work on the sesquicentennial. Rice was then in the office of Le Corbusier, but Kahn did not make an effort to see the modernist's work.[20] More impressive to him was the vital energy of the Parisian metropolis—what he later called its "will to live"—and the integrity and completeness of its classical architecture and city planning. "For pure form (city form)," he said, "you can't beat that city."[21]

In April 1929 Kahn sailed for home. He found work immediately in the office of his revered teacher, Paul Cret, and his proposal of marriage was accepted by Esther Israeli (b. 1905), a beautiful research assistant in the Department of Neurosurgery at the University of Pennsylvania. He had met Esther at a party before sailing to Europe, intrigued her with talk about a newly acquired book on Rodin, and given her the book as a gift; they rapidly fell in love.[22] But Kahn did not write her from

4

abroad, and she became engaged to someone else during his travels. Upon his return they argued, but reconciliation came after they saw each other in the audience at the Academy of Music, listening to the Philadelphia Orchestra. Kahn proposed to her during a visit to the Rodin Museum (designed by Cret), and they were married on August 14, 1930.

Kahn's position with Cret was junior, and he was overshadowed by the senior members of the office, John Harbeson, William Hough, William Livingston, and Roy Larson. He worked on most of their major commissions during that period, which ranged in style from Cret's increasingly simple classicism—like the uncolumned Folger Library in Washington—to the jazzy modernity of his design for the General Exhibits Building at the Century of Progress Exhibition in Chicago. It must have been very provocative work for Kahn, who found himself, like most intelligent young architects of the time, torn between the lessons of the past and the enticements of the present. Here he could see his own teacher dealing intelligently with the same dilemma.

The romantic and artistic sweetness of those first months back in America diminished as the Depression settled over the country in the wake of the crash of 1929. Kahn and his fiancée put off plans to travel to Europe after their wedding, he to learn more about Walter Gropius and she to study with Freud, and within a year even Cret's office was starved for work. Kahn left before being asked to leave. Cret managed to arrange a place for him in the office of his friend Clarence Zantzinger, whose firm, Zantzinger, Borie, and Medary, had landed one of the first big Depression-era public works projects, the Treasury Building in Washington. A chameleon-like design with staid facades on the major thoroughfares and exuberant, Art Deco detail elsewhere, the Treasury Building was another work of transition. Kahn labored

5

4. *Porte delle Torri, Spoleto, 1928.*
5. *Sketch of cathedral at Assisi, Winter 1928–29.*

on it until February 1932, when, at the very nadir of the Depression, he found himself out of work again.

Depression Modern

Kahn was unemployed for most of the next four years, supported by his wife and living with her parents, as they had since their marriage. But along with financial hardship came an unusual kind of architectural opportunity: the chance to pause and come to a new understanding of the role of his art at a time of great social demand and new technical and aesthetic potential. Philadelphia was an advantageous place in which to take that kind of holiday. In the bright shadow of George Howe and William Lescaze's Philadelphia Savings Fund Society Building (1929–32)—America's most visible contribution to international modernism—the Quaker city hosted a vigorous but gentlemanly debate about the future of architecture. The forum for much of that discussion was the *T-Square Club Journal of Philadelphia*, a new magazine, funded by Howe, which began publication in December 1930 and lasted for not quite two years.[23] In that short time, opinion was exchanged among many of the major forces in modern architecture. There was first of all George Howe himself, who, before his mid-life turn to modernism, had been trained in Paris and successfully established himself as one of the premier designers of Philadelphia's distinctive stone suburban houses—by turns inspired by low-slung Cotswold cottages and high-roofed French farms. There were also progressive Beaux-Arts architects, drawn from Penn's faculty and Cret's partnership—Harry Sternfeld, William Hough, Roy Larson, and John Harbeson—and Cret himself, all of whom contributed to or were profiled in *T-Square*. And there were essays by the leading Art Deco protagonists—the New York skyscraper builders Ralph Walker, Ely Jacques Kahn, and Raymond Hood and Philadelphia's

Howell Lewis Shay. Finally, one could find the opinions of the more extreme modernists of every stripe: Frank Lloyd Wright, Richard Neutra, Rudolph Schindler, Norman Bel Geddes, Le Corbusier, Philip Johnson, and Buckminster Fuller (who took over the magazine and renamed it *Shelter* for its last three issues). No other magazine in America offered anything like this range of advanced opinion.

Kahn's classmate Norman Rice, having returned from his stint with Le Corbusier, was among the contributors, and his article "This New Architecture" (March 1931) offered one of the first careful expositions by an American of what, in the wake of the exhibition that opened at the Museum of Modern Art on February 10, 1932, would be christened the "International Style." (That show came to the Philadelphia Museum of Art in April.) Kahn himself published "The Value and Aim in Sketching" in *T-Square* in May 1931, illustrated with some of his Italian drawings.

Kahn organized another center for the discussion of modern architecture in Philadelphia, the Architectural Research Group (ARG). In 1931, while still working in the Zantzinger office, he and Dominique Berninger, an unemployed French architect, assembled a group of about thirty young designers, most of whom were also out of work. They rented cheap rooms, borrowed drawing tools from the school board, and set to work. When he lost his job, Kahn devoted all his energies to the group, which once a week indulged in lunch at Ethel's Restaurant, a favored daily eating place among architects who were lucky enough to have jobs. David P. Wisdom, who was later to work for Kahn for many years, remembered seeing him for the first time in that setting: "this little guy who held forth" at the center of a group of admirers.[24]

Kahn now became a modernist. He studied intensely what was going on abroad, paging through the publications of Le Corbusier's work for the first time, and over the next two decades his architecture echoed many of the major themes of the International Style.[25] Most important to him were the new compositional strategies that it introduced, including open planning, and its emphasis on the social responsibility of the architect. He also participated in the widespread modernist experimentation with new building technologies.

It was social responsibility, and in particular the problems of mass housing, that was the chief concern of Kahn's Architectural Research Group. This issue was well established at the center of the discussion of modern architecture in Europe, but it still had a small following in the United States. Awareness grew, however, as slum conditions worsened because of the Depression. Philadelphia was the site of the first modernist *Siedlung* to be built in America, the Carl Mackley Houses, designed for the Full Fashioned Hosiery Workers Union by a pair of young émigré architects, Oscar Stonorov (1905–1970) and Alfred Kastner (1900–1975),[26] who had taken second place in the 1931 competition for the Palace of the Soviets in Moscow. The Mackley Houses were initially funded by a loan from Hoover's Reconstruction Finance Corporation, and they were taken over in the summer of 1933 as the first project in the much more ambitious program of Roosevelt's Public Works Administration.

Exhibited in a preliminary form during the Philadelphia stopover of the Museum of Modern Art's modern architecture show in 1932, the four long, tile-faced buildings were redesigned in 1933 and under construction in 1934. With their high standard of design and construction and such generous amenities as garages and a swimming pool, the Mackley Houses attracted nationwide attention.

Within a few years Kahn would work with both Stonorov and Kastner, but in the meantime his research group did its best to stay busy and attract local attention. In April 1933

they placed a model in the Better Homes Exhibition that showed their proposed rebuilding of a typical tract of South Philadelphia slum. Like the Mackley Houses, it consisted of four long buildings (their kin in Germany were called *Seilenbauten*) placed within a parklike setting.[27] The ARG scheme had been Americanized, again like the Stonorov and Kastner design, with garages and generous recreation facilities.

The ARG also put forward a proposal later in 1933 when the PWA launched its housing subsidy program.[28] Submitted on behalf of the Northeast Philadelphia Housing Corporation, their plan placed a variety of buildings within a network of gently curved, limited-traffic roads on a substantial, fifty-four-acre tract. The buildings included long apartment blocks, like those planned for South Philadelphia, and also row-house strips and four-unit, windmill-plan clusters designed by Kahn *(fig. 6)*. With their corner windows and floating roof slabs, the windmill houses demonstrated the architect's familiarity with some of the signature details of modernism. But the rather conservative and placid facade composition was more like contemporary English work than the livelier avant-garde architecture on the Continent, and Kahn's unsureness can also be seen in the overt artifice of the unusual plan, with its cramped, enclosed stairhall. With the exception of the Mackley Houses, the PWA denied funding to all twelve of the schemes submitted by Philadelphians in 1933, and the members of the Architectural Research Group went their separate ways in May 1934.

In part, the breakup of the ARG had to do with the advent of the New Deal's work projects for architects. Kahn himself took a position as the head of a research "squad" under the coordination of Philadelphia's weak City Planning Commission. Partnered with the established firm of Henry Magaziner and Victor Eberhard (which had also sponsored the Architectural Research Group), he authored a proposal for building on another site in Northeast Philadelphia, adjacent to the main Pennsylvania Railroad right-of-way.[29] Called St. Katherine's Village, it made use of the same mixture of building types that had been devised for the Northeast Philadelphia Housing Corporation.

At the same time, Kahn began to build, albeit very modestly, with clients coming from the socially and artistically progressive Jewish community in which he and his wife had many friends. Harry ("Mish") Buten, who owned a paint company, had Kahn modernize his store in Germantown in 1934. The work was carried out in partnership with Hyman Cunin, a Penn classmate who had also worked for Cret and been a member of the ARG (see *fig. 2*). Cunin had apparently secured the architectural registration that Kahn still lacked. In 1935, when Kahn had obtained his own credentials, the congregation of Ahavath Israel came to him for a new building to be inserted in a row of two-story houses close to the northern boundary of the city. For them he produced a plain, brick-faced box, pierced by factory-style steel windows and with a main sanctuary of notable and (at the time) refreshing austerity.

The generally slow pace of Depression-era work for Kahn was interrupted by more than a year of intense activity as an architect for the Division of Subsistence Homesteads. He was called to Washington in December 1935 by Alfred Kastner, a Hamburg-trained architect and one of the Mackley Houses designers, who had himself been recruited from Philadelphia to rescue a program called Jersey Homesteads. This was a scheme to relocate the families of 200 Jewish garment workers from New York to a site near Hightstown, New Jersey.[30] Benjamin Brown, a Ukrainian-born proponent of cooperative industry and a leader of the Jewish back-to-the-land movement, spearheaded the project,

which was to include a cooperative clothing factory and a cooperative farm. Brown believed that the combination of these two seasonal enterprises would make the community self-sustaining; in addition, each house was to stand on enough ground to permit large-scale gardening. Supported by the International Ladies Garment Workers Union (ILGWU) and endorsed by Albert Einstein (who had taken up residence in nearby Princeton), the project advanced quickly during the first years of Roosevelt's administration. A design with Cape Cod-style cottages was worked out during the first half of 1935 and the pouring of foundation slabs begun, all under Brown's supervision.[31] But the Division of Subsistence Homesteads was moved into the Resettlement Administration in May 1935, and there the project came under sharp scrutiny. It was noted that Brown had not yet reached an agreement on the details for operating the factory with ILGWU president David Dubinsky, and it appeared that the houses would be very expensive. Rexford Tugwell, the "brain truster" whom Roosevelt had appointed to head the Resettlement Administration, decided to place the project more directly under federal supervision, and Kastner and Kahn (who carried the titles principal and assistant principal architect) were given the job.

In December 1935 the two young architects moved into offices in one of the World War I "temporary" buildings on the Mall. Their orders were to push the project ahead, and they were encouraged to utilize prefabricated construction. They used these demands to convert Jersey Homesteads into an ambitious experiment with adapting new technology and the modernist idiom of Europe to the needs of the American suburb. Robert W. Noble, who worked in their office, later observed, "Little cinder block houses held down by concrete slabs were never more completely studied."[32]

Kahn served as the head of the drafting

room, submitting weekly reports and playing a role that he always called "co-designer."[33] Indeed, although junior architects in the office were given credit for four of the twelve house types worked out during the first months of 1936, it is evident that a single coordinating intelligence lay behind their variety of forms (fig. 7).[34] The numerous, predominantly one-story house plans were contrived to allow the pairing of units in an almost endless number of combinations. Economical construction with concrete slab roofs and floors and cinderblock walls (adopted after experiments with precast concrete wall sections ran into construction and licensing problems) allowed for a surprising number of luxuries. These included wood-block floors laid on top of the concrete, as well as carports. The plans were also generous, with many three- and even four-bedroom units designed for large families. Rooms were flung outward to create irregular plan perimeters that were more like the picturesque tradition of the American suburban house than modern, European-style workers' housing. It was a highly ambitious project, and when the house designs were displayed in the "Architecture in Government Housing" show at the Museum of Modern Art in June and July 1936, Lewis Mumford singled them out as "the most adventurous, the most stimulating" on display.[35] Others, however, were less infatuated with what the *Philadelphia Inquirer* called a "commune" headed by "a Russian-born little Stalin" (i.e., Benjamin Brown).[36]

Despite initial construction delays, the first houses at Jersey Homesteads were occupied in the early summer of 1936, only about six months after Kastner and Kahn had begun work. When the clothing factory opened in August, however, there was not yet enough housing for the work force, although most of the houses were ready by January 1937.

In the fall of 1936 the architects began to plan the school, which was also to serve as a community center. Kahn studied several

6

7

8

6. *Project for Northeast Philadelphia Housing Corporation, 1933. Bird's-eye perspective of windmill-plan house.*
7. *Jersey Homesteads, Roosevelt, N.J., 1935–37. Houses under construction, July 1936.*
8. *Jersey Homesteads. Perspective and plan of school, Fall 1936.*

possible *partis*. These designs reflected his increasingly confident use of the Le Corbusian vocabulary, replete with slabs supported on slender *pilotis* and curvilinear walls that exploited the possibilities for free planning within such a structural system *(fig. 8)*.[37] The school was still under study when Kahn was furloughed early in 1937, and Kastner decided its final design in May, settling on a composition that was much less extroverted than those sketched by Kahn.[38] The painter Ben Shahn received his first major commission for a large mural in the school lobby, depicting immigration and labor history, and he moved to Jersey Homesteads in 1938.

After Kahn returned to Philadelphia, he again found himself without steady employment, although he was now supervising the construction of Ahavath Israel. Together with Henry Klumb, a former assistant of Frank Lloyd Wright's whom he had met while working in Washington, he used his free time to study the possibilities of prefabricated steel housing.[39] Their work was supported by Samuel S. Fels, the soap maker and philanthropist, and in part they collaborated with Louis Magaziner, who provided Kahn with a mailing address and a drafting table in his office at 1701 Walnut Street. The steel construction system severely limited the architects' freedom, and some of the designs were very conservative, with pitched roofs. But Kahn wrung more out of the problem than most could have done, notably in a series of designs for small row houses that used a mid-roof monitor to light the upper halls and bathrooms.

The architectural doldrums of 1937 were interrupted in September when Congress passed the Wagner-Steagall Act, ending a two-year battle over public housing. The act put housing—and, with it, modern architecture—on a new, higher footing within the New Deal and promised increased opportunities for architects. Partly in response to a negative evaluation of the PWA program (which had

built only one additional project in Philadelphia after the Mackley Houses), the act created the more powerful United States Housing Authority.[40] A parallel local movement gave birth to the Philadelphia Housing Authority in August 1937, also designed to build more vigorously.[41] Kahn, who had become a recognized authority on housing matters, found employment with both the USHA and the PHA.

It was the Philadelphia Housing Authority that offered the first opportunities, conducting a competition in 1938 to select architects.[42] A team assembled by George Howe, with Kahn and Kenneth Day (1901?–1958) as its designers, won the right to design a project to eradicate the densely inhabited alleyways in the Southwark section of South Philadelphia, adjacent to historic Gloria Dei ("Old Swedes' ") Church. Day claimed to have been responsible for the plan of the 950-unit project, which placed smaller apartments in towers and larger apartments in low rises, with a view to maintaining the high density of the site.[43] Kahn by himself designed another 1,500-unit PHA project, begun in 1939 for vacant land in West Philadelphia owned by the Pennsylvania Hospital for Mental and Nervous Diseases (called "Kirkbride's" after its founder, Dr. Thomas Kirkbride). In this time of matter-of-fact segregation, Old Swedes' was to be a project for whites and Kirkbride's was to be for blacks.

Federal funds were approved for both designs ($5,551,000 for Old Swedes'; $7,881,000 for Kirkbride's), but intense opposition came from members of the close-knit Italian community of Southwark, who did not want to be displaced from their small but generally well-maintained homes, and from the builders and real estate men who did not want the government to become more deeply involved in the housing market.[44] In a conference with federal and city housing officials on May 30, 1940, Mayor Robert E. Lamberton announced his own opposition to the plans.

Calling public housing an untested social experiment, he opined, "Slum areas exist because some people are so utterly shiftless that any place where they live becomes a slum, and others are so poor that they cannot afford to live anywhere else."[45] The City Council declined to take the matter further.

This setback contributed to Kahn's politicization. He had come to recognize that housing was more than a matter of architectural design, and for the next decade he was an activist. Kahn had already spent five months in 1939 working with Catherine Bauer and Frederick Gutheim on a public education campaign launched by the United States Housing Authority to counter exactly the kind of concerns that had been raised in Philadelphia. He had first prepared the illustrations for some of the small pamphlets issued by the USHA to explain its mission and the character of public housing in general, and he then worked on the USHA's "Houses and Housing" exhibition, mounted at the Museum of Modern Art in New York. The show was designed in part to make up for the absence of public housing in any of the several future-oriented dioramas at the New York World's Fair that summer. Kahn's contribution was a large panel entitled "Housing in the Rational City Plan," which analyzed the problems of Philadelphia and proposed remedies at every scale, ranging from the demolition of large parts of Center City and their replacement with clusters of towers (like those in Le Corbusier's most extreme proposals for Paris) to the efficient, zoned organization of the ordinary house plan.[46]

With this training, Kahn joined wholeheartedly in the campaign to reverse Philadelphia's official opposition to federally funded housing. But he and all those who had fought for decades for the establishment of the Philadelphia Housing Authority found their position complicated by the war clouds that began to sweep in from across the seas during that dark summer of 1940. On the one hand, Philadelphia's swelling population of war industry workers and servicemen had already begun to overtax the supply of housing, and Congress passed the Lanham Act in October, aimed at meeting this shortage. On the other hand, the legislation did not endorse projects like Kirkbride's and Old Swedes', planned by the PHA, for funding by the USHA. Most Lanham Act money was allocated for wartime, emergency shelter only, and it was administered through the Federal Works Agency, the USHA being rightly suspected of seeking a permanent government presence in the housing market.

In an effort to steer wartime funding toward projects of lasting social value, Kahn allied himself with the Philadelphia Housing Guild, and with support from the Philadelphia Housing Association, the American Institute of Architects, the Tenants' League, and labor unions, he helped to organize a citywide protest meeting on December 10, 1940.[47] Kahn chaired the publicity committee, which made posters and educational exhibits for the meeting, and Edmund Bacon, having recently arrived in Philadelphia on the first step toward his long and celebrated tenure as executive director of the Planning Commission, headed the program committee. Their efforts, and efforts like theirs, helped to redirect some of the first Lanham Act money toward the construction of real communities.

Architecture at War

Kahn was himself soon working for the war effort. He spent most of 1941 and 1942 designing seven workers' communities, five of which, totaling more than 2,200 units, were built.[48] The projects were caught in a constant crossfire between those, like Kahn, who wanted a national housing program and critics who could tolerate government involvement in the housing market only because of the wartime emergency and who sought to keep that involvement at a minimum. Despite this sniping, the projects afforded Kahn a rich opportunity to test solutions to basic problems in something like a laboratory environment. It may have been in the course of this testing that he began to have doubts about the functionalist course of modern architecture.

As the threat of war loomed, George Howe, who had assembled the team for Old Swedes', approached Kahn with the suggestion that they form a partnership and go after government work.[49] With his impeccable architectural credentials and social connections, Howe was an ideal partner, and he and Kahn had obtained the first of their wartime commissions, for Pine Ford Acres in Middletown, Pennsylvania, within days of the creation of the Division of Defense Housing within the Federal Works Agency on April 5, 1941. By midsummer 500 units at Pine Ford Acres and 1,000 units at Pennypack Woods, close to the St. Katherine's Village site in Northeast Philadelphia, were under construction, and Pine Ford Acres was occupied by fall. The firm sometimes employed as many as two dozen designers and draftsmen, and although there was no official hierarchy among them, Frederick Savage, Joseph N. Lacy, Charles Abbe, and David Wisdom served successively as informal "head draftsman" during the war years, a position Wisdom also held during all the years of Kahn's independent practice. They occupied George Howe's offices on the top floor of the old *Evening Bulletin* Building, whose public spaces and ground floor facade had been sleekly modernized by Howe in 1936.

Within stringent financial limits (the average unit cost for these first projects was below $3,000), Howe and Kahn set out to build model communities that might set the standard for postwar planning. Like virtually all the wartime projects, theirs were built on open land rather than slum clearance sites, and despite the lack of single-family houses, they offered an appealing evocation of a sub-urban future. However, the most progressive feature of their work—the placement of housing within the greenery of superblocks, served by limited access roads—was lost on those who built postwar America.

Architecturally, the challenge thrown up by wartime housing was to introduce external variety without the kind of energetic (and expensive) planning that Kastner and Kahn had utilized at Jersey Homesteads. Wartime houses were necessarily more compact, and the profiles of buildings blockier. With their means thus limited, Howe and Kahn experimented chiefly with variations on two building types: two-story row houses with two and three bedrooms, arranged in flat-roofed strips that resembled *Seilenbauten*, and single-bedroom apartments stacked in four-unit buildings. At Pine Ford and Pennypack, the row houses adopted the shallow plan that Kahn had used for his prefabricated houses in the 1930s, designed to allow good cross ventilation *(fig. 9)*. The buildings with one-bedroom apartments differed slightly in the two projects, offering variations on a common theme. The architects introduced varied coloring and used two widths of wooden siding in order to animate the facades; at Pine Ford the skylines were broken by peaked roofs—added to satisfy conservative critics.

While work was progressing on these first projects, Howe began to do an increasing amount of consulting work on housing in Washington, and he and Kahn added Oscar Stonorov to their partnership to help take up the load.[50] Stonorov had been one of the editors of the first volume of Le Corbusier's *Oeuvre complète*, and he had been paired with Kastner in the design of the Mackley Houses for the Full Fashioned Hosiery Workers. He had continued to strengthen his connections with organized labor during the thirties, attaching himself particularly to labor leaders who were interested in housing, like John Edelman of the Hosiery Workers, and he had advised Edelman in setting up Philadelphia's Labor Housing Conference in 1934.[51] This became one of the most effective groups in pushing for passage of the Wagner Act and the creation of the USHA, and it was Stonorov who suggested that Catherine Bauer, an eloquent propagandist of the housing movement, be brought to Philadelphia as its director. He made room for her and the fledgling organization in his office. Stonorov is not remembered as playing a key role in the design end of his partnership with Howe and Kahn, although he did handle a number of jobs himself on the side for friends and old clients.[52] But his activism and union connections transformed the shape of the practice.

The firm continued to explore the variations possible within the established housing types, and by the end of 1941, in time for Pearl Harbor, they had adopted a strong new arrangement for the multibedroom, row-house building. This was first seen in their designs for Carver Court, a 100-unit project for black steelworkers just outside Coatesville, Pennsylvania (fig. 10). They realized that by lifting all of the living quarters to the second floor, they could free the ground floor to provide ample storage and a carport that might easily be converted into one or more extra rooms. This "essential space," as they called it, was what made working class homeowners put up with the other deficiencies of speculator-built, "dickey-front houses," and it was what was missing in government-built housing.[53] They did not claim authorship for the "ground-freed" house, which had clear antecedents in the *piloti*-lofted designs of Le Corbusier and many predecessors in American practice as well. But Carver Court was well publicized. With its cleanly detailed units gathered happily around a loop road at the foot of a wooded hillside, it was a special favorite of the organizers of the show "Built in USA, 1932-1944" at the Museum of Modern Art. It was with this design that Kahn first began to gain wide-

9

10

9. Pennypack Woods, Philadelphia, Pa., 1941–43. Family seated in front of row houses, ca. 1942.
10. Carver Court, Caln Township, Pa., 1941–43. Ground-freed and one-story buildings, ca. 1942.

11

12

11. *Pine Ford Acres, Middletown, Pa., 1941–43.*
Community building, ca. 1943.
12. *Lily Ponds Houses, Washington, D.C.,*
1942–43. Houses, ca. 1943.

spread attention. The ground-freed formula was immediately adopted by him for the Stanton Road Dwellings—300 units in Washington, D.C.—and for a second, 150-unit Coatesville project for white workers called Lincoln Highway, for which designs were prepared in late spring 1942.

But artistic merit did not guarantee that these works would be built, and an almost equal amount of energy had to be devoted to the political fight for public housing. Here, the old battlelines were still being contested, with conservatives loath to have the government build anything out of permanent materials or with lasting social value. At both Pine Ford and Pennypack, opposition forces delayed the construction of community buildings and stores—amenities that were sorely needed by the inhabitants of the relatively isolated settlements. Both Coatesville projects were fought in their entirety by local interests, who were especially opposed to the black housing. In combating this, Stonorov proved to be an effective lobbyist, convincing, for instance, his labor friends to "raise plain hell" over the Coatesville developments.[54]

In the end, the contested housing and community buildings were completed, and the latter showed what Kahn and his colleagues could accomplish when they faced fewer constraints *(fig. 11)*. In the community buildings the picturesque tradition of the American suburb was infused with an angular new geometry. The plans were frequently terminated or divided by oblique walls, and even the rectangular-plan units slid by each other on nonorthogonal trajectories that were, in turn, reflected in staggered, sloping rooflines. The dynamism of these buildings seemed to express the feelings of an architect who was freed, at least for a moment, from the stringent requirements of wartime housing.

By the time these projects were complete, George Howe was no longer in Philadelphia, having left the partnership in February 1942 to accept an appointment as supervising architect of the Public Buildings Administration, the highest architectural post in the federal government. At the same time, Kahn and Stonorov's division of labor between design work and political work seems to have become increasingly clear. It was Stonorov, for instance, who led them into the most dramatic political battle to be fought over war housing, the great clash over the construction of a "Bomber City" for the workers at Henry Ford's Willow Run airplane factory, near Ypsilanti, Michigan.

The battleground had been chosen by Ford, who early in 1941 undertook to build a factory just outside Detroit's Wayne County in Washtenaw County, where he apparently reckoned that conservative rural politicians would help him fight the United Auto Workers.[55] The UAW's Walter Reuther was a friend of Stonorov's, and together they immediately hatched a plan to outflank Ford: they would get the government to build a large workers' city near the new plant, putting union members on the poll lists in Washtenaw County and creating a model for postwar planning at the same time.[56] President Roosevelt gave his blessing to the plan in November, and by December, Howe, Stonorov, and Kahn had built a model of such a community of 20,000 residences.[57] Stonorov had also begun to draw up a list of architects who might be asked to collaborate on the design, working in consultation with the architect Eero Saarinen, whose practice was located in nearby Bloomfield Hills, Michigan.[58] After powerful lobbying in Washington by the UAW, a site was selected, and in late May 1942 five architectural teams—including Stonorov and Kahn—were chosen to design five housing neighborhoods (now reduced to a total of 6,000 units). Saarinen and Swanson were put in charge of the community center. In June, Henry Ford announced that he would use every legal means to block the plan; great confusion was

sown by Ford about the number of workers at the plant and the number of permanent, post-war jobs that it would provide. The federal government accordingly reduced the project in August to three 1,200-unit neighborhoods, and Stonorov and Kahn were told that only 900 of theirs would be built in the first phase.[59]

In the meantime Kahn had overseen the design of eight building types for Willow Run, including a ground-freed model, adjusting the design as needed to allow for the growing shortage of timber.[60] He and Stonorov had to defend these designs against the fierce and essentially antimodernist criticism of Otis Winn, an architect who was originally retained to design one of the housing neighborhoods and was kept on as an advisor to the government after his neighborhood was cut. Winn apparently bore a grudge against Stonorov, and he shrewdly presented his criticism to the housing committee of the UAW, where underlying sentiments favored traditional, single-family houses. Stonorov argued back that Willow Run "should be a symbol of things to come and a prophetic statement in terms of housing and not an imitation, and a bad one at that, of what the operative builders are selling to the workers now."[61] But his defense was in vain, and, despite his friendship with Reuther, the UAW dismissed him from the advisory position that he had held with the union.[62] In October 1942 the entire project was canceled—replaced by temporary dormitories designed by Saarinen and Swanson. The collapse can be blamed on the diminution of union support.

As Willow Run was being killed, work was just beginning on the 475 units of the Lily Ponds Houses in Washington, D.C., identified from the start as a "demountable" project. It was composed entirely of clever one-story buildings with four small apartments whose bathrooms were backed up against each other beneath a gull-wing monitor (fig. 12). The exteriors were partly faced in rough tile, and the bare wood of the interior walls and ceilings was left unfinished. The rustic materials and reverse-pitch roof were evidence of Kahn's growing familiarity with the range of Le Corbusier's recent work, including his simple, quasi-primitive houses like the Sextant Villa, a summer cottage built for the Peyron family in La Palmyre-Les Mathes in 1935. It had been well illustrated in the third volume of Le Corbusier's *Oeuvre complète* (1939).

Kahn undertook one further wartime housing commission in 1944–45, a thorough redesign of the still unbuilt Stanton Road Dwellings. The concrete needed for ground-freed units was now unavailable, and so he had to devise a large number of other types, including relatively conventional brick row houses and three-story apartment buildings— rare in wartime. He took special pains over the site plan, which created many small, semiprivate courtyards between the buildings. George Howe, who had retained an interest in this long-developing project during his service in Washington, reviewed Kahn's design and praised it. But he also expressed reservations, in words that could probably have been echoed by any of the talented architects who labored on wartime housing:

> I must say . . . that as I get further and further away from the engrossing work of solving a series of practically unsolvable problems, the more [the] unsatisfactory nature of housing project programs in general impresses me. The basis of city requirements for street widths, set backs, etc., is so rigid, extravagant and oppressive as to doom all solutions to comparative negation. This is all part of the general planning problem which faces us and which if we do not approach with imagination and freedom from restriction, we can make little progress in architectural design in general.

He added, "Do look me up. I miss you constantly."[63]

Plans for 194X

Stanton Road remained unbuilt, a victim of the impending peace. But the prospect of peacetime work also began to offer some of the freedoms that Howe missed. As the quantity of war work declined sharply in 1943–45, Stonorov and Kahn found themselves increasingly engaged in a series of imaginative projects, designed to shape the character of postwar architecture.[64] With the sponsorship of magazines and manufacturers of building materials, they designed houses, hotels, stores, office buildings, and entire neighborhood redevelopment projects. This farsighted work continued for several years after the war, and it brought with it a substantial involvement in social activism: in housing, city planning, trade unionism, and architectural politics. It also brought them some real commissions.

The most complex and widely recognized of Stonorov and Kahn's postwar-oriented projects was a pair of booklets on urban neighborhood planning that they prepared as part of an advertising campaign for Revere Copper and Brass. Written just as the Philadelphia City Planning Commission was being reincarnated with greater powers in 1943, the pamphlets used Philadelphia neighborhoods as examples of possible action. Stonorov was in charge of most of this work, but Kahn certainly did not dissent from the message the booklets conveyed, and his hand can be seen in some of the illustrations.

The work began in April 1943, when Stonorov was introduced to Revere's advertising representatives by Howard Myers, publisher of *Architectural Forum*. Revere was sponsoring a series of booklets on postwar architecture that they hoped would promote the use of their materials, although the advertising message in Stonorov and Kahn's work was very restrained. Also in the series were Lawrence Kocher's *Homes to Enrich Our National Standard of Living* and Serge Chermayeff's *A Children's Center or Nursery*

School. Stonorov and Kahn were commissioned to make a plan that would "integrate four existing city blocks into a community by providing it with a neighborhood nursery and playground, including a store."[65] A section of South Philadelphia was chosen for this exercise, and the partners rapidly designed the new facilities, including a small component of public housing. The nursery, combined with an activities center for teenagers, was to be a building of explosive constructivist geometry *(fig. 13)*. It was probably Stonorov's work, as he claimed for the whole commission.[66] But the underlying premise of the project, that old neighborhoods ought to be preserved and strengthened rather than demolished and rebuilt, seemed to reflect Kahn's experience with Old Swedes', where he had discovered to his surprise that residents did not want to leave their old houses. The booklet argued for "*conservation* and not outright destruction" and described new schools, shopping centers, and open spaces as the "protective armor" with which to preserve "worthwhile older residential neighborhoods."[67] Most importantly, it called for grass roots citizen participation in the planning process, with powerful neighborhood civic organizations to guide the professionals. The booklet was called *Why City Planning Is Your Responsibility.*

Announced on July 3, 1943, with a full-page advertisement in the *Saturday Evening Post* that invited readers to request copies, the booklet was an enormous success. It satisfied an evident hunger for information about post-war planning, and within a month Revere had distributed 110,000 copies.[68] This achievement seems to have whetted the architects' appetite for such work, and in the fall they joined a team of other Philadelphians in developing a cognate project, designing an educational model that could be used to show how another sample South Philadelphia neighborhood might supply itself with their "protective armor." Edmund Bacon spear-

13

13. *Axonometric of teen and nursery building, for* Why City Planning is Your Responsibility, *April–May 1943.*

GIVE EVERYBODY A
CHANCE TO SPEAK UP—
RESOLVED:
TO FORM
A NEIGHBORHOOD
PLANNING COUNCIL

14

15

14. *A neighborhood organizational meeting, illustration for* You and Your Neighborhood: A Primer for Neighborhood Planning, *1944.*
15. *Illustration for* You and Your Neighborhood: A Primer for Neighborhood Planning, *1944.*

headed this effort, and the model was built by the Architects' Workshop, set up by the local chapter of the American Institute of Architects in cooperation with a host of other Philadelphia groups. By means of replaceable parts, the model showed the effects of the kind of work described in the Revere booklet. Kahn and Stonorov demonstrated it before the planning commission, the Philadelphia AIA, the League of Women Voters, and many city and neighborhood civic organizations during 1944. Photographs of it were also included in that year's "Look at Your Neighborhood" show at the Museum of Modern Art.

The model, in turn, formed the basis of Stonorov's proposal to Revere Copper for a second, more ambitious pamphlet. This was under discussion in the fall of 1943, and in February 1944 Revere Copper agreed to pay $5,000 for a community planning "primer."[69] The new booklet, which appeared in October, was vastly more sophisticated than their first effort, with many more illustrations (most by Stonorov) and a lively scenario. *You and Your Neighborhood: A Primer for Neighborhood Planning* followed the story of a neighborhood improvement campaign from its beginnings in a single family's dinner-table conversation. It told of the creation of a "neighborhood planning council" and the development of a plan (embodied in the model), and it explained how such a plan could be presented to the city planning commission *(fig. 14)*. It went on to discuss how an entire city might be planned with concern for each of its neighborhoods, and it very elegantly explained how, in the accommodation of different activities and in the separation of incompatible uses, "the plan of a city is like the plan of a house" *(fig. 15)*. This notion of the indissoluble bond between architecture and city planning was to be a hallmark of Kahn's mature work.[70]

The second booklet was also hugely successful, with distribution continuing for years. Its engaging narrative structure seemed to suggest itself for dramatic presentation, and, indeed, Stonorov campaigned for it to be made into a film.[71] Kahn sketched out an elaborate outline for the script, entitled "Can Neighborhoods Exist?" but, while the Museum of Modern Art and Revere expressed interest, the project came to nothing.[72]

The commitment to an alliance between architecture and community activism that underlay the Revere project was more Stonorov's than Kahn's, but, like Stonorov's engagement in union affairs, it was a commitment that Kahn appreciated and participated in insofar as he was able. Indeed, Kahn himself was active during the immediate postwar period in a number of political and social service organizations, including the Independent Citizens Committee of the Arts, Sciences, and Professions, a group dedicated to a liberal agenda on atomic energy, race relations, full employment, and a national health and welfare program.[73] Kahn faithfully served as a member of the board for the Philadelphia division of the committee, to which he was elected in 1946, although stories later abounded about his unwillingness to do political work. In 1946 he was also named to the Building Bureau of the National Jewish Welfare Board, which was charged with overseeing the architectural component of Jewish social services, and throughout the late forties and fifties he was a member of the Welfare Board's executive committee.[74]

In matters closer to real architecture, Kahn brought out of the war years an even greater commitment to involvement. In April 1945 the Federal Public Housing Agency (successor to the USHA) established the Architectural Advisory Committee, with eight regional sub-units. Kahn was made a member of the committee and elected chairman of region two, which reached from New York to Washington. Here again he was conscientious, organizing a survey of existing housing projects with a view to improving standards for future construction.[75] Kahn continued to serve on the successor committee that advised the Public Housing Agency in the early fifties, and he joined the mass resignation from that committee in November 1951 to protest the deficiencies of the federal program.[76] In a related project, he chaired a committee of the Philadelphia AIA that prepared a report on housing in 1947, aimed at stimulating larger government involvement.[77]

Kahn's greatest political energy was devoted to the American Society of Planners and Architects.[78] He attended its preliminary meetings in 1944 at the Museum of Modern Art in New York and at Harvard, and he was also in attendance at the first general meeting on January 27, 1945, when George Howe gave the keynote address.[79] Modeled on CIAM (the Congrès Internationaux d'Architecture Moderne), the ASPA was set up to provide American modernists with an activist alternative to the AIA and to build stronger ties between city planning and architecture. The membership list brought together the radical forces in American architecture, from German émigrés to the homegrown ranks of housing advocates, and included Howe, Walter Gropius, and G. Holmes Perkins—modernists who were or would soon be in charge of the architecture programs at Yale, Harvard, and the University of Pennsylvania. Kahn was elected vice president for 1946 (Joseph Hudnut, the Harvard dean, was president), and in 1947 he served as president. Perkins was secretary/treasurer in both years. Kahn's involvement in the ASPA focused on the great debate over the selection of the site and the design of the headquarters building for the United Nations.[80] Jointly with the American branch of CIAM, the ASPA fought for an open and systematic planning process, but the possibility of this was forever lost in the turmoil that followed John D. Rockefeller's gift of the adopted site on the East River. Kahn, who had also participated in the campaign to bring the

16

17

16. Jewish Agency for Palestine Emergency Housing, Israel, 1949. Perspective (detail of sheet). Inscribed Lou K.
17. Memorial Playground, Western Home for Children, Philadelphia, Pa., 1946–47. Axonometric. Inscribed Louis I. Kahn '46.

UN to Philadelphia, must have felt doubly thwarted by this turn of events.

On September 20, 1947, during Kahn's presidency, the ASPA annual meeting was held in Philadelphia; the highlight of the event was a reception at Stonorov's house in the country. The organization virtually ceased to exist after that date, perhaps a sign that modern architecture in America no longer needed a special advocate.

The tangible, architectural corollary of these years of quite intense social and political involvement was a group of modest commissions, largely undertaken after the frenzy of war housing had diminished. Many were for labor unions, for which Stonorov's responsibility was great, although the first such work predated Stonorov's partnership: a modest row house remodeled as the headquarters of the Battery Workers Union in 1940. Other union projects included the interior renovation of a health clinic for the International Ladies Garment Workers Union (1943–45), the remodeling of the headquarters of the shipyard workers union in Camden, New Jersey (1943–45, largely by Stonorov), an unbuilt headquarters building for the Moving Picture Operators' Union (1944), a rustic lodge for the Philadelphia members of the ILGWU at a camp in the Pocono Mountains (1945–47), two dormitories at a union-sponsored children's camp in Bucks County, Pennsylvania (1945–47) and another clinic renovation, for the American Federation of Labor at St. Luke's Hospital (1950–51). The client liaison for many of these commissions was garment workers leader Isidor Melamed, who would later hire Kahn to build his first prominent building in Philadelphia, the AFL Medical Services Building on Vine Street (1954–57).

Another small group of postwar commissions sprang from Kahn's involvement with Jewish social service activities. These included the Jewish Community Center of New

Haven (discussed in 1948 and designed in 1950) and a place on the team that went to Palestine in 1949 to advise on emergency housing. The trip to Israel gave Kahn a chance to revisit Paris, and it also enabled him to return to the problems of prefabrication, an area of concern that he had ceded to Stonorov since their partnership. For Israel he proposed houses assembled from parabolic concrete sections, and, with the overconfidence that was to characterize many of his large, later projects, he exhorted the new settlers to "Turn the Building Emergency into a Major Industry" and make their homeland "the center of Building Fabrication of the Near East" *(fig. 16)*.[81]

Of all these idealistic projects, the one that perhaps best captures the hopeful spirit of the time was the playground Kahn designed and built in 1946–47 for the Western Home for Children, an orphanage *(fig. 17)*. It was located just around the corner from the Graphic Sketch Club, where he had spent so many boyhood Saturdays. His design possessed all the happy clichés of the era: its play yard perimeter was defined by jaunty angles and surrounded by a curving walkway, there was an outdoor hearth sheltered by a horizontal roof slab, and in the rear corner stood a biomorphic concrete "fun sculpture" whose shapes were echoed in a mural on the wall of an adjacent building. It must have seemed perfectly complete when the pleased sponsor told Kahn that he had seen "little Brownie Scouts hopping gleefully around your fireplace."[82] In those years Kahn was himself the new father of a daughter, Sue Ann.

In addition to doing community and socially oriented work during the mid-forties, like many American architects Stonorov and Kahn joined in the discussion of the future of more mundane architectural forms—the miscellany of useful buildings that would shape postwar America. They produced imaginary designs for a number of these pragmatic types, many

of which were sponsored by the architectural magazines, hungry to fill pages during the war and, like everyone, eager to look beyond its privations.

Architectural Forum, which had followed Kahn's housing work closely, invited him to submit a design for their "New House 194X" feature, to appear in September 1942. With its announced emphasis on prefabrication, this project interested both Stonorov and Kahn, but work on Willow Run kept them from meeting the deadline.[83] They were luckier in making their submission for another "194X" project, sponsored by *Forum* in 1943, when they were among those invited to design an array of buildings for a medium-size postwar city. Their assignment was a 200-room hotel, for which they proposed a 13-story slab with aluminum sunshades, marble cladding, and "plastic exterior veneer" on all other surfaces.[84] Inside, everything was also up-to-date: the public spaces were full of curved and diagonal walls, placed with studied casualness, and the guest rooms were equipped with molded plywood furniture and smoothly curved, prefabricated bathroom units. This was also the sleek vocabulary for the model glass-fronted furniture and shoe stores they designed in 1944 for a Pittsburgh Plate Glass publication.[85]

The largest concentration of this kind of speculative architecture was in the design of houses—the postwar home of the GI—for which the need was reckoned to be enormous. Stonorov and Kahn applied themselves assiduously to the "Design for Post-war Living" competition, sponsored by *California Arts and Architecture* in the spring of 1943. Their unsuccessful entry was a single-family version of the ground-freed house, developed directly out of their war housing work.[86]

Much more ambitious was the Parasol House system they devised in 1944 at the request of Hans Knoll, the furniture manufacturer. He invited them and six other architecture firms to

18

19

18. Parasol House, 1944. Bird's-eye perspective.
19. Parasol House, Plan.
20. Pennsylvania Solar House, 1945–47.
Perspective from southwest. Inscribed
Louis Kahn '46.

20

join a "planning unit," set up to study the needs of contemporary households and devise new "equipment for living"—essentially furniture and appliances—for his clients to manufacture.[87] These were then to be placed within an ideal architectural environment. Kahn and Stonorov submitted drawings for molded plywood cabinets, a prefabricated stair, and bathroom and kitchen units—including the Thermostore refrigerator they had already mocked up for Gimbels department store in 1942–43.[88] But they put most of their effort into the architecture. Their proposed houses were defined by a roofing system that consisted of square slabs (apparently of steel construction) held aloft on slender columns. These parasol-like units were then stacked to make two-story houses or assembled to form the sheltering canopy for great strips of one-story row houses (fig. 18). Beneath this covering, with its insistent rational gridding, non-load-bearing walls were placed with the contrasting, somewhat cranky angularity that Kahn seems to have adopted as a badge of his freedom from the limitations of war housing (fig. 19). While many precedents for this form of free planning existed, including Le Corbusier's Dom-ino-type buildings and Mies van der Rohe's courtyard houses, and while the umbrella roof was predated by Wright's lily-pad columns for the Johnson Wax Administration Building, the synthesis of these elements was fresh and unencumbered by any obvious sense of quotation. Unfortunately, the architects' ambitions outpaced Knoll's, and they were not asked to develop any of their ideas further.

The last of these postwar-oriented house projects was commissioned in August 1945, ten days after VJ Day, when Stonorov was informed by Libbey-Owens-Ford Glass Company that he had been selected by a jury to design the Pennsylvania house in their forty-eight-state solar house program.[89] The design work was carried out by Kahn, assisted by Anne Griswold Tyng (b. 1920), a recent graduate of Gropius's Harvard program who had just joined the office.[90] Most of the other designers produced conventional houses with increased glazing toward the south, but Kahn and Tyng took the solar heating issue more seriously. During the spring of 1946 they created a trapezoidal house plan that carefully oriented three of its facades to face the sun in its arcing passage across the sky (fig. 20).

More significant probably than the solar house design itself was the destructive effect it had on the partnership of Stonorov and Kahn. Libbey-Owens-Ford had commissioned the house for use in a book, and in January 1947, with publication approaching, they telegrammed Stonorov to inquire how the design should be credited. His reply, requesting that the byline "carry both our names," seems to have roused Kahn to anger. But while the answer that Kahn rushed off began "I do not agree with the general tone of Mr. Stonorov's telegram," he concluded by apparently asking for the same thing: shared credit.[91] In the end, the Pennsylvania solar house was published as the work of "Oscar Stonorov and Louis I. Kahn Architects," but the nasty tone of this now obscure argument reflected the rift that had opened between two contrary personalities.[92] With little housing work being done, the teaming of Stonorov's political acumen with Kahn's increasingly independent design sense had less to recommend it. They agreed to split amicably, dividing up the small number of commissions then under way, and on March 4, 1947, the movers transported Stonorov's papers to the Broad Street Station Building while Kahn moved to 1728 Spruce Street, a town house where George Howe also kept a small office.[93] Kahn, just turned forty-six, was now on his own.

The House

For the next few years the backbone of Kahn's work was single-family houses, which in some ways fulfilled the promise of the "194X" pro-

21

21. *Oser house, Elkins Park, Pa., 1940–42. Front facade, 1990.*

jects. They also reestablished the trajectory he had set for his practice on the eve of the war, when he had built a small house for his longtime friend Jesse Oser and his wife, Ruth *(fig. 21).*[94] While the Oser house was one of Kahn's first independent commissions, it was a confident design, reflecting the extensive experience he had amassed since graduating from architecture school in 1924. It is also clear that in 1940, when the Oser house was designed, Kahn had come under the powerful influence of George Howe, whom he was about to join in a partnership to build wartime public housing. Although the Osers had limited funds, Kahn worked wonders to imitate for them the effect of Howe's great house of 1932–34 for William Stix Wasserman, which had been given the evocative modernist name Square Shadows. Kahn's homage to Howe can be seen in the modern steel casements—tugged to the corners of the facades—the projecting horizontal roof slabs, the staggering of exterior wall planes (achieved despite the compact plan required by the budget), and the carefully contrived juxtaposition of these avant-garde details with the traditional building stone of the region. Inside, beige woodwork of tough gum wood joined sleek built-in furniture in a modernist composition around the hearth, but the fireplace itself was faced with irregular Mercer tiles that bespoke contrasting, Arts and Crafts ideals. This complexity of meaning was characteristic of Howe and much of the best American architecture in this transitional period.

The Oser house was already under construction at the time of Pearl Harbor, and it was completed in 1942 despite wartime shortages. Not so lucky were Louis Broudo and his wife, friends of Esther Kahn's parents, for whom Kahn designed a similar small house for a lot close to the Osers'. Contract drawings and specifications for their house, with its more conservative peaked roof, were just being finished in December 1941 at the time of the Japanese surprise attack, and the project had to be abandoned.[95]

Aside from some renovations, which Kahn disliked cordially, and the imaginary projects sponsored by magazines and manufacturers, there was no more single-family house work for the duration of the war, and wartime, multi-unit housing did not offer the artistic opportunities of even the modest Oser house. But after VJ Day business slowly began to pick up as predicted. First to reach the office, in 1945–46, were several ambitious additions to suburban houses. Stonorov and Kahn added a two-story wing—based on the ground-freed model—to B. A. Bernard's handsome house overlooking French Creek in Kimberton, Bucks County. (This job probably came to them through Stonorov, whose own house was nearby.) They also designed a new, one-story wing for the Ardmore house owned by Lea and Arthur Finkelstein, both radiologists, whom Esther had met fifteen years earlier in her work at the University of Pennsylvania. The Finkelsteins had become close family friends, and, along with Jacob and "Kit" Sherman, the Finkelsteins and Kahns had vacationed together for many summers, including sojourns to Nova Scotia and more sedentary holidays in the house rented by the Finkelsteins at Lake Placid. Kahn could rarely take more than two weeks away from the office, but Esther usually spent a month with the two other couples. The Finkelstein project was the subject of long discussion, including a major redesign in 1948, but nothing was built. The same fate befell the largest of these first postwar house jobs, an enormous one-story wing containing a new dining room, playroom, guest suite, garage, and horse stall that Kahn designed in 1946 for the Baltimore house of Mr. and Mrs. Arthur Hooper. Kahn arranged the new rooms to shelter the backyard within an architectural ell, a formula that Frank Lloyd Wright had established in his house for Herbert Jacobs (Westmoreland, Wisconsin, 1937) and that

Richard Neutra also adopted in his postwar work.

This somewhat desultory rate of work accelerated rapidly after Stonorov and Kahn ended their partnership early in 1947. Over the next eighteen months, Kahn was engaged in the design of five substantial houses, three of which were built. His office staff during this period was very small, with David Wisdom and Anne Tyng being his principal assistants, and the work was shaped by Kahn's close artistic and growing romantic ties with Tyng.

The first of these houses to reach the design phase was a commission from Harry and Emily Ehle. It was brought to Kahn by Abel Sörensen, who had worked in the office during the Kahn-Stonorov partnership and joined the headquarters planning staff of the United Nations on Long Island after the war. In May 1947 Sörensen sketched the plan of an ell-shaped house, wrapped around a large patio, for the Ehles' site in suburban Haverford. This he sent to Kahn, who studied the elevations and imparted more energy to the rather conventional scheme during June, raising a butterfly-roof clerestory over the living room and establishing a vigorous interplay between masonry and wood-framed wall elements.[96] The result was too expensive for the Ehles, and during the first months of 1948 the Kahn office eliminated the garage and maid's quarters and reduced the size of living room. But this, too, exceeded the budget of the client.

In early 1948, just as the second version of the Ehle house was being worked out, Kahn and Tyng were launching two other house projects. Carried through to quick completion, these departed decisively from the rather lackluster Ehle design, and they were full of the evidence of the two architects' sometimes diverging ideas. The first was a house for Dr. and Mrs. Philip Roche on a site just beyond the northwest boundary of Philadelphia in Conshohocken.[97] The Roche plan pulled all of the living quarters together into a compact rectangle, zoned for sleeping at one end and daytime functions at the other. Tyng was devoted to the planning discipline that she had seen at Harvard, and she seems to have contributed the defining 3'9" modularity of the design, while Kahn's diagonalism reemerged in the broken-backed mountain of chimney that erupted obliquely through the living room wall.[98]

The balance of ideas shifted more decisively toward Tyng in the almost exactly contemporary Weiss house, located further west of Philadelphia near Norristown.[99] Its more sharply bifurcated plan, worked out during the first half of 1948, bore the unmistakable impress of the "binuclear" division between daytime and nighttime activity that was associated with the work of Marcel Breuer, one of the leading members of the Harvard faculty during Tyng's study there *(fig. 22)*. The sweeping reverse-pitch roof was also Breueresque, although Kahn had been experimenting with this form throughout the decade *(fig. 23)*. Distinctively Kahn's own was the ingenious system of double-hung windows and shutters, which could be slid up and down to vary the lighting, privacy, and view. He had already sketched a related system of wall panels of varied opacity for the Parasol House, but now it was worked out in the complex detail needed to make it weatherproof and buildable. These designs marked the beginning of his decades-long experiment with the manipulation of natural light.

Kahn insisted that the Weiss house, with its bold use of local stonework and untinted wood, was "contemporary but does not break with tradition."[100] Citing the example of Pennsylvania barns in support of this position, he argued that "the continuity between what was valid yesterday and what is valid today is considered by every thinking architect." Many of his contemporaries did cast an admiring glance toward the past, but for Kahn this was to become an increasingly serious endeavor.

When he and Tyng returned to the Weiss house some years after it was completed to paint a mural next to the craggy stone fireplace, they borrowed many of their motifs from the simple architecture of the Pennsylvania countryside. But also evident in the mural were the profiles of the Egyptian pyramids Kahn had visited early in 1951. He had begun to see that great architecture had to be of its own time and imbedded in the deeper historical stratigraphy of human achievement as well.

Kahn designed two other houses in the late forties, beginning both early in the summer of 1948, just after the plan of the Weiss house had been finalized. These houses showed a stronger assertion of Kahn's exuberance. The unbuilt project for Dr. and Mrs. Winslow Tompkins pushed its living room and dining room to the very brink of a precipitous, wooded slope that descended to Wissahickon Creek in Philadelphia. The dining room was cradled in a massive serpentine masonry wall, and the sleeping quarters, conceived as one block in the first plans of June, were split into two staggered units when a final set of finished drawings was made in September.[101]

At the same time, Kahn and Tyng were at work on a house in suburban Wynnewood for Samuel Genel, who had once dated Esther Kahn and whose sister was Esther's classmate and a member of her sorority at the University of Pennsylvania.[102] The first plan in the summer of 1948 was a squat tee, with its stem pointed down a gentle hill that allowed the split-level placement of the garage underneath the bedrooms.[103] As developed during the first months of 1949, the plan grew into a lopsided binuclear arrangement with the garage relocated downhill in a structure of its own and replaced on the ground floor of the main house by a playroom. An energetic interplay of ramping roof surfaces was introduced at this point, amplifying the effect of the terrain *(fig. 24)*. The most striking component of the plan was the ell of masonry that rose between the living room and the front hall, framing the fireplace. This piece of elemental composition could also be read in elevation, where the marble-clad chimneystack rose in calculated juxtaposition to the brick and wood of the house *(fig. 25)* Even the exterior masonry was now executed in roughly squared stone, answering to a new sense of order. Kahn's interest in such abstraction can be attributed in part to Anne Tyng's influence and also to the studio work he had seen at Yale, where he had begun teaching in 1947.

The jostling of Kahn's freer planning against Tyng's sense of geometrical order continued in the two buildings he designed and built for the Philadelphia Psychiatric Hospital in 1948–52.[104] This was a project with a long prehistory. In 1937–38 he had studied the possibility of altering several buildings on a site in West Philadelphia for the hospital. In 1939 he had designed an entirely new building for a different site, only to have the client reject his work because of its cost and turn to another architect, with whom the project went ahead.[105] And in 1944–46 he and Stonorov had designed a large addition to that small building.

This third design, initiated during the final year of the war and the first year of peace, paved the way for the work done in 1948–52, but it got off to a slow start. The client was not sure of the program, and Kahn and Stonorov were beginning to be busy with small residential jobs, all of which was frustrating to Isadore Rosenfield, the hospital design consultant who teamed with them for this and the final project. Kahn tried to make light of their harried state in a letter to Rosenfield: "We are going crazy in our own little architectural hospital, doctoring up old buildings, handling our own psychiatric clients, appeasing our erratic and temperamental personnel. It all adds up to fine experience which can be applied to the hospital, so really no time is lost."[106] Rosenfield was

22

23

22. *Weiss house, East Norriton Township, Pa., 1947–50. Plan, ca. 1948.*
23. *Weiss house. Front facade, ca. 1950.*

unamused, and throughout their relationship he continued to criticize what he called their "strange and unprofessional conduct."[107]

The design that was worked out during the spring of 1946 provided a vast new ward block, a semidetached convalescent pavilion, and a hammerhead-shaped entrance pavilion with state-of-the-art insulin and electric-shock treatment rooms on its top floor *(figs. 26, 27)*. In the oblique placement of building units across the site, the hospital recalled Kahn's wartime community centers, and it also seemed to reflect the calculated casualness with which the slabs of Alvar Aalto's famous tuberculosis sanatorium were clustered on their wooded hilltop at Paimio, Finland (1928–33). The sanatorium had been included in the 1938 Aalto show at the Museum of Modern Art, and there Kahn also seems to have encountered the auditorium of Aalto's Viipuri library, which he used as an example of the ideal neighborhood meeting room in the second Revere Copper pamphlet. But regardless of its sophistication, this design, too, was rejected because of its cost.

The Philadelphia Psychiatric Hospital was a member of the Federation of Jewish Charities, and Kahn's long work on the commission, despite its rocky moments, helped to cement his relationship in those circles. He also established a warm if combative friendship with Samuel Radbill, the president of the hospital board. During the time of the 1944–46 design, Kahn was simultaneously at work on alterations to the offices of the Radbill Oil Company and overseeing the installation of air-conditioning and the modernization of a bathroom in Radbill's house in Merion. The latter was subject to delays due to Kahn's increasingly famous perfectionism and procrastination, and Radbill, in frustration, canceled part of the work.[108]

The underlying strength of Kahn's relationship with his clients was sufficient for him to be called back in 1948 to direct the work that was finally executed for the hospital. Designed in 1949, this scheme consisted of a three-story, crook-necked block, attached at its bend to the existing hospital to create a Y-shaped building, and a separate, one-story auditorium and occupational therapy building. The new entrance facade of the Radbill Building, as the larger unit was named, was a serene modular composition, rendered in slate and stratified by horizontal sunshades *(fig. 28)*. These shades were regularly perforated by what appeared to be ordinary flue tiles, but the terra-cotta inserts were actually custom-made. The entrance itself was sheltered by a triangular canopy—a piece of abstract collage suggested by Anne Tyng.[109] The occupational therapy building, named the Pincus Building in honor of a major donor, was a simple structure whose flat roof was supported on exposed steel trusses. It employed a double-hung window/shutter system like that just devised for the Weiss house, allowing the careful adjustment of lighting and privacy.

Monumentality

Although the psychiatric hospital was Kahn's largest building to date and one with an important public face, it was essentially private and residential in character. It did not provide a testing ground for a final facet of the future-oriented speculation that had occupied him during the war. This was the question of how modern architecture, whose accomplishments in the prewar period had been concentrated in housing projects and houses, could embody public or institutional values and advance the larger aspirations of a human community. In the vocabulary of the day, how could modern architecture achieve "monumentality"?

Kahn's own work was a mirror of the problem he perceived. Since working for Cret and Zantzinger—and since giving up their modernized classical vocabulary—Kahn had devoted

24

25

26

27

28

24. *Genel house, Wynnewood, Pa., 1948–51. East elevation, early 1949. Inscribed Lou K.*

25. *Genel house. Entrance hall with back of fireplace, ca. 1951.*

26. *New wing, Philadelphia Psychiatric Hospital, Philadelphia, Pa., 1944–46. Perspective. Inscribed Louis I. Kahn '46.*

27. *New wing, Philadelphia Psychiatric Hospital. Second-floor plan.*

28. *Radbill Building, Philadelphia Psychiatric Hospital. Front facade, ca. 1954 (entrance canopy now removed).*

virtually all his energy to housing. He had spent years making, or trying to make, functional residential architecture, and, like George Howe, he had come to know the artistic limitations of functionalism, and to see that few transcendent ideas could be expressed with that vocabulary. Accordingly, as the end of the war approached and Kahn looked ahead to projects such as the United Nations that would demand distinctive treatment, he began to wonder aloud about the possibility of redirecting the course of modern architecture. This was a question that arose simultaneously in the minds of many during the war, and it had reached a kind of intellectual flash point by 1943, when the architectural historian Sigfried Giedion (whose *Space, Time and Architecture* had appeared in 1941), the architect José Luis Sert, and the painter Fernand Léger met in New York. They had each been invited to contribute to a publication planned by the pioneering American Abstract Artists, and they agreed that they should jointly address the fact that modernists in all media had achieved little outside the realm of domestic architecture and private art. What was needed was a "new monumentality," they decided, one capable of satisfying "the eternal demand of the people for translation of their collective force into symbols."[110] Giedion became a tireless champion of this idea, speaking on the subject on both sides of the Atlantic, and his 1946 lecture in London sparked the *Architectural Review* to take up the issue, eventually hosting a symposium and becoming one of the staunchest advocates of this redirection of modern design.[111]

When the planned publication by the American Abstract Artists failed to materialize, Giedion placed his essay in a volume assembled by Paul Zucker in 1944. This had an entire section called "The Problem of a New Monumentality," and it was here that Kahn also published his first extended theoretical paper, titled simply "Monumentality."

Giedion and Kahn approached the question

from opposite points of view. Whereas the Swiss scholar argued that the search for "emotional expression" demanded a recognition that "architecture is not exclusively concerned with construction," Kahn began by proclaiming that "monumentality in architecture may be defined as a quality, a spiritual quality inherent in a structure which conveys the feeling of its eternity, that it cannot be added to or changed."[112] Moreover, while Giedion lamented that the abusive eclecticism of the nineteenth century had poisoned the well of historical examples for the modern architect, Kahn forthrightly accepted the usefulness of history. The "monumental structures of the past," he wrote, "have the common characteristics of greatness upon which the buildings of our future must, in one sense or another, rely."[113]

In his twin fascination with structure and history, Kahn was returning to principles that he had been taught at the University of Pennsylvania. His teacher Paul Cret's philosophy had been developed on the side of the École des Beaux-Arts that favored the strong French tradition of structural rationalism, and Cret had also believed unswervingly that modern architecture could be made without rejecting the past.

What Kahn now proposed was that the starting point for monumental architecture could be discovered in history and then made modern by the application of new technology. In particular, he argued that the "spiritual quality" needed by monumental buildings was to be sought first in the "structural skeleton" of the Gothic and in the Roman dome, vault, and arch—forms whose influence had "etched itself in deep furrows across the pages of architectural history."[114] These forms were now to be modernized by the introduction of the steel frame. Kahn, who had taken a course in steel ship design in 1942, observed that "Beauvais cathedral needed the steel we have," and he recommended special attention to the use of welded tubular construction, curved to imitate the "graceful forms which the stress diagrams indicated."[115] Thus would "the ribs, vaults, domes, buttresses come back again only to enclose space in a more generous, far simpler way and in the hands of our present masters of building in a more emotionally stirring way."[116] Kahn predicted that new materials would lead the modern architect to "the adventures of unexplored places."[117]

Despite the talk of Roman architecture, Kahn's recipe produced a kind of modernized Gothic. This was clearly prefigured by the work of Eugène-Emmanuel Viollet-le-Duc, whose Gothic rationalism had been admired in Cret's circle at the École, and it was also related to the analytical drawings of structure published by Auguste Choisy, another favorite of Cret's. Kahn used Choisy's analysis of Beauvais as an illustration of his argument. Supporting Kahn's text were his own sketches for an urban cultural center, with a theater and a museum framed by the kind of sinuous steel skeleton he recommended (fig. 29).

This ferrous medievalism seems unrelated to the great masonry buildings, with their classical overtones, that were to dominate Kahn's mature work. But by then he had been diverted: the steel shortage of the postwar period helped to turn him back toward brick and concrete, and during that time he also rediscovered the power of ancient Rome at first hand. But although transmogrified, history and structure were to remain Kahn's watchwords.

The years immediately after the end of the war offered a few important opportunities for Kahn to develop this new vocabulary for monumental architecture. Together with Stonorov, he was appointed in October 1946 to the team of architects charged by the City Planning Commission with the creation of a master plan for the vast tract of central Philadelphia called the "Triangle." This was bordered on its three sides by the infamous "Chinese Wall" (the soon-to-be-demolished viaduct that had brought the Pennsylvania Railroad into the very heart of the city), the Schuylkill River (the western boundary of Center City), and Philadelphia's City Beautiful boulevard, the Benjamin Franklin Parkway. Kahn provided the planning team with illustrations for their report, issued in January 1948, and he made some of the drawings that guided the builders of an enormous model of Philadelphia that was created for the "Better Philadelphia" exhibition at Gimbels Department Store in October 1947. The model contrasted conditions before and after the implementation of the master plan by means of large panels that flipped over dramatically to reveal the city of the future (fig. 30). It was the centerpiece of the exhibition and exceedingly popular, and the fact that Stonorov (who had already done a good deal of remodeling work for Gimbels) shunted Kahn aside in order to coordinate the show himself seems to have contributed to their falling-out. Most of the buildings drawn by Kahn—office blocks, apartment buildings, and low-rise cultural institutions alike—took the by then familiar form of the Le Corbusian prism supported on pilotis (fig. 31). There was, however, some "monumental" use of steel in a sports arena suspended beneath four parabolic arches, and several large pieces of biomorphic sculpture embodied the "graceful forms" Kahn had recommended in 1944.

A simultaneous project with explicitly monumental content was Kahn's entry in the first phase of the Jefferson National Expansion Memorial competition, which led ultimately to the construction of Eero Saarinen's "Gateway Arch" in St. Louis. Kahn's design of 1947 would have covered both banks of the Mississippi River with a mixture of horizontally and vertically oriented slabs set atop an elaborate system of railroad and highway connections. There was to be more of the steel architecture foreseen in 1944, most notably a vast open-plan Laboratory of Education containing exhibition galleries and a theater and covered by a raking steel-frame roof. Kahn was not, however, selected to continue

29

30

31

29. *Model civic center illustrating "monumentality," 1944.*
30. *Philadelphia model from the exhibition "A Better Philadelphia Within Your Grasp," Gimbels Department Store, Philadelphia, Pa., 1947.*
31. *Triangle Redevelopment Project, Philadelphia, Pa., 1946–48. Bird's-eye perspective of Schuylkill River apartment buildings. Inscribed Louis I. Kahn, '47.*
32. *Christmas card showing Kahn at Yale, by David Wisdom, 1947.*

in the second phase of the competition, and this was a keen disappointment. Luckily, he began teaching at Yale in the same week the results were announced.

Yale

Kahn had actually been teaching for years; the members of the Architectural Research Group had hung on his words, and the large staffs assembled for Jersey Homesteads and the wartime housing projects had been treated like the malleable young artists they were. Before the fall of 1947, however, Kahn's natural talents as a teacher had not been formally employed. He had been invited a year earlier to teach at Harvard, then by far the leading school for modern architecture, but he turned down the appointment, largely because he could not bear to leave his native Philadelphia.[118] Yale was a different matter. Kahn was to be one of the visiting critics—they were the mainstay of studio instruction at Yale—with responsibilities limited to two days a week. That meant he could commute to New Haven by train. He accepted, and Yale became the forum for the ideas he had not yet been able to convert into real architecture.

Yale was an exciting place in 1947 (fig. 32).[119] A new dean, Charles Sawyer, had just come on board in the summer before Kahn began to teach, and together with architecture chairman Harold Hauf he was working to consolidate the decisive turn toward modernism that had begun under Wallace Harrison, the chief critic in 1939–42. This was now continued under Edward Durell Stone, who held the same position. Kahn undoubtedly came to their attention because of his well-published war work and his highly visible role in the American Society of Planners and Architects. At the same time, Sawyer had offered an associate deanship to Holmes Perkins, another prominent member of the ASPA, but Perkins had elected to remain with Gropius at Harvard.[120]

Kahn's appointment at Yale in the fall semester of 1947 was moved up because of the delayed arrival of another visiting critic, Oscar Niemeyer, the already renowned Brazilian disciple of Le Corbusier whose Communist sympathies had aroused the suspicions of immigration officials. Like most practicing architects who are part-time teachers, Kahn designed many of his studio problems to mirror his own work, and during his first stint he assigned a suburban shopping center like the one for which he was serving as a consultant in Greenbelt, Maryland.[121] Despite its relevance to postwar conditions, this was probably not a very challenging project for the Yale students, but Kahn's talent for teaching was evident, and Hauf asked him to return. He taught in both semesters in 1948–49 and took over the duties of coordinating the visiting critics from Stone. Among the visitors that year were Hugh Stubbins, Pietro Belluschi, and Eero Saarinen.

In his second year at Yale, Kahn was also put in charge of realizing Sawyer's favorite educational innovation, the "collaborative problem," for which student architects, painters, and sculptors were assembled into teams. Collaboration per se was also one of the hallmarks of Gropius's teaching at Harvard, where he organized his own private practice as The Architects' Collaborative in 1946. But teaming up with painters and sculptors was not usually attempted at Harvard, which had no real fine arts program. While such cooperation was achieved at specialized art schools like Cranbrook, the Yale system was rightly recognized as distinctive among university programs.

In the fall of 1948 the collaborative problem was the design of an exhibition hall for an imagined headquarters of UNESCO, the United Nations Educational, Scientific, and Cultural Organization.[122] Kahn located the project in Philadelphia's Fairmount Park, on the site he had promoted for the entire UN two years earlier. (During the same semester he presented an advanced design problem that was even more directly related to his own practice—a suburban residence modeled, down to the client biography and street address, on the Genel house.[123]) Leaving the creation of a huge UNESCO mural to the painters and the treatment of "the vertical circulation element" (i.e., stairway) to the sculptors, he made the team architects responsible for the master plan and for engineering the vast exhibition hall—200,000 unobstructed square feet beneath an 80-foot ceiling. Here was a chance to see his notions of monumentality fulfilled, for he specified that the skeleton frame of the exhibition hall be left undisguised. Several of the teams devised structures suspended on steel cable, while others cantilevered stupendous trusses over the hall. The project attracted national attention.[124]

Kahn's teaching in the spring semester of 1949 was interrupted by his trip to Israel. But his administrative involvement increased, and he championed the appointment of his old friend George Howe as chairman of architecture when Hauf resigned to become editor of *Architectural Record*. After Sawyer wired Yale's offer to Howe, who was then newly in love and very comfortably ensconced as resident architect at the American Academy in Rome, Kahn wrote his own powerful letter. "George, the school needs your personality and your kind of leadership," Kahn entreated, and he described the attractions of Yale:

> The school is progressive, and in the state of constant change and development. There is no dictation from above. Everyone seems to like the results although there is no particular order or ideology followed. You can make the school what you want it to be and Ed [Stone] Chris [Tunnard, head of city planning] and I who know you best feel that you can give it the guidance which would continue the existing free spirit and better the results, thru your experience culture and wisdom.[125]

Howe accepted, agreeing to take up his new responsibilities in January 1950.

At the same time, Kahn and Sawyer convinced the former Bauhaus painter Joseph Albers (1888–1976), who had transplanted many Bauhaus ideals to America, to come as a visiting critic for the collaborative project in the fall of 1949. This time the program was an "Idea Center for Plastics," intended to serve the design staff of a manufacturer.[126] Albers liked Yale, and Sawyer, strongly supported by Kahn, liked him. They arranged for him to join the faculty permanently in the fall of 1950 as head of a newly organized department of design, subsuming and radicalizing the old programs in painting and sculpture. Although Sawyer did not entirely succeed in creating what he had hoped would be a broad collaborative environment, framed by architecture under Howe and design under Albers, the almost simultaneous appointment of two artists of such high caliber moved Yale to the forefront of American art.

Albers had commenced the painstaking chromatic investigations of his "Homage to the Square" series just before his first teaching at Yale, and Kahn was evidently impressed. The painter's work may have helped to spark his own exploration of the underlying order of things, and Albers' aphoristic poems may also have shaped Kahn's later word compositions. In a typical poem Albers proclaimed:

> To design is
> to plan and to organize, to order, to relate and
> to control
> in short it embraces
> all means opposing disorder and accident.
> Therefore it signifies
> a human need
> and qualifies man's
> thinking and doing.[127]

When Kahn was designing a wall hanging for his First Unitarian Church in Rochester, New York, he turned to Albers's wife, Anni, a famous weaver, for its execution.

Architecture students did not study directly

with Albers, however. For first- and second-year students (who were in the third and fourth years of the combined B.A./B.Arch. program), Howe created a separate basic design studio, headed by the almost mystical Eugene Nalle. Nalle's emphasis on personal discovery and on sensitivity to materials recalled the teaching of Johannes Itten during the earliest years of the Weimar Bauhaus. In the first volume of *Perspecta*, the Yale-based journal that Howe launched in 1952 as a vehicle for architectural debate, Nalle explicated his philosophy in typically opaque terms:

> "Whole Design" in architecture, with its irrational complex yet deep roots of personal discipline, demands an extremely broad and viable outlook. It must encompass intuitive sensibility to the immediate situation observable in short range fact; this must be combined with a "moral behavior" (in the largest sense of the word) beyond egocentric sentimentality which demands a continual intellectual wrestling with theory—a philosophic study of relationships between the inner and outer worlds of reality.[128]

Kahn, who had his own streak of obscurantism, tolerated Nalle, but he concentrated with Howe on overseeing the advanced end of the program, where the established Yale model of visiting critics was continued. Philip Johnson and Buckminster Fuller were prominent visitors, and they were joined on juries by members of an art history faculty, notably Vincent Scully, who took their studio obligations seriously. Scully's passion for making students see the patterns of intention within the art of all periods served as a refreshing antidote to the kind of historical oblivion in which many young architects believed that modern architecture had to be created. This, of course, was entirely in keeping with Kahn's conviction about the necessity of history, and he and Scully became good friends. Yale students, who had this panoply of ideas before them, were watching the beginning of a new era in architecture.

Howe faced mandatory retirement at the end of the fall semester of 1953, and he may have considered Kahn as his own successor, but the chairmanship passed instead to Pat Schweikher, who had been an effective visiting critic. Schweikher lacked Howe's ability to keep a stable of visitors happy while ensuring that Nalle was properly appreciated by his sometimes jaundiced students. Kahn was uncomfortable under the new regime, and he quit in the spring of 1955. The architectural accrediting board smelled the blood of faculty dissension in the water, and it threatened loss of accreditation and put Yale on probation in 1955–56. Schweikher and Sawyer were compelled to resign.

Scully was among those who convinced Yale president Whitney Griswold to invite Kahn to become chairman in 1956, and Kahn was sorely tempted.[129] But he recognized that it was a decision that would keep him from at last expanding his architectural practice to match the size of his reputation as a teacher. Although he returned as a visiting critic in Yale's new master's program in the late fifties, he turned down the chairmanship. In a sense it was Yale itself that convinced him to reject the very position that it now offered, for the university had also given him the first great commission of his career, the Yale Art Gallery extension (1951–53). The enthusiasm for his built work that had begun with the completion of the new gallery gave Kahn the courage to say no.

D.B.B.

Chapter 2

The Mind Opens To Realizations

Conceiving a New Architecture, 1951–61

33

33. Pyramids, Giza, January 1951.

When Louis Kahn received the commission for the Yale Art Gallery in 1951, he was a well-respected but hardly famous architect. Few besides those who worked with him sensed the potential that would, within the decade, lead to international acclaim. Yet in the relatively brief span of ten years following the Yale commission, he evolved an original vocabulary that responded to concerns being voiced by an entire generation of architects. And in the years remaining before his death in March 1974, he worked with that vocabulary to reshape architecture.

By no means was Kahn alone among his contemporaries in seeking change. But like Frank Lloyd Wright before him, he seemed to be the first of his generation to express through actual building what others had been able to suggest only through words, and Kahn, too, thus began a new architecture. In his persevering search for the very beginnings of architectural form, Kahn readily sacrificed visual charm. Considerations of site and materials—issues of primary importance to Wright—would for Kahn become secondary, although he used materials with an equal appreciation of their inherent qualities. He was less daring in his use of exotic geometries and innovative structure than Wright; in his determination to achieve the timelessness of great architecture, discovery became more important than invention. Whether the architecture that Kahn began should continue to be called modern or should be characterized by some other term would in itself have seemed of little consequence to Kahn—indeed, he once claimed, "there is no such thing as modern since everything belongs to architecture that exists in architecture and has its force"[1]—yet he wrought significant change of the sort that readily leads to such speculation.

When word came of the Yale commission, Kahn was a Resident of the American Academy in Rome, where, like so many architects before him, he no doubt welcomed the respite from practice to reconsider the direction of his work. His stay there was relatively brief—only three months—yet it seemed to have effect, for afterward the direction of his work began its decisive change. Clearly the physical presence of Rome, which offered fundamental lessons of history, was overwhelming. Shortly after his arrival he wrote to his office colleagues in Philadelphia:

> I firmly realize that the architecture in Italy will remain as the inspirational source of the works of the future. Those who don't see it that way ought to look again. Our stuff looks tinny compared to it and all the pure forms have been tried in all variations. What is necessary is the interpretation of the architecture of Italy as it relates to our knowledge of building and needs. I care little for the restorations (that kind of interpretation) but I see great personal value in reading one's own approaches to the creation of space modified by the buildings around as the points of departure.[2]

Traveling the next month in Greece and Egypt, he remained enthusiastic as he visited sites suggesting the very beginnings of monumental architecture (fig. 33).[3] Confirming his interest in history when other architects still tended to question its value, he later said, "The architect must always start with an eye on the best architecture of the past."[4]

Regarding specific impressions of Rome Kahn left few clues. Other than one or two tentatively identified sketches, no drawings of Roman ruins seem to exist. In his notebooks he wrote only that "the Romans introduced brick used elementally[?] with facing of marble."[5] As to specific monuments, he mentioned only two with any regularity: the Pantheon and the Baths of Caracalla.[6] Although his statements suggest it was the Pantheon to which he was most drawn, it was the Baths of Caracalla he formally identified as his favorite building: "It is ever a wonder when man aspires to go beyond the functional. Here was the will to build a vaulted structure 100 feet high in which men could bathe. Eight feet would have

sufficed. Now, even as a ruin, it is a marvel."[7] Yet, however scant the evidence, Kahn's later work suggests that he benefited greatly from what he saw. Clearly he appreciated the massive, brick-faced ruins that characterized the ancient city. With its applied decoration missing, Roman architecture was revealed as pure geometric volumes shaped by powerful walls and concrete vaults. Depictions of Rome that Kahn had long known no doubt strengthened his perceptions. Among these, as identified by Vincent Scully in his seminal monograph, were drawings by Auguste Choisy and Giovanni Battista Piranesi.[8] Choisy's illustrations reduced buildings to their structural and volumetric essence, and Piranesi's reconstructed views of Rome enlarged upon the fantastic geometries that lay beneath its ancient ruins.

Determining what Kahn actually read while in Rome, or, indeed, in any later period, is more problematic than determining what he saw. He always claimed never to have read, and there is no reason not to believe him.[9] For example, to a group of architecture students he once said, "I consider myself a rather interesting kind of a scholar because I don't read and I don't write."[10] Yet he constantly examined books and listened perceptively. At Yale he frequented Scully's classes on the history of architecture, and at the American Academy he reportedly conversed at length with Frank E. Brown, the resident historian and archaeologist whose own appreciation of Roman architecture paralleled Kahn's.[11]

Kahn's travel sketches, even if not of Roman subjects, reveal a strong sense of ancient architecture that would also be reflected in his later work. Regarding travel sketches, he had written in 1931 that if such a drawing "discloses a purpose, it is of value," and, further, that following conventional rules of perspective or composition was unnecessary, for each drawing should reflect of its subject "that element of the feeling for its design, and the lyrical rhythm and counterpoint of its mass."[12] Kahn's later

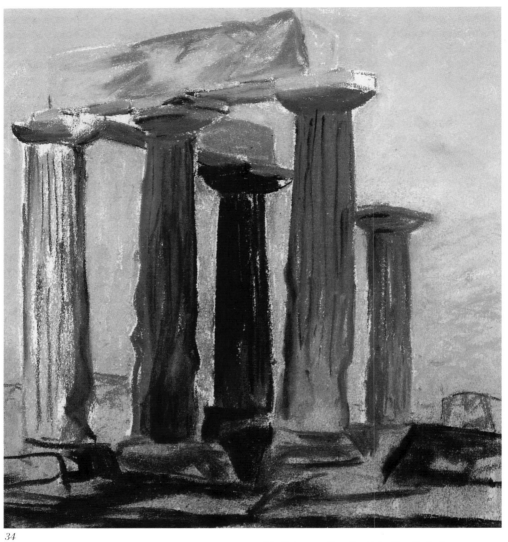

34

34. Columns, Temple of Apollo, Corinth,
January 1951.
35. Acropolis, Athens, January 1951.
36. Temple interior, Karnak, January 1951.

35

36

37

37. *Yale University Art Gallery, New Haven, Conn.,*
1951–53. View from north, 1953.
38. *Yale University Art Gallery. Entrance.*

Following pages
39. *Yale University Art Gallery. Gallery.*

drawings of Greek columns *(fig. 34)*, done after his stay at the academy, render their mass with an animated vigor not apparent in earlier depictions, and his sketch of the Athenian acropolis *(fig. 35)* signals a new appreciation of the mass and symbolic force of sacred terrain. The abstract, geometric power of architectural form is even more dramatically revealed by his sketches of Egyptian pyramids and temples *(fig. 36)*. Together these drawings reflected discoveries of ancient form that could still evoke the highest aspirations of humanity.

Reintroduction of Mass

Only a few weeks after returning from Rome, Kahn presented his first ideas for the Yale Art Gallery. By June 1951 his proposal was approved; essentially a loft building with entire walls either glazed or closed, it affirmed Kahn's adept handling of a modernist vocabulary and linked smoothly with his work before 1950. Yet it also gave evidence of his first major departure from that vocabulary, for in the subtle play of stringcourses along the brick plane of the main facade *(fig. 38)*, and more emphatically in the almost three-foot-thick system of concrete floor slabs *(fig. 37)*, Kahn had reintroduced the antique notion of mass with structure openly depicted as bearing weight. Certainly he was not the first to elect this course—Le Corbusier was one of several European contemporaries who had long since led the way—but in America the gallery's appearance had impact, when completed in 1953.

Kahn has often been described as approaching modernism uneasily, yet there is no record of his actually speaking against it. Instead he rethought it by dealing with its parts, and in so doing came ultimately to change it as a whole. Beginning with aspects of mass, he later examined aspects of spatial division, of openings, of interior and exterior correspondence, so that in the end nothing

40

40. *Yale University Art Gallery, New Haven, Conn.,*
1951–53. Reflected ceiling plan.
41. Stairwell, looking up.

remained the same. At this stage of his career, however, little of this was apparent.

The hard, exposed structure of Kahn's gallery, which harbored exposed utilities, did not go unnoticed abroad as a departure from the smoother, seamless volumes of orthodox modernism. In England the gallery was seen as the best American example of New Brutalism, a briefly fashionable term that captured only a single dimension of Kahn's purpose.[13] Reflecting American bewilderment, Philip Goodwin, who had earlier proposed a design for the gallery and who, with Edward Durell Stone, had designed one of the icons of modernism in New York's Museum of Modern Art (completed in 1939), thought Kahn's building was "excellent, especially on the outside. I have some reservations on the ceiling treatment."[14] As these views suggest, Kahn had joined those architects of the 1950s wishing to free themselves from the constraints of the International Style without inclining toward the equally limiting approach of Wright. At the time, Eero Saarinen was regarded as more successful in this pursuit; Yale students were in fact unhappy that he had not gotten the gallery commission.[15] Like Kahn, Saarinen sought inspiration in both history and new building technologies, yet he approached those sources more as a means to surface decoration and superficial complication. By failing to question fundamental aspects of modernism, Saarinen, like so many of his equally restless contemporaries, romanticized architecture but did not change it.[16] That achievement lay with Kahn.

The ceiling treatment that had troubled Goodwin was, of course, crucial to Kahn's conception, for in answering both structural and mechanical needs in such an orderly manner as to leave structure and utilities exposed, he achieved architecture as basic and timeless as that which he had come to appreciate in Rome. Moreover, the insistent pattern of the ceiling's triangulated ribs sug-

gested a differentiation of space below in a manner sympathetically aligned with Roman vaulting *(fig. 39)*. In such ways Kahn brought fundamental aspects of history to bear on his architecture, combining them with an image of advanced technology—in this case, the ceiling system—that spoke strongly of its own time. It was a system related to Buckminster Fuller's space frames, which Kahn had transformed from a lightweight to a visually heavy structure, thus balancing history and technology, as Kenneth Frampton would note of his later buildings:

> Kahn's work presents us with two complementary yet utterly opposed principles. The first is categorically anti-progressive and asserts the presence of a collective abstract architectural memory in which all valid compositional types are eternally present in their disjunctive purity. The second principle is vehemently progressive and pursues the renovation of architectural form on the basis of advanced technique. It seems that Kahn believed that this second principle, as it responded to new tasks and uses, would be able to lead, when combined with the first, to an appropriate architectural expression, resynthesizing fresh poetic and institutional values in terms of concrete form. [17]

On closer inspection, Kahn's approach seems characterized not so much by a pairing of history with advanced technique as by the pairing of history with a superimposed geometric order that gave the impression of advanced technique. In publications of his work Kahn favored the gallery's reflected ceiling plan *(fig. 40)*, which indicated the stair enclosure as a pure cylinder, rather than plans showing the actual, only partly cylindrical form. And when compliance with local building codes forced Kahn to redesign the space frame so that it became a more conventional system of inclined "T"-beams, he complicated its appearance to preserve the dramatic look of the earlier system, leaving the hollow, three-sided pyramids—for Scully,

a strong reminder of Kahn's recent Egyptian trip—intact as bracing elements. [18] Reinforcing the sense of this shape as an aesthetic choice is the dramatic stairwell, where the triangular plan of the stairs echoes the triangular coffer of the ceilings, thus amplifying the building's geometric theme *(fig. 41)*.

The ordered geometry of the Yale Art Gallery reflects the continuing critical influence of Anne Griswold Tyng, [19] who had earlier explored similar systems. She saw the gallery as a turning point in Kahn's career, one that she helped inspire and that sparked his awareness of "the archetypal order of geometry." [20] Something of Tyng's influence in this regard can be guessed from Kahn's reaction to Le Corbusier's Chapel at Ronchamp (1951–55): "I fell madly in love with it. . . . It is undeniably the work of an artist. . . . Anne is not satisfied . . . by form making not derived from an order. . . . [She] claims that if Le Corbusier had a growth concept of structure as I and she understand it, Le Corbusier himself would not be satisfied with his work." [21] Later he wrote that Tyng "knows the aesthetic implications of the geometry inherent in biological structures bringing us in touch with the edge between the measurable and the unmeasurable." [22] Tyng also formed an effective bridge between Kahn and Buckminster Fuller. She and Kahn had met Fuller in 1949, [23] and Fuller came to respect her ideas, praising her "superbly crafted and original scientific work which discloses her discovery of Golden-mean relationships between the whole family of Platonic solids. These relationships, according to the records, have not been previously known by man. . . . Anne Tyng has been Louis Kahn's geometrical strategist." [24]

Geometric order persisted in Kahn's work, as did an expressive use of masonry structure to impart a feeling of architectural mass. This can be seen in two somewhat conservative designs for Philadelphia begun in these years: the Mill Creek project (1951–56) and the

American Federation of Labor Medical Services Building (1954–57). The Mill Creek project (to which a second component was added in 1956–63) embodied Kahn's ongoing efforts to design low-cost housing whatever the constraints. The resulting complex of high-rise and low-rise units (with most of the latter added in 1956–63), reflecting a long and bureaucratic process of compromise, is understandably subdued *(fig. 42)*. The AFL building is the one other project in these years to link strongly with Kahn's pre-1950 work. Like the Yale Art Gallery, the AFL building made use of an exposed concrete structure to achieve a distinguishing appearance as well as to provide for an integrated system of mechanical services *(fig. 43)*. The Vierendeel trusses that span between the widely spaced columns are cut with hexagonal openings, distantly recalling the geometry of the gallery, and inside, behind glass and stone panels sheathing the smooth, volumetric exterior, the resulting sense of mass was more appreciable. Yet by the time the AFL building was dedicated in February 1957, it was clearly out of phase with Kahn's other, more publicized work, and when in 1973 it was demolished to make way for a new expressway, there was little outcry.[25]

42

43

42. Mill Creek Project, Philadelphia, Pa., 1951–56. Community center and high-rise apartment buildings, ca. 1956.
43. American Federation of Labor Medical Services Building, Philadelphia, Pa., 1954–57.

Differentiation of Space

Kahn's pursuit of an idealized geometric order, informed by his sense of historic architecture, seemed to draw him toward the differentiation of space, and the modernist ideal of spatial continuity was soon challenged. Traffic movement studies that he conceived for Philadelphia from late 1951 to mid–1953, while completing the design and supervising the construction of the Yale Art Gallery, forecast such ordered separation. Unbound by the sort of restraints that had so affected his design for the Mill Creek project, Kahn prepared these visionary studies for a committee of the Philadelphia Chapter of the

44

45

44. *Philadelphia Traffic Studies, Philadelphia, Pa., 1951–53. Proposed traffic pattern.*
45. *Fruchter house, Philadelphia, Pa., 1951–54. Plan, ca. 1952–53.*

American Institute of Architects. He began by differentiating individual elements in his remarkable representations of urban movement, following the long tradition of first analyzing a problem by identifying its component parts, in this case individual vehicles and people, each designated by an arrow of different size or intensity to suggest relative scale and speed. Next these elements were reassembled into a more ordered totality that provided the appropriate harbor or channel of flow for each component, so that a persuasive unity was achieved without a loss of individual identity *(figs. 44, 46)*. Other perspectives recall Le Corbusier's idealized city images but happily lack the threatening presence of hovering airplanes and death-defying landing strips.

Anne Tyng recalled that "Lou always wanted a distinction between things,"[26] referring primarily to his way of detailing, but it was the same at a larger scale. For Kahn such uncompromising reduction and reassembly was a viable means of beginning, and he next applied it to architecture. The plan of the H. Leonard Fruchter house (unbuilt, 1951–54) shows this approach at a preliminary stage *(fig. 45)*. Commissioned by a New York businessman and his wife in September 1951 as designs for the Yale Art Gallery ceiling were being refined, it was not designed until spring of the following year, with additional modifications in the first months of 1953.[27] Each primary function was given an independent geometric unit, yet in their reassembly Kahn seemed less drawn to discovering unique relational order than to amplifying his earlier configuration of the Yale gallery stair. He must have found the plan device of a triangle inscribed within a symmetrical enclosure compelling, for within the next year three other projects reflect its ordering pattern. Beneath their visual similarities lie diverse unidentified sources.

In April 1953, not long after stopping work on the Fruchter house, Kahn diagrammed a

46

46. *Philadelphia Traffic Studies, Philadelphia,*
Pa., 1951–53. Perspective, ca. 1953.

47

48

49

47. *Adath Jeshurun Synagogue and School Building, Philadelphia, Pa., 1954–55. Plan, 1954.*
48. *Civic Center on the Schuylkill River, 1951–53. Bird's-eye perspective, ca. 1951–52.*
49. *Civic Center, Philadelphia, Pa., 1952–57. Perspective showing City Tower, ca. 1952–53.*

circular enclosure of hotel rooms superimposed over a triangular department store as part of his visionary Philadelphia Civic Center. Claude-Nicolas Ledoux's project for an inn, ca. 1785, published in a Philadelphia journal in 1952, must have reinforced his fascination with this geometric combination.[28] Next he exploited this device in the layout for the Adath Jeshurun Synagogue and School Building (1954–55, unbuilt), now assigning the triangular shape to the sanctuary and placing it within a partially embanked, circular enclosure *(fig. 47)*.[29] For its structure he envisioned an open, triangulated space frame that recalled the idealized structure he had drawn around 1953 to show how the Yale Art Gallery might have been; as he wrote to Walter Gropius: "My work on the Yale Art Gallery has led me to think about three-dimensional construction and its implications architecturally. I failed to command the forces which could have produced a truly significant building."[30] In the synagogue Kahn explored the potential of columns—sometimes angled in response to the frame—to be joined together in clusters that could define places for stairs within the larger volume.[31] Kahn's synagogue was planned for a site on York Road in North Philadelphia near Elkins Park, not far from the site where Frank Lloyd Wright's Beth Sholom synagogue (1954–59) would shortly rise. Kahn had kept clippings illustrating Wright's hexagonal plan;[32] in his own design he effectively rationalized Wright's romantic essay.

A third related design (developed in collaboration with Anne Tyng) exploited space-frame technology even more dramatically. For what came to be called the City Tower, Kahn and Tyng had indicated a simple prismlike triangle, shown as a component of the Civic Center studies around 1952 *(fig. 48)*. By 1953, drawings record its early development as a triangular space frame with angled, faceted walls *(fig. 49)*.[33] Its design might reflect the influence of the French engineer Robert Le Ricolais (1894–1977), who, like Tyng and Fuller, advocated such technology. Le Ricolais had written Kahn in April 1953, sending copies of two papers that explained his concepts. In these he argued poetically that hexagonal space frames could enhance spatial and structural efficiency in multistory buildings.[34]

Typically, Kahn sensed wide-ranging, less technological advantages, as he had earlier with his steel-frame experiments of the 1940s. In 1953 he wrote: "In Gothic times, architects built in solid stones. Now we can build with hollow stones. . . . The desire to express voids positively in the design of structure is evidenced by the growing interest and work in the development of space frames."[35] The clustered columns of Adath Jeshurun were a variation, with the void expanded to encompass circulation elements. Kahn's interest in space frames soon waned, but he continued to explore the interstitial spaces that he discovered within other structural systems. This became a means of defining relationships between spaces according to a visible, rational pattern, and a way of invigorating traditional, wall-bearing structure in a manner suitable to his own time. Ultimately he achieved the organic interrelatedness of parts that marks great architecture.

Kahn's preoccupation with the Yale Art Gallery extended to more than idealized amplifications of its structure and geometry, for his investigations into the rational division of space stemmed also from a growing dissatisfaction with how its open plan could be too freely changed. At first he thought his system of movable partitions had solved the problem by allowing controlled flexibility within the open plan of the gallery, explaining on the occasion of its opening, "A good building is one which the client cannot destroy by wrong use of space."[36] Inevitably other partitions were substituted; Kahn protested to Yale's president that his design was being compro-

mised.[37] He had come to define architecture as "the thoughtful making of spaces"[38] and later said: "If I were to build a gallery now, I would really be more concerned about building spaces which are not used freely by the director as he wants. Rather I would give him spaces that were there and had certain inherent characteristics."[39] The Fruchter house had indicated the direction of this approach, yet its implications were at first left unexplored. In the Francis Adler house (1954–55, unbuilt), which he developed in September 1954, he initiated a more decisive course of action, one that led directly to a fully realized example of differentiated space in the Trenton Bathhouse of early 1955.[40]

The fall of 1954 was a time of relative calm in Kahn's office, encouraging concentrated effort. The Yale Art Gallery had been finished the previous year, the AFL building was at last under construction, the first phase of Mill Creek was very nearly done, and the final presentation of Adath Jeshurun had just been made. Kahn was rejoined by Anne Tyng, who was back from Rome, where their daughter, Alexandra Stevens Tyng, had been born. In these months Kahn's persistent questioning of his own beliefs seemed recharged. As he approached the design of smaller houses with new ideas, so he also began to formulate his distinction between ideal form, or what a building "wants to be," and design, what actually emerges as a result of specific circumstance. At first he used the terms "order" and "design" to differentiate: "I believe that we are speaking about order when we are speaking about design. I think design is circumstantial. I think order is what we discover the aspects of."[41] No longer did he refer to order in the usual sense of superimposed geometric pattern, but rather as a preexisting, Platonic ideal. The measure of his designs depended, then, on the degree to which they participated in that discovered ideal.

Mrs. Adler had become impressed with

Kahn while serving on the mayor's committee overseeing Philadelphia's Penn Center, and she encouraged Kahn to break with convention in the house she and her husband wished to build in the Chestnut Hill section of the city.[42] This Kahn did in simple, almost diagrammatic terms *(fig. 50)*. Specified uses were each housed in individual structural units so that spatial and structural division corresponded; the open plan so characteristic of modernism had been reconfigured. Walls continued to be mostly glazed or solid, but the corner piers themselves were planned as massive masonry elements. In the visible joining of parts Kahn seemed also to sense a potential for ornament; while designing the Adler house he said:

> The feeling that our present-day architecture needs embellishment stems in part from our tendency to [furr] joints out of existence—in other words, to conceal how parts are put together. If we were to train ourselves to draw as we build, from the bottom up, stopping our pencils at the points of pouring or erecting, ornament would evolve out of our love for the perfection of construction and we would develop new methods of construction. [43]

This statement, so indicative of Kahn's celebratory articulation of parts, would continue to figure in his thinking and was much repeated, with only minor variations. How well he had come to understand the origins of ornament and of the classical orders that apotheosized the joining of parts.

When zoning problems caused the Adler project to falter early in 1955,[44] Kahn adapted the concept for the Weber DeVore house in Springfield Township, Pennsylvania (ca. 1954–55). Again he composed the house of informally grouped pavilions, each a twenty-six-foot square, but now subdivided by two additional columns to better facilitate internal divisions *(fig. 51)*. In both the Adler and DeVore projects, sketches record a variety of groupings as Kahn tried different relation-

ships between each pavilion and the adjoining terrain.

The DeVore project was apparently shorter lived than the Adler,[45] but the bathhouse that was part of the Jewish Community Center near Trenton, New Jersey, provided a third opportunity to develop a pavilion plan. Kahn received the commission in February 1955, and preliminary plans indicate a bathhouse of no particular distinction. Then, on February 15, he presented his Greek cross scheme of four symmetrically placed, pyramidal pavilions *(fig. 52)*. A simple structure, it was built rapidly, within a few months *(figs. 53, 54)*. There the balance of parts and the architectural hierarchy of what Kahn came to call "served" and "servant" space is clearly resolved, for the piers of the Adler project have been enlarged and made hollow, resulting in small, symmetrically placed rooms that contain toilet facilities or serve as vestibules. More extraordinary, perhaps, is the visual clarity of the building, for each functional unit is distinctly defined by its own structural volume.

The Trenton Bathhouse became widely acknowledged as a key point of transition in Kahn's work. Looking back, Kahn reflected, "If the world discovered me after I designed the Richards towers building, I discovered myself after designing that little concrete-block bathhouse in Trenton."[46] At the time of its design in 1955 he had already begun to perceive its implications, recording in a section of his notebook titled "Compartmented Spaces": "Space made by a dome then divided by walls is not the same space. . . . A room should be a constructed entity or an ordered segment of a construction system."[47] He then commented on the great architects of his day in a way suggesting self-evaluation:

> Mies's sensitivities with creation of space reacts to imposed structural order with little inspiration drawn from what a building 'wants to be.' Corbusier feels what a space 'wants to be,'

50

51

52

53

54

50. Adler house, Philadelphia, Pa., 1954–55.
Plan, ca. Fall 1954.
51. DeVore house, Springfield Township, Pa., ca.
1954–55. Plan, ca. 1955.
52. Jewish Community Center, Ewing Township,
N.J., 1954–59. Roof plan of bathhouse. Published
in Perspecta in 1957.
53. Jewish Community Center. Central courtyard
of bathhouse, ca. 1957.
54. Jewish Community Center. Bathhouse, ca.
1959.

55

56

55. Adler house,
Philadelphia, Pa.,
1954–55. Sketch plan
(detail of sheet), ca. 1954-55.
56. Jewish Community
Center, Ewing Township,
N.J., 1954–59. Plan.
Inscribed Louis I.
Kahn–Architect/Nov. 3,
1955.
57. Morris house, Mt.
Kisco, N.Y., 1955–58.
First-floor plan, Summer
1955. Inscribed Lou.
58. Jewish Community
Center. Elevation
Inscribed LIK '56.

57

58

passes through order impatiently and hurries to form. In Marseilles order was strong. . . . At Ronchamp order is only dimly felt in form born of dream. Mies's order is not comprehensive enough to encompass acoustics, light, air, piping, storage, stairs, shafts, vertical and horizontal and other service spaces. His order of structure serves to frame the building but not harbor the servant space.

Next he praised Wright's early work as "the most wonderfully true architecture Amerique" but added, "The imitators of F.LL.W are of a lesser strata than imitators of Corbu. Wright is more arbitrary, personal, experimental and disdainful of tradition."

Kahn concluded his notebook entry with a section titled "The Palladian Plan" that clarified his sense of historic precedent:

I have discovered what probably everyone else has found, that a bay system is a room system. A room is a defined space—defined by the way it is made. . . . To me that is a good discovery. . . . Someone asked me how one may carry out the room idea in the complex problems of house. I point to the DeVore house which is strictly Palladian in spirit, highly ordered for today's space needs. . . . The Adler house [is] stronger in order.[48]

Thus Kahn questioned the convention of open planning in light of a more antique sensitivity. To identify Palladio as the intermediary provides a clue to one source of this departure: Rudolf Wittkower's influential treatise *Architectural Principles in the Age of Humanism*, a book with which Kahn had earlier been familiar, even if, as colleagues claim, he mainly studied the illustrations.[49] Wittkower's diagram of Palladian villas, with clearly ordered "served" and "servant" spaces, would in itself account for his calling his own designs Palladian. Missing in the Adler and DeVore plans is the symmetrical balance of Palladio, yet in one of the first conceptual sketches for the Adler house (*fig. 55*), before specific circumstance reshaped its

perfect symmetry, Kahn seemed to begin with a very Palladian plan indeed—what he would later use for the Trenton Bathhouse.

One final statement in Kahn's 1955 notebook linked the differentiated, Palladian plan with two later designs that he also began that year, the Lawrence Morris house in Mt. Kisco, New York (1955–58, unbuilt), and the intermediate scheme for the main building of the Jewish Community Center: "The community center in Trenton and the Morris house in Mt. Kisco promise to be worthy variations of the room-space concept. There the supports are rooms serving the larger living spaces with the needed stairways, washrooms, closets, [illegible], entrances, etc."[50] Kahn began sketching his first scheme for the Morris house during the summer of 1955, but laid it aside during 1956. His preliminary plan (*fig. 57*), which corresponds to his notebook description, could almost be a conceptual sketch for the Richards Medical Research Building at the University of Pennsylvania (1957–65), his most noted example of differentiated space in these years, which he began in 1957.[51]

Reinforcing Kahn's Wittkowerian ties at mid-decade was a prolonged conversation late in December 1955 with one of Wittkower's most brilliant students, Colin Rowe.[52] The specific references to Palladio in Kahn's notebook may, in fact, have been entered after that meeting. Within a few weeks Rowe sent Kahn a new copy of *Architectural Principles*, saying, "I think that you may discover attitudes with which you are profoundly in sympathy."[53] Rowe may have had more in mind than Palladian parallels, for Kahn had earlier begun to differentiate ideal order from achievable shape in a manner recalling Wittkower's quotation of Barbaro: "The artist works first in the intellect and conceives in the mind and symbolizes then the exterior matter after the interior image, particularly in architecture."[54] Later, when Kahn came to speak of "the great event in architecture when the walls parted and columns became," he again recalled Wittkower's text, for he mythologized history in a manner not unlike Alberti as quoted by Wittkower: "A row of columns is indeed nothing else but a wall, open and discontinued in several places."[55] Both statements would have reinforced Rowe's appreciation, for he saw Kahn as a neo-humanist at the same time that Reyner Banham saw him as a New Brutalist; by then, however, Kahn had risen above both conventions.

The intermediate scheme for the Jewish Community Center that Kahn mentioned in his notebook and on which he worked from November 1955 into March 1956 is more startling in its diagrammatic rigidity than his other work of the time (*fig. 56*). Here the hand of Anne Tyng can again be sensed, and even more strongly in an elevation study (*fig. 58*) that resembles a drawing in D'Arcy Thompson's *On Growth and Form*. It seemed to illustrate her belief that architects should "conceive of forms in building which create their own *terrain* based on truly three dimensional relationships rather than on two dimensions simply extended upward. . . . From a comprehension of the geometries of close-packing may be developed forms which are most effective in creating spaciousness where populations are dense."[56] About similar polygonal solids Thompson had said that "in close-packed association" they could "enclose space with a minimum extent of surface."[57]

Tyng's collaboration was more openly acknowledged in the final version of the City Tower (1956–57), a 616-foot-high structure developed for Universal Atlas Cement as one of a series meant to stimulate far-reaching uses of concrete (*fig. 59*). A model of the highly articulated structure was exhibited at the Museum of Modern Art in 1960, where it was described by one critic as "a tottering, concrete Erector set."[58] The triangular geometry now seems firmly Tyng's, but Kahn's earlier sketch of San Marco records a sympathetic view of masonry frames. Other designs incorporating triangular geometries—like the Wharton Esherick Workshop addition (1955–56) or the Fred Clever house (1957–62)—were also much guided by Tyng.[59] And she contributed to the unbuilt design for the General Motors Exhibit at the 1964–65 New York World's Fair on which Kahn worked briefly between December 1960 and February 1961.[60] He experimented with centralized and even spherical structures, but settled on loosely grouped inflated pavilions (*fig. 60*). Tyng's own scheme brought to these the geometric regularity that she more consistently sought, for while Kahn absorbed such elements within a broader framework, Tyng remained more focused."[61]

In these years Kahn's commissions were so paced that he could focus on each individually, at least for a period of weeks. Thus as he was completing work on the octagonal scheme for the Jewish Community Center, an invitation came in February 1956 to enter the limited competition for the Washington University Library in St. Louis; when that was submitted in May, office records show that his attention turned to the Research Institute for Advanced Science near Baltimore, which had been commissioned in 1955 but awaited his efforts. When his final drawings for the research institute were completed in November 1956, he turned again to the Jewish Community Center, and between November and June 1957 he prepared his third and best-known proposal for that commission.

In both the library (*fig. 61*) and the research institute (*fig. 62*), Kahn continued to explore the Greek cross as a plan device appropriate to ordered, differentiated space, although now for programs of far greater complexity than that of the Trenton Bathhouse. The images that Kahn favored for publication minimized the necessary maze of partitions, particularly in the

59

59. *City Tower, Philadelphia, Pa., 1952–57. Model, 1956–57.*
60. *General Motors Exhibit, New York, N.Y., 1960–61. Bird's-eye perspective.*
61. *Washington University Library, St. Louis, Mo., 1956. Perspective, February–May 1956. Inscribed Lou K.*
62. *Research Institute for Advanced Science, near Baltimore, Md., 1956–58. Model.*
63. *Civic Center, Philadelphia, Pa., 1956–57. Bird's-eye perspective. Inscribed Lou K '57.*
64. *Jewish Community Center, Ewing Township, N.J., 1954–59. Model, November 1956–June 1957.*

60

61

62

63

64

library. Such elimination of specifics reflected one means by which Kahn approached his universal truths: the program guided but did not command. As Kahn said of his design for Washington University, "A library should offer a system of spaces and their consequent form as a building should originate from broad interpretations of use rather than the satisfaction of a program for a specific system of operation."[62] Later he added, "It is the duty of the architect to find what is this thoughtful realm of space . . . not just take the program of the institution but try to develop something which the institution itself can realize is valid."[63] In this he became ever more firm: "I never read a program literally. . . . It's like writing to Picasso and saying, 'I want my portrait painted—I want two eyes in it—and one nose—and only one mouth, please.' You can't do that, because you're talking about the artist."[64] He approached his third proposal for the Jewish Community Center in the same way (*fig. 64*), for beneath the ordered, pyramidal pavilions are a variety of uses and spaces not always in congruence with the architectural shapes that contain them. Space was now particularized according to a general pattern of differently proportioned elements that facilitated minor shifts of function without impairing architectural character.

Unlike his commissions for actual buildings in these years, Kahn's visionary proposals for Philadelphia that he now initiated on his own (May 1956 through much of 1957) provided space for dreams. Perspectives of Philadelphia (*fig. 63*) show a fantastic landscape of powerful forms reminiscent of Piranesi's Rome. The Roman quality, in fact, seems stronger here than in earlier work and may reflect the influence of Robert Venturi. Kahn, impressed with Venturi's thesis at Princeton, had recommended him to Eero Saarinen, with whom he worked before going to the American Academy in Rome. Upon his return from the academy in 1956, Venturi joined Kahn's office; later, when he began to practice independently in 1957, they continued to exchange ideas.[65] Kahn's letters of recommendation for Venturi document close ties and deep appreciation,[66] and it was surely Venturi's perceptive comprehension of personal mannerisms and specificity in architecture that came to loosen Kahn's growing inclination toward highly controlled, even compulsively ordered designs. Within the very shadow of the pure logic cast by the City Tower project, Venturi, in his sketch of the plaza, invoked the emotionally charged spirit of Michelangelo's Campidoglio. If Anne Tyng can be said to have strengthened Kahn's tendencies toward abstract geometric order, then surely Venturi provided the means by which that order could be made poetic.

Venturi was not alone among those who helped lead Kahn toward solutions. About his informally organized office much has been said in this regard,[67] for he benefited greatly from those who worked with him to develop his sketches into more finished drawings, and he depended heavily on a few more experienced colleagues who maintained some sense of conventional office routine. In a like manner he worked with students and faculty at Yale or the University of Pennsylvania or at other schools where he taught. After September 1955 his teaching was mainly at Penn, although he taught for short periods at both MIT and Princeton. He was recruited to Penn by G. Holmes Perkins, then dean of the school, as part of Perkins's farsighted development of that institution. There Kahn was primarily involved with advanced students working toward a second professional degree. He had begun to disengage from Yale just as Paul Rudolph began teaching. The problem of a "roadside frozen custard stand" that Rudolph assigned his studio may have contributed to Kahn's ultimate departure, especially when Kahn was curtly requested to serve on the reviewing jury.[68] Kahn's interest lay with deeper issues, and he identified problems accordingly. Often he assigned his own commissions, always in a spirit calculated to encourage wide-ranging inquiry. At Penn he organized his studio in the manner of a seminar, engaging in open discussion with both students and his fellow teachers, Robert Le Ricolais and a former classmate, Philadelphia architect Norman Rice. As Kahn said near the end of his life, "I come much more refreshed and challenged from the classes. I learn more from the students than I probably teach."[69] He encouraged students to join with him in discovering the ideal form for each problem. In one instance the universal ideal was determined to be a sphere; how each student arrived at something approaching its shape was the measure of individual distinction.[70]

As Kahn's earlier connection with Yale led to the Yale Art Gallery commission, so his affiliation with the University of Pennsylvania led to the Richards Medical Research Building commission in February 1957 (figs. 65, 66, 67, 68). By the time of his first presentation in June 1958, he had developed a basic scheme of three laboratory towers grouped asymmetrically about a fourth service tower. That summer the commission was expanded to include laboratory facilities for biology, and these Kahn added as two additional towers (fig. 69). Various fenestration patterns were proposed, some with arcuated elements recalling Roman motifs, and the service towers were much studied as to profile and shape; but the plan itself held, and ultimately its clear resolution honored both structural and compositional logic.

More fully than any of his previous designs, the Richards Building embodied Kahn's developing sense of differentiated space shaped by visible, rational, individualizing structure. By the time of the building's dedication in May 1960, critics sensed that a new synthesis was emerging, one that seemed to derive partly from Mies van der Rohe and the International Style, partly from Le Corbusier, and partly from Frank Lloyd Wright, but with an individual quality uniquely its own.[71] Kahn's clear articulation of separate components and his emphatic distinction between servant and served spaces were judged to be his strongest departures from accepted norms. These were generally explained as rational responses to specific demands of the program, in particular the need to designate separated areas for animals and to provide for the complicated systems of air supply and exhaust. In retrospect these demands seem almost incidental. Such pavilion plans were then well established as a theme in his work, and in the Trenton Bathhouse of 1955 his urge to clarify service elements had been made evident. It was a concept he readily acknowledged as stemming from his Beaux-Arts training.[72] He also wrote, "The nature of space is further characterized by the minor spaces that serve it. Storage-rooms, service rooms and cubicals [sic] must not be partitioned areas of a single space structure, they must be given their own structure."[73] In the Richards Building Kahn's sensitivity to human feelings seems more crucial to his concept than functional need:

> The Medical Research Building . . . is conceived in recognition of the realizations that science laboratories are studios and that the air to breathe should be away from the air to throw away. The normal plan of laboratories . . . places the work areas off one side of a public corridor [with] the other side provided with the stairs, elevators, animal quarters, ducts and other services. . . . The only distinction between one man's spaces of work from the other is the difference of the numbers on the doors.[74]

In his building Kahn not only provided for these differentiated areas that honored human effort, he also grouped them so that a sense of working among a community of scientists could be appreciated (fig. 70).

The Richards Building's concrete structure, elegantly expressed in juxtaposition to the

66

Preceding pages
65. *Richards Medical Research Building,*
University of Pennsylvania, Philadelphia,
Pa., 1957–60. Towers from northeast.

66. Richards Medical Research Building.
View toward entrance.
67. Richards Medical Research Building.
Biology Building towers.

visually more inert surfaces of red brick, was
also much celebrated at the time of its completion. As in the Yale Art Gallery, an experimental system was exploited to order space,
but now that order was more clearly defined
and the spatial divisions within it more directly
outlined by a system of interlocking precast,
post-tensioned beams. Collaborating on its
design was August Komendant, who since
1956 had been a frequent consultant.[75]
Komendant, described by Kahn as "one of the
rare engineers qualified to guide the architect
to develop meaningful form,"[76] proved himself
an able contributor. He recalled introducing
Kahn to the structural potentials of precast
concrete, and less generously said that Kahn
"was completely ignorant of engineering. He
lacked the basic knowledge of structures and
structural materials. . . . He hid his lack of
structural knowledge behind arrogance and
his position. . . . Kahn's attitude about engineering changed drastically after close association with Robert Le Ricolais and myself."[77]

Various visual sources have been suggested
for the Richards Building, ranging from the
medieval towers of San Gimignano to facades
by Mies van der Rohe.[78] Wright's Larkin
Building (1904), which Scully suggested as an
influence early on, provides a more convincing
precedent and brings into sharper focus the
question of Kahn's relationship to that architect.[79] Typical of his generation, Kahn had
little praise for Wright's later designs, favoring
instead the more rigorously intellectual work
of Le Corbusier. Yet Kahn's work in these
years suggests deeper understanding than is
generally acknowledged.

Documented evidence of ties between
Wright and Kahn is slight. His connection
with Henry Klumb (1904–1984), a former
associate of Wright's and a staunch supporter
of his ideals, is noted in chapter 1.[80] In 1952
Kahn and Wright both attended a convention
of the American Institute of Architects,[81] in
1955 (as previously noted) Kahn praised

69

70

68. *Richards Medical Research Building and
Biology Building, University of Pennsylvania,
Philadelphia, Pa., 1957–65. Entrance tower,
corner detail.*
69. *Richards Medical Research Building. Typical
floor plan.*
70. *Richards Medical Research Building. View
between towers, ca. 1961.*

Wright's early work, and when Wright died in 1959 Kahn wrote in tribute, "Wright gives insight to learn/that nature has no style/that nature is the greatest teacher of all/The ideas of Wright are the facets of this single thought."[82] Scully recalls that later that same year Kahn made his first visit to a Wright building, the S. C. Johnson and Son Administration Building (1936–39), where, "to the depths of his soul, [he] was overwhelmed."[83] In view of the Richards Building, one further tie seems of special interest. In 1953, rebutting Pietro Belluschi's criticism that Wright's 1947 research tower for Johnson and Son did not function as a laboratory, Kahn said, "The Tower was done with love and I should say it is architecture. . . . Architecture should start a new chain of reactions. It shouldn't just exist for itself; it should throw out sparks to others. . . . If the Tower has this power . . . then I believe it functions."[84] Such could also be the defense for Kahn's similarly criticized research towers.

In seeking logical definition of spaces within, Kahn may also have respected Wright's approach to fenestration, for Wright varied openings systematically and effected dramatic balance between glazed and masonry surfaces. Nowhere is this better demonstrated than in the Richard Lloyd Jones house (Tulsa, Oklahoma, 1929), in which alternating bands of glass and masonry block reconfigure conventional enclosure. As one of Wright's most abstract and scaleless buildings, lacking the romantic contrivances typical of his later work, it may have held special appeal for Kahn, who seems to have taken it as his model for the reworked Morris house. At first its plan (see *fig. 57*) had anticipated the Richards Building, as noted. After putting the house project aside for more than a year, Kahn resumed work during the summer of 1957, while refining his design for Richards.[85] Drawings again reveal similarities between the two designs, and later perspectives of the

Morris house closely resemble the towered massing of the Richards Building. But as the lower, more open pavilions and hipped roofs of earlier versions gave way to a stronger depiction of mass (*fig. 71*), it began to recall Wright's Jones house. In plan the two designs also drew together, for in the final version of the Morris house (*fig. 72*) the pavilions had coalesced, and volumetric divisions were achieved by internal piers.

However much Kahn may have drawn from Wright, the two remained divided in fundamental attitudes. Both believed in order as a fundamental principle, but they saw it as differently generated. As Scully summarized, Kahn believed that order was a "cultural construction and its archetypes are therefore to be found in human history";[86] or as Kahn said, "Architecture is what nature cannot make."[87] Wright believed that order was derived from nature. Both architects also sought ideal form, but Wright found patterns in earthly models, while Kahn searched for cosmic inspiration.

One last pavilion scheme, the day camp for the Jewish Community Center in Trenton, had been designed in June 1957, just as the Richards design was being readied for presentation and before work on the Morris house resumed. Designed and built with uncharacteristic speed, it is essentially a group of simple, open units that seem more like a quick sketch than a finished design. Of interest is the plan (*fig. 73*), for in the angled, informal play of the individual units an element of geometric complexity new to Kahn's work is suggested. This approach to planning would not be further explored until 1959, in the M. Morton Goldenberg house (unbuilt). But in the fall of 1958, when work on the Morris house had stopped and other projects were inactive, elevation studies that Kahn began for the Tribune Review Building show a similar sense of geometric freedom. It is tempting to link these variations as a group to ideas that Robert Venturi may have helped to stimulate,

for in Kahn's immediate work to follow are
even stronger reflections of what Denise Scott
Brown has claimed: "Lou learned from Bob
about Mannerist exception, distortion, and
inflection in form. . . . Through Bob, he inves-
tigated the layering of enclosed spaces and
the layered juxtaposition of walls and openings, and he discovered that windows could
be holes in the wall again."[88]

Layered Juxtapositions

In the fall of 1958 Kahn began work on the
Tribune Review Publishing Company
Building, planned to accommodate a local
newspaper in Greensburg, Pennsylvania
(1958–62).[89] Its basically rectangular plan
was relatively conventional, with two open
bays joined by a central line of services, but
in detailing its enclosing walls Kahn experimented with openings shaped in response to
light. Only months before, Kahn had been
forced to eliminate window blinds and other
light-controlling devices in the Richards
Building, and it was perhaps with this in mind
that he sought a more integral control of natural light, conceiving devices less subject to
elimination when the inevitable problems of
cost arose. He studied windows with shapes
that were foreign to modern architecture but
suited to masonry walls, for whether arched or
corbeled, such openings could be framed
without steel lintels and were thus more natural to brick construction. By positioning the
larger openings within the upper part of the
wall and leaving only narrow slots below, he
was able to moderate glare without blocking
views. In appearance these windows recall
Roman prototypes like those Kahn had seen
at Ostia. Critics came to call them "keyhole"
windows, and Kahn was not alone in using
them; a simply grasped element, they soon
became a much employed device in the hands
of other architects. By the fall of 1959, when
construction began on the Tribune Review
Building, other light-moderating elements

71

72

73

71. *Morris house, Mt. Kisco, N.Y., 1955–58.*
Model, ca. 1957–58.
72. *Morris house. Plan.*
73. *Jewish Community Center, Ewing Township,*
N.J., 1954–59. Plan of day camp, ca. June 1957.

74

75

76

77

78

74. *Tribune Review Building, Greensburg, Pa.,
1958–62.*
75. *Fleisher house, Elkins Park, Pa., 1959. Model.*
76. *Fleisher house. Plan, ca. January–March
1959.*
77. *Goldenberg house, Rydal, Pa., 1959. Model.*
78. *Goldenberg house. Plan.*
79. *First Unitarian Church and School, Rochester,
N.Y., 1959–69. Plan diagram, ca. January 1961.*

79

that Kahn had proposed, including projecting bays and hoods, had been eliminated, but the keyhole windows, simplified in shape, remained (fig. 74).[90]

Kahn developed his keyhole windows more extensively in the Fleisher and Goldenberg projects, both designed in the first months of 1959, while he was simplifying the Tribune Review Building in an effort to lower costs. The Robert H. Fleisher house for Elkins Park, Pennsylvania (1959, unbuilt), is a complete essay in the keyhole, with arcuated openings defining each of its square bays (figs. 75, 76).[91] At each end of the house, terminating units are left unroofed to serve as walled gardens. As if subjected to compacting pressure, the loosely arranged pavilions of the earlier Adler and DeVore projects are now densely ordered, and the Palladian aspect is made more apparent. In this design Kahn suggested two further departures from modernist norms that he would later examine in greater detail: exaggeratedly thick walls—for here his plan inclines away from the planar modularity of Brunelleschi toward the more three-dimensional units employed by Alberti—and the visual separation of outer layers of enclosure, signaled in the Fleisher house by the hypaethral garden rooms abutting the ends of the house.

In the M. Morton Goldenberg house, Rydal, Pennsylvania (1959, unbuilt), Kahn again relaxed the plan, not by dispersing individual elements but by exploring radiating, 45-degree diagonals as a means to less constrictive unity (figs. 77, 78).[92] For Kahn, such expressive reconfiguration of a square enclosure went beyond artistic choice: "I felt this was rather a discovery in the desires of interiors-interior spaces . . . a house is a building which is extremely sensitive to internal need. In this satisfaction there was an *existence will* of some kind . . . but there was an *existence will* for this house not to be disciplined within a geometric shape."[93] On one level, the

diagonal framing elements satisfied Kahn's demand for variety based on demonstrable logic rather than personal choice. As something generated more readily by square rather than polygonal geometry, the 45-degree diagonal was also in sympathy with a preference he later stated: "I always start with a square, no matter what the problem is."[94] In the hands of other architects, such diagonals became an architectural cliché of the 1960s. As with certain of H. H. Richardson's details some eighty years earlier, the appropriation of Kahn's more obvious elements gave an impression of newness, however shallow the thought behind their use.

The First Unitarian Church and School in Rochester, New York (1959–69), which Kahn began to design in June 1959 after work on the Fleisher and Goldenberg projects was largely completed, also, like the latter, began as a square, or so he claimed. Before his final scheme was approved in early 1961 he had tried several variations, but the centralized form that Kahn believed to be essential was ultimately honored (fig. 79). It was Kahn's first commission for a church, and Wittkower's discussion of ideal Renaissance churches must have been of interest. Wittkower had explained that Alberti recommended nine symmetrical shapes, beginning with the circle and the square, and further demonstrated the importance of centralized planning as honoring geometrical perfection: "No geometrical form is more apt to fulfill this demand than the circle or forms deriving from it. In such geometrical plans the geometrical pattern will appear absolute, immutable, static and entirely lucid. Without that organic geometrical equilibrium where all parts are harmonically related like the members of a body divinity cannot reveal itself."[95] Kahn's first known drawing for the Unitarian Church conforms remarkably with Wittkower's illustrations of centralized churches by Leonardo da Vinci (fig. 80). Centralized planning itself was hardly new to

Kahn's work—Adath Jeshurun was one of several earlier designs in which such rules had been followed. What was new was the extension of that centralized shape through juxtaposed units of sympathetic, but distinctly different, configuration. For the first time in his post-1950 phase Kahn seems to be dealing with supporting elements of the program in a more exploratory manner, dissolving thereby the modernist expectation of conventional geometric coherence. It marks an advance from the subdivided bays of the Washington University Library scheme, and also from the simple duplication of identical shapes that characterizes so many earlier projects. Different variations were developed for the Rochester commission, some as fully symmetrical as his first drawing, and others sympathetic to Wright's Unity Temple, as recorded in his conceptual diagrams (see *fig. 79*). With each developed version Kahn provided ambulatories that enriched the Renaissance prototype:

> The ambulatory I felt necessary because the Unitarian Church is made up of people who have had previous beliefs. . . . I drew the ambulatory to respect the fact that what is being said or what is in a sanctuary was not necessarily something you have to participate in. And so you could walk and feel free to walk away from what is being said. And then I placed a corridor next to it—around it—which served the school which was really the walls of the entire area.[96]

The bottom image of Kahn's conceptual diagrams for the Unitarian Church corresponds most closely to the built version (*fig. 81*) and introduces another, more passive kind of geometric juxtaposition. The shapes no longer conform to a preconceived pattern but rather reflect specific demands of individual use, and the resulting profile seems more distant still from conventional modernist planning. The precedents now are not Renaissance as much as late Roman, or more specifically Early Christian, for in plan Kahn's design recalls fourth-century funerary

basilicas. Such basilicas were a relatively new archaeological discovery, only fully identified after the Second World War.[97] Given his fascination with beginnings, it seems possible that Kahn, perhaps through Frank Brown, was familiar with this early, short-lived building type.

In his final schemes for the Unitarian Church, designed during the spring and summer of 1960, Kahn not only reestablished the central focus of his first scheme but also conceived the enclosing walls in terms of a perceivable, faceted thickness, infusing his building with a quality of exaggerated mass that was new even to his work (*figs. 82–86*). His design of the Margaret Esherick house in Chestnut Hill (1959–61) may have contributed to this result, for its walls, designed just before those of the Unitarian Church, are similarly conceived though less emphatically massive (*figs. 87, 88*).[98] A single-person dwelling, the house was designed for the niece of the sculptor Wharton Esherick, whose studio Kahn had designed in 1955. In his first plan of late 1959 Kahn had combined square units in a manner recalling the Adler project, but in the first months of 1960 he consolidated these into a compact rectangular enclosure.[99] Both the Esherick house and the Unitarian Church reflected Kahn's continued study of openings that moderated light, and in each instance built-in furniture was inserted to justify the extra thickness: bookcases in the house (*figs. 89, 90*) and window seats in the church. He described the effect in Rochester as "very Gothic," and in February 1961—the very month he completed the design of the facades—he said:

> Before [in the second scheme] the window's punched out of the walls. We felt the starkness of light again, learning also to be conscious of glare every time. . . . This [final scheme] is the beginning of a realization that the reveals are necessary. And this came about also because there was a desire to have some window seats. . . .

80

81

82

80. *First Unitarian Church and School, Rochester, N.Y., 1959–69. Sketch plan and elevation, June–July 1959.*
81. *First Unitarian Church and School. Plan, ca. June 1961.*
82. *First Unitarian Church and School. North elevation, ca. January 1961.*

Following pages
83. *First Unitarian Church and School. Rear facade of church.*

85

84. First Unitarian Church and School, Rochester,
N.Y., 1959–69. Front facade of church.
85. First Unitarian Church and School. Entrance.

Following pages
86. First Unitarian Church and School.
Auditorium.

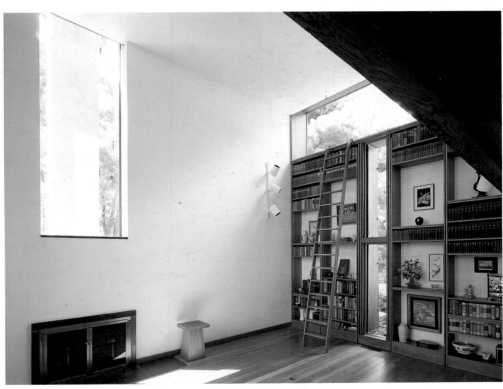

89

Preceding pages
87. Esherick House, Philadelphia, Pa., 1959–61.
Rear facade.

88. Esherick House. Front facade.
89. Esherick House. Living room.
90. Esherick house. First-floor plan, redrawn 1990.

This window seat had a lot of meaning and it became greater and greater in my mind as meaning associated with windows.[100]

The Unitarian Church may also owe something to Kahn's well-known fascination with plans of Scottish castles, a source more often linked to his later design for the Erdman dormitory (1960–65). Recalling his interest in 1973, he wrote: "The Scottish Castle. Thick, thick walls. Little openings to the enemy. Splayed inwardly to the occupant. A place to read, a place to sew. . . . Places for the bed, for the stair. . . . Sunlight. Fairy tale."[101] The result indeed recalls images of another time, its already complicated profile further exaggerated by light hoods rising above the parapet. Kahn had made these light-giving elements an integral part of the roofing structure, which was further enriched by inclined ceiling planes that configured the space below *(fig. 86)*. Typically Kahn's rejection of the conventional and more readily achievable flat roof reflected a pervasive rethinking of how spaces might be more expressively shaped. Frank Brown's lucid discussion of Roman vaulting may have encouraged Kahn in his own search.[102]

During 1960, as Kahn realized his thick walls in the Esherick and Unitarian Church commissions, he took the momentous step of consciously separating interior and exterior surfaces in his project for the Luanda Consulate. He had begun discussions with the State Department in October of the previous year and signed a contract for the consulate's design in December. In January 1960 he traveled to Angola to study conditions in accord with State Department policy, which urged some visible reflection of local climate and site.[103] Still, Kahn delayed in designing, and in March 1960 he had only his sketches of the site to submit as proof of work. Over the next three months he conceived his approach: to protect against intense glare, the chancellery and adjoining residence would each be enclosed by a second system of walls, and to

help cool the buildings a second roof would be erected to provide a ventilating layer of shade. Officials at the State Department were alarmed by Kahn's first drawings, finding the roof "bizarre" and fearing the buildings would seem "windowless," adding, "the whole concept is rather cold and formidable."[104] During the fall Kahn refined his design *(fig. 91)*; keyhole windows that he had added to the outer wall, a simplified roof structure, and clarified plan arrangements were more favorably received, but his seeming inability to meet deadlines, together with the State Department's changing political objectives, led to the cancellation of the commission in August 1961.[105] Kahn clung to the project; a model was completed later that same month *(fig. 92)*, while formal termination of the contract was pending, and Kahn did not submit his final bill until December 1962.[106]

The Luanda plans are clearly organized but not particularly remarkable. In the separation of walls and roofs, however, Kahn initiated an approach that for the time was revolutionary. Again work by Le Corbusier provided a precedent, for example the sunscreens shading the High Court at Chandigarh (1951–56), but a more remote and, for Kahn, less agreeable precedent, as he felt the problem of glare was unresolved by such devices. Even more emphatically he reacted against the sort of filigreed sunscreens popularized by Edward Durell Stone in the mid 1950s, for he sought an architectural rather than decorative solution. As he explained, "I thought of the beauty of ruins . . . the absence of frames . . . of things which nothing lives behind . . . and so I thought of wrapping ruins around buildings."[107] What began as the addition of one series of walls to another Kahn soon came to regard as one irreducible element, a hollow wall with the potential of two quite distinct interior and exterior profiles. This he first demonstrated in the Salk Institute for Biological Studies.

91

91. *U.S. Consulate, Luanda, Angola, 1959–62. Isometric diagram of wall and roof detail, Fall 1960.*
92. *U.S. Consulate. Model, ca. August 1961.*
93. *Salk Institute for Biological Studies, La Jolla, Calif., 1959–65. Plan of meeting house, Fall 1960–Spring 1961.*

92

93

94

94. *Richard Neutra. Kaufmann house, Palm Springs, Calif., 1946. Plan.*

Resolutions of Form and Design

Rarely has the beneficial effect of a sympathetic, collaborative client been better demonstrated than in the extraordinary commission given to Kahn by Jonas Salk. It was Kahn's first real opportunity to conceive the very nature of an institution itself, the tabula rasa he had long sought, and with his resulting design it is possible to define the beginning of a later, more mature phase of his career. In this context the commission will be more fully discussed in chapter 4. But the design for the unbuilt meeting house that Kahn initiated in the fall of 1960 *(fig. 93)* also brought to a conclusion the development of a formal vocabulary that Kahn had initiated with the Yale Art Gallery in 1951, for disparate elements of earlier work were now joined in one project. The meeting house is strongly, almost aggressively massive. Its interior spaces are differentiated according to use and defined by individualizing structure. These units of varied shape are juxtaposed in plan without an extrinsic management of form, resulting in a geometrically varied profile. This profile is further complicated by portions of walls enclosing differently shaped interior volumes, for in addition to passively juxtaposed shapes, other, more complicated shapes are juxtaposed through superimposition: squares enclosing circles, circles enclosing squares.[108] Although the similarity is surely coincidental, these configurations recall Renaissance diagrams of the Vitruvian man. Wittkower had described how these diagrams, inscribed within a superimposed square and circle, served "as a proof of the harmony and perfection of the human body . . . [and] seemed to reveal a deep and fundamental truth about man and the world."[109] What better symbol for Salk? For Kahn, the double layers generated by these superimposed shapes illustrated the different natures of inside and outside surfaces, which he diagrammed to accompany the first publication of the design in April 1961.[110] A few months later he wrote: "Because a wall has an interior which is different from an exterior . . . we have come to the point where this realization now can separate an exterior wall from an interior wall . . . and create space between them that you could walk between, that which you couldn't do with a solid stone wall."[111]

A comparison of the meeting house plan with Richard Neutra's Kaufmann house (Palm Springs, California, 1946, *fig. 94*) shows how far Kahn had progressed in the fourteen-year period since that much-praised example of American modernism had been completed. Kahn's plan is rendered to emphasize an ordered assembly of separate spaces, each firmly and clearly enclosed, while Neutra's emphasizes the opposite effect of freely disposed, flowing spaces with lines of enclosure purposely obscured. No governing logic seems to guide dimension or shape in Neutra's design; rather, the scheme reflects an unstructured freedom of what was rapidly becoming another age.[112] Wright's plans in these years exhibited more rigorous organization, but the differentiation of space was implied rather than explicit, and shapes were woven into unified, concordant tapestries.

Major periods of architectural history have often been defined by alternating manifestations of massive or volumetric shape, differentiated or open space, juxtaposed or unified geometries, and layered or exposed profiles. Similar characteristics, differently balanced, have been cited to demonstrate stylistic shifts from imperial Roman to Late Antique architecture, from Renaissance to Baroque, from premodern to modern, and so on. It could be argued that Kahn, beginning with the meeting house, redirected architectural style in the twentieth century through similar means. Yet to judge his work solely in physical terms obscures its deeper meanings, even if at this secondary level his measurable influence has been more immediate. But like Wright before him, Kahn projected an influence so pervasive as to defy concise summary. By reconnecting architecture with the fundamentals of history, he revitalized its primary forms and principles, and he awakened an entire generation of architects who followed. For some of those architects, less drawn to principles, this encouraged an almost picturesque application of specific historic motifs; for others, it led toward a profound exploration of spatial configuration. It would be premature to judge the former as a secondary phenomenon; work by Michael Graves and Robert A. M. Stern, among others, exhibits a warmth that comes from the familiarity of historic associations and should not be denied. But in the architecture of such diverse figures as Mario Botta and Tadao Ando, a deeper influence can be detected, one rooted in the freedom to reconsider the underlying aspects of design in the light of history.

Before Kahn's debt to history was openly acknowledged, critics tended to praise his work to the degree that it upheld standards of modernism, and they hesitantly excused his unusual, expressive forms as specific responses to tightly defined, conventionally narrow functions. They soon saw otherwise, among them Sibyl Moholy-Nagy, who wrote after visiting Kahn's office: "I was very much impressed with the first sight of the Philadelphia sketches till I realized . . . that these . . . towers are not the uniquely adequate solution of this and no other building, but are your trademark now: impartially imposed on everything you design. That is when I liked the [Mikveh Israel] Synagogue less."[113] Kahn indeed imposed inventive, sometimes historically inspired devices— keyhole windows, diagonal elements, circular towers—on whatever commission he was designing at any given time, irrespective of specific function. As he evolved his approach he was not bound by standard typologies. Historic precedents could suggest physical patterns and provide models for organizing space that were new to the twentieth century, but they were a means rather than an end.

The seriousness of Kahn's intent can be sensed in his brief, often repetitive writings. One article in particular stands out as summarizing his attitudes in the 1950s: "Form and Design," which he presented in an early form at the 1959 CIAM conference, then revised for delivery in California in April 1960, and further revised for a Voice of America broadcast in November 1960. With minor revisions this last version was much published, first by the Voice of America and shortly after by *Arts and Architecture* and *Architectural Design*.[114] To those requesting copies of his writings, "Form and Design" was most often sent; as a colleague explained, "It was worked on painstakingly by him over a period of several months and embodies, as nothing else he has written, his current thinking and ideas."[115]

In "Form and Design" Kahn described his work more as the discovery of some ideal, preexisting "form" than as the invention of something new:

> When personal feeling transcends into Religion (not a religion but the essence of religion) and Thought leads to Philosophy, the mind opens to realizations. Realization of what may be the *existence will* of, let us say, particular architectural spaces. Realization is the merging of Thought and Feeling at the closest rapport of the mind with the Psyche, the source of *what a thing wants to be*.[116]

Kahn's distinctions between "form" and "design," now matured from his first statements of 1953, thus offered a means of disciplining personal choice: "Form has no shape or dimension. . . . Form is 'what'. Design is 'how'. Form is impersonal. Design belongs to the designer. Design is a circumstantial act. . . . Form has nothing to do with circumstantial conditions."[117]

Until he discovered the Platonic image for any given problem, questions of materials and site remained secondary in importance,

as he explained in an earlier version of "Form and Design": "What material you use is circumstantial; it is a design problem. . . . The realization of what is an auditorium is absolutely beyond the problem of whether it is in the Sudan, or in Rio de Janeiro."[118] He reinforced this neo-Platonic view by likening form and design to ideas of "spoon" versus "*a spoon*," "house" versus "*a house*," and "school" versus "*a school*": "A School or a specific design is what the institution expects of us. But School, the spirit school, the essence of the *existence will*, is what the architect should convey in his design. And I say he must, even if the design does not correspond to the budget."[119] Regarding sources and extensions of Kahn's neo-Platonism there has been much thought, most of it necessarily speculative, as Kahn left few specific references. How he came to these ideas is thus somewhat uncertain, although such sources as Egyptian hieroglyphics and German romanticism have been suggested.[120]

Elsewhere in "Form and Design" Kahn partly explained his urge to differentiate space, and to relate that space to structure:

> A teacher or a student is not the same when he is with a few in an intimate room with a fireplace as in a large high room with many others. . . . Space has power and gives mode.

> Each space must be defined by its structure and the character of its natural light. . . . An architectural space must reveal the evidence of its making by the space itself.[121]

After mentioning selected projects, Kahn concludes "Form and Design" by discussing his unified vision of the city:

> The motor car has completely upset the form of the city. I feel that the time has come to make the distinction between the Viaduct architecture of the car and the architecture of man's activities. . . . The Viaduct architecture includes the street which in the center of the city wants to be a building. . . . The distinction between the two

95

96

95. *Market Street East Studies, Philadelphia, Pa.,
1960–63. Model, ca. January 1962.*
96. *Market Street East Studies. Bird's-eye perspective of inner viaduct, looking north, ca. 1961–62.*

architectures, the architecture of the Viaduct and the architecture of the acts of man's activities, could bring about a logic of growth and a sound positioning of enterprise.[122]

The designs for viaduct architecture that he envisioned for Philadelphia from 1959 to 1962 provided an outlet for explorations parallel to his writings. As rendered, they reflect an abstract mastery of Roman forms parallel to the much smaller Salk meeting house (*figs. 95, 96*). Like Piranesi, Kahn had reconfigured reality. But unlike Piranesi, he would in the years to follow transfer these monumental urban images to other, more realistic commissions.

Others besides Kahn were reexamining history at this time. Buildings by Philip Johnson, Eero Saarinen, and Minoru Yamasaki were among those in America sporting various historic motifs, but these motifs were applied primarily as surface decoration without ties to deeper principles of spatial configuration or structural integrity.[123] Kahn alluded to this issue in criticizing Saarinen's MIT Chapel (1950–55) in "Form and Design."[124] Elsewhere Kahn was critical of what he characterized as "chaotic permissiveness," and he spoke of the need for "an anchoring course of logic."[125] By 1961, following his critical decade of development, his innovative forging of that logic was beginning to be widely recognized, and he came to be acknowledged as the leader of what was termed the Philadelphia School. Referring to this school, which included such architects as Robert Venturi, Romaldo Giurgola, and Robert Geddes, all loosely allied through affiliations at the University of Pennsylvania, one writer stated: "The sixties, it appears, began without any coherent ideologies and systematic disciplines; instead, a strange free-for-all is the admitted, accepted, and defended design approach. There are indications, however, that among this confusion there is already in existence a new design movement with a powerful ideology and a clearly defined design approach."[126]

Kahn's dedication to conceiving buildings that symbolized human beliefs and aspirations, and to providing places where such values could flourish, guided later achievements. As he advised the Kennedy family in their planning for the John F. Kennedy Memorial Library:

> Every building that is built is dedicated to the man. It is a way of life. It is the first duty of an architect in order to know in what way to express this. I am hoping that a commitment here will be made to the well being of man. There are many ways to express this. Buildings are based on beliefs—that is the material you need to know, to know how to express it. This is the most important thing.[127]

As these words imply, Kahn believed it was imperative to identify human beliefs in order to discover ideal form, and to this end he rejected conventional typologies, which he suspected of subverting such investigation by supporting a routine response. As he had earlier observed: "The Air Force Academy [Skidmore, Owings, and Merrill, 1957ff] is a design based on building types accepted by the profession to date as appropriate. In a phenomenally short time the Academy was given form. . . . It would have taken Corbusier many months more than was apparently allowed the architects to conceive the Academy."[128]

As has been much noted, Kahn sought beginnings, designing each building as if it were the first of its kind. His often-cited example was that of the first school:

> Schools began with a man under a tree. . . . Soon spaces were erected and the first schools became. The establishment of school was inevitable because it was part of the desires of man. Our vast systems of education, now vested in Institutions, stem from these little schools but the spirit of their beginning is now forgotten. The rooms required by our institutions of learning are stereotype and uninspiring.[129]

He later added, "So I believe the architect somehow must hark back to the time of the beginning."[130] In the Salk Institute Kahn had the rare opportunity to actually conceive a new institution, but in other instances he simulated the effect of origination by reducing programs to their most basic human elements. This process of reduction seemed to relate very much to concerns for the single, essential use that gave meaning to any building. By examining these aspects it is possible to suggest a broad pattern of less conventional typologies that draw closer to Kahn's own objectives. Sharp divisions are necessarily arbitrary, for such typologies lack exclusivity. Yet in the 1960s, as Kahn's commissions increased to a degree not experienced in his earlier years, the linear development of an evolving vocabulary that characterized his work in the 1950s seemed to give way to parallel campaigns devoted to these typologies of use, and differences were clarified.

When Kahn wrote, "space has power and gives mode," and discussed how that power could impose patterns of use, he provided one clue to his manner of conceiving typologies: spaces providing for one person differed fundamentally from those for many. One typology seemed, then, to derive from the creation of individual places, or studies, which were strongly related whether they served laboratories or monasteries. These will be discussed in chapter 4. An opposite typology was guided by the need to create places for meeting or assembly, conceptually similar whether secular or religious, as examined in chapter 3. Kahn discussed ideal images of each: for study, the St. Gall plan, which diagrammed a series of extended, separated spaces for a monastery; and for assembly, the Pantheon, with its single holistic space.[131] Each defined the terminus of a continuum of possible spatial configurations.

A third typology, the subject of chapter 5, dealt with more complicated problems, with assemblages of components lacking any simple, single focus. For Kahn these resulting complexes were analogous to cities, and like cities they were meant to provide frameworks for more varied human use, for individual choice, and for the resources that he often termed "availabilities." In this way he seems to have rethought such ubiquitous problems as fine arts centers and commercial developments, finding within them unexpected bonds of human endeavor.

Near the end of his career, when Kahn defined the three major human inspirations as "learning, meeting, and well being," the basic typologies relating to study, assembly, and the availabilities seemed firmly established.[132] By then his richly complex, almost baroque solutions had been much publicized. At about this time he seems also to have considered a fourth typology, one that honored both ideas and things and that led him to simpler resolutions. Related in this way were libraries and museums as well as commemorative monuments, all providing spaces for experiencing the achievements of others. Perhaps his commitment to the Kennedy Memorial Library had first inspired the joining of these otherwise disparate types.[133] Later he used the term "treasury space" to characterize his project for the De Menil museum, again enlarging meaning.[134]

Very much a part of these honorific designs were Kahn's later writings relating silence and light, as discussed in chapter 6. How appropriate, then, that he sketched his concept for the Franklin Delano Roosevelt Memorial (1973–74) at the bottom of notes for a talk on silence and light.[135] For in conceiving his design together with ideas of eternity and creation, he reminds us that the simple placement of stones, like the room, is a beginning of architecture.

D.D.L.

Chapter 3

Assembly . . . a Place of Transcendence

Designs for Meeting

97

97. *Mikveh Israel Synagogue, Philadelphia, Pa., 1961–72. Sketchbook studies, ca. August 1962.*

Following pages
98. *Sher-e-Bangla Nagar, Dhaka, Bangladesh, 1962–83. National Assembly Building, seen from west hostels.*

Buildings dedicated to assembly provided Louis Kahn with extraordinary opportunities to express his beliefs. For him, places of meeting shared essential qualities that rendered differences between secular and religious use secondary in importance, and commissions as diverse as the Mikveh Israel Synagogue in Philadelphia (1961–72, unbuilt), the National Assembly Building at Sher-e-Bangla Nagar in Dhaka (1962–83; *fig. 98*), and the Palazzo dei Congressi in Venice (1968–74, unbuilt) thus drew together as a common endeavor. Few of these designs were realized, but in those that were, his visions of eternal, timeless principles assumed tangible form, and the promise of a new architecture, so fervently sought by his fellow architects, was fulfilled. This he accomplished despite the demands of more commissions than he could readily manage, commissions often made difficult by bureaucratic complexity and extensive travel to unfamiliar climes. With his growing fame, invitations to speak came even more frequently than in the previous decade, and these he continued to accept, for, however pressed, he remained unremittingly generous in sharing his ideas. Perhaps this very activity also proved stimulating, for it required that he focus on essentials and seemed to encourage a clarification of differences.

Kahn had first recorded his thoughts about assembly in 1955 when speaking of his design for the Adath Jeshurun synagogue (1954–55, unbuilt): "It is what the space wants to be: a place to assemble under a tree" (see *fig. 47*).[1] This sense of the historic origin of assembly he later elaborated by explaining his triangular synagogue as "free from a single traditional plan, free from a space everyone remembers as typical."[2]

In his next design for assembly—the First Unitarian Church in Rochester (1959–69), designed while he was still developing his mature vocabulary—he discarded the triangular shape, but not the centralized plan, which remained a constant. Theaters or lecture halls Kahn approached differently; performance—whether speech or music—differed by nature of its predictability, and a passive audience did not constitute true assembly: "With only one other person one feels generative. The meeting becomes an event. The actor throws aside the lines of his performance. The residue from all his thoughts and experiences meets the other on equal terms."[3]

Beginning in 1961, within a few weeks of receiving the commission for Mikveh Israel, Kahn began to speak more frequently of assembly and of beliefs that transcended conventional religion. Declining to enter the proposed competition for the state capital of Gandhinagar in India, Kahn explained: "The beginning of any work must start from Belief. . . . I distrust competitions because the design is unlikely to stem from Belief which is of religious essence out of a commonness sensed from other men."[4] Whether a particular use was religious or secular became incidental to the nature of assembly, which Kahn believed embodied a broader concept than either alone could command. This view was reflected in his frequent references to the Pantheon, for him an archetypal image: "It was a kind of conviction, a belief on the part of a man who said that this, because of its shape, presents a statement in form of what may be a universal religious space."[5] Later he described the Pantheon as "a kind of institution"[6] and then as "a world within a world. The client . . . saw the demand of this pantheonic requirement of no religion, no set ritual, only inspired ritual."[7] Centralized shapes—preferably circular rather than triangular—best served this end; thus the Pantheon was "a circular building from which one could derive a formalistic ritual."[8] Kahn developed his ideal prototype by adding an ambulatory. As eloquently explained in regard to the design of the Unitarian Church, the form of centralized volume was thus modified to allow participants to elect degrees of commitment. Kahn seemed drawn less to centralized churches of the fourth and fifth centuries than to their pagan prototypes; perhaps the particularized provisions for religious ritual and established axial hierarchies of those churches defeated the participatory experience he sought to foster.

In his first proposal for Mikveh Israel, presented in December 1961, Kahn began with a square sanctuary. Its ambulatory, slight at first, gradually expanded in later proposals until it came to have its own definition. From the outset he firmly separated the place for religious assembly from places for other uses, resisting the creation of any multipurpose spaces, however much later economy would seem to dictate. In Kahn's mind space dedicated to a single, elevating purpose was evidently essential to assembly, and in this he did not waver.

As a specific design, Mikveh Israel is better known for its "window rooms," the extraordinary cylindrical, open towers that Kahn derived from diverse sources but persuasively synthesized, so that ultimately they came to characterize one aspect of his inventive genius. They first appeared in plans dating from August 1962, spaced along the perimeter of a square sanctuary. Undated pages from Kahn's notebook suggest how he began their design: as light-filtering elements generated by a plan fully regulated according to circular modules (fig. 97). Brunelleschi's plan of Santo Spirito (Florence, 1434–82), although emphatically longitudinal, was similarly planned, and was originally to be bounded by continuous, semicircular niches that were meant to be seen from the outside.[9] Kahn's own design for the Salk meeting house of 1960 offered a closer precedent, both for cylindrical elements serving to modulate light and for the concept of separating interior and exterior walls. With Mikveh Israel, Kahn developed the circular unit as a space in itself, opened to

the inside and linked by passages so that the ambulatory assumed an architectural presence.

When Kahn gave the sanctuary an octagonal configuration in October 1962, he intensified its centralized focus. Its shape was slightly elongated in his scheme of the following year, but without a loss of centrality (*fig. 99*), and it was this version and its model (*fig. 100*) that Kahn preferred to illustrate in publications of his work.[10] As others have noticed, the plan resembles a cabalistic image of a Tree of Life that depicts ten aspects of God;[11] its symbolism would have been appropriate, but Kahn's knowledge of the image remains uncertain. Regarding the architect's approach to such obscure sources he stressed visual aspects alone: "He doesn't *read* the thing anyway. If it is in Latin, it is just the same as if it was in English, because he will see the pictures. He will see what he sees, what his mind tells him it is. . . . What you *think* it is, is absolutely as important as what the man *writes* it is."[12]

In appearance, Mikveh Israel understandably elicited comparisons with various medieval fortifications, yet the familiar gateways of ancient Rome's Aurelian walls would have provided an even earlier antecedent. Other buildings that Kahn designed also bore something of a castle air, and many of these were for assembly. Kahn admitted fascination with castles (see chapter 4), and the layered composition he defined for the synagogue visually ennobled its broader purpose as perceived from without. Perhaps more essentially, it strengthened the creation of the "world within a world" that Kahn so admired in the Pantheon and that he seemed to envision for Mikveh Israel (*fig. 101*). There, apart from the outer world yet within natural light seemingly generated by the building itself, assembled members of the congregation appear not as mute spectators but as participants actively seeking common understanding.

As with Jonas Salk, Kahn again benefited from an understanding client in Mikveh Israel, and while Dr. Bernard Alpers (for whom Esther Kahn worked) chaired the building committee, the design progressed. Kahn's proposal for Salk and Mikveh Israel —both resulting in construction estimates far beyond the original amounts available—were part of a pattern from which he rarely deviated: the refusal to be bound by conventional economic restraints. For Kahn, such restraints had no bearing on the ideal form each building should approximate. By discovering that form and giving it tangible shape, he understandably felt that he had fulfilled a primary obligation, and that somehow the means to realization would be found. Yet the degree of client support necessary to assemble the vast sums that were usually required was seldom sustained. Inspired by such commitment, Salk heroically jeopardized his institution and proved the rightness of their shared vision. With committees Kahn was ordinarily less fortunate, and at the very least defeating compromises resulted. Two extraordinary exceptions—both commissioned in the fall of 1962—were the Indian Institute of Management in Ahmedabad (1962–74; discussed in chapter 4), and Sher-e-Bangla Nagar in Dhaka (1962–83), originally commissioned as the legislative capital of East Pakistan. On the subcontinent Kahn's philosophic approach seemed more widely appreciated than in his own country. In the latter commission that appreciation was facilitated by the firm and continuing support of Dhaka's preeminent architect, Mazharul Islam, who actively supported Kahn's design throughout its long course.

Kahn received the Ahmedabad and Dhaka commissions at a time of unusual activity in his career. Only months before, in March 1962, he had moved his Philadelphia office for what would be the last time, from 138 South 20th Street to a more central location at 15th

99

100

99. *Mikveh Israel Synagogue, Philadelphia, Pa., 1961–72. Plan. Inscribed 10-29-63.*
100. *Mikveh Israel Synagogue. Model, January 1964.*
101. *Mikveh Israel Synagogue. Perspective of sanctuary, 1963.*

101

and Walnut. In addition to Mikveh Israel and Salk, Kahn was already involved with designs for the Erdman dormitory, the Fort Wayne cultural center, and the Levy Memorial Playground, as discussed in later chapters. His schedule was further complicated by the birth of a son, Nathaniel Alexander Phelps Kahn, in November that same year. Robert Venturi had introduced Kahn to Nathaniel's mother, Harriet Pattison, around 1959. She had a diverse background in theater, philosophy, and music, and had studied at Yale and in Edinburgh.[13] She and Kahn developed a close relationship that was to last until his death and that was to involve her as a professional associate, for after Nathaniel's birth she studied landscape architecture first as an apprentice to Dan Kiley, then at the University of Pennsylvania. During the last years of Kahn's life, she described herself as a "companion for his thoughts," and continued to offer influential support as he developed his ideas.[14] His sensitivity to the landscape grew, and he sought intellectual parallels between their relationship and that between Edwin Lutyens and Gertrude Jeckyll: "When I think of how sensitive a person must be in regard to human agreement, I think of Gertrude Jeckyll, who was a great landscape architect who worked with Lutyens, who was a great architect. . . . She was . . . very responsive to what would sympathize with his architecture."[15]

Kahn deferred work on the Dhaka commission until January 1963, when he traveled to the subcontinent to inspect the site and began designing one of his most important works: the capital district of what later became the independent nation of Bangladesh. Distinguished by the name Sher-e-Bangla Nagar, meaning "the city of the Bengal tiger," it lies on the outskirts of the city of Dhaka. He was to be occupied with this commission for the remainder of his life, yet when he returned from his first trip to Dhaka in early 1963, he already had the

guiding idea in mind. Referring to its beginnings, he explained to his students at the University of Pennsylvania:

> On the night of the third day, I fell out of bed with the idea which is still the prevailing idea of the plan. This came simply from the realization that assembly is of a transcendent nature. Men came to assemble to touch the spirit of commonness, and I thought that this must be expressible. Observing the way of religion in the living of the Pakistani, I thought that a mosque woven into the space fabric of the assembly would have such effect.[16]

From a long list of building requirements that he had been given, Kahn had already identified those essential components that could give meaning to his design:

> The relationship of the assembly, mosque, [supreme] court, and hostels in their interplay psychologically is what expresses a nature. The institution of assembly could lose its strength if the sympathetic parts were dispersed. The inspirations of each would be left incompletely expressed.
>
> What I'm trying to do is establish a belief out of a philosophy I can turn over to Pakistan so that whatever they do is always answerable to it.[17]

Kahn's dedication to the Dhaka commission was intense, and within a matter of days following his return he assigned it to his class as their studio problem. Forgotten was the earlier assignment of a new design for Market Street East that the dean of the school had urged Kahn to undertake; the greater and more realistic challenge of significant, city-scaled design in Dhaka now eclipsed hypothetical reworkings of Philadelphia.[18] With the class he continued to explore the underlying meaning of assembly, speaking of it as having "a religious atmosphere" and defining the sense of religion as "a realization that you are responsible beyond your own selfish self—the kind of thing that makes people group together to form a mosque or form a legislature. . . . Kinship, a simpler word than religion, comes from the same inspiration. . . . Because architecture has enclosure, it has the power to evoke a feeling of kinship when [one] enters the spaces."[19] Kahn's belief in the sacral meaning of secular assembly remained firm; he later said, "A house of legislation is a religious place,"[20] and, of the commission as a whole, "The stimulation came from the place of assembly. It is a place of transcendence for political people. . . . The assembly establishes or modifies the institutions of man."[21]

On the program he received during his first trip to Dhaka in early 1963 Kahn sketched his ideas.[22] He indicated positions for major elements within the site, emphasizing the geometric motif that would shape the joined assembly and mosque: two squares, one turned obliquely to the other. In March, during the spring break at the university, he returned to Dhaka to make his first presentation. The obliquely placed square of the assembly was diagrammed with a low dome near its center, and angled spurs representing minarets expanded the square mosque it touched (*fig. 102*). To give some shape to the largely featureless terrain and to guard against floods, Kahn proposed embanked roadways and geometrically shaped mounds of earth; on these he placed related elements, partly framed by a lake that he "employed . . . as a discipline of location and boundary."[23] At the opposite end of the expansive site he located schools, libraries, and other facilities, grouped as his Citadel of Institutions to balance the Citadel of Assembly.

Le Corbusier's work at Chandigarh (1951–63) must have been in Kahn's mind. He had visited that new capital during his first trip to India in November 1962, when he began work on the Indian Institute of Management, and later he urged his students to study it as they began their individual designs for Dhaka.[24] Yet however much he admired Le Corbusier, he also harbored

doubts about Chandigarh. Earlier he had praised Le Corbusier's buildings for their beauty, but he had also claimed that they were "out of context and had no position."[25] At Dhaka, Kahn's buildings were emphatically positioned so they formed a single, interconnected composition; an urge for connection seemed basic to his approach.

Nowhere was Kahn's urge for architectural connection more apparent than in the joining of mosque and assembly, the central focus of his plan for Dhaka. As a conscious motif, the linking of one square at its corner to a second, diagonally aligned figure had no exact parallel in his earlier work, nor was it a familiar plan elsewhere. At Dhaka, Kahn devised a forceful, active juxtaposition of parts that differed from both the more passive and the more sympathetic juxtapositions discussed in the previous chapter, for they were neither a loosely joined arrangement of differing shapes, as in later plans for the Unitarian Church (see *fig. 81*), nor a more formal grouping of similarly shaped, hierarchically stabilized units, as in an earlier scheme for that same project (see *fig. 80*). Dhaka's strongly wrought exterior differed also from cohesive shapes that Kahn had juxtaposed through superimposition, as in the Salk meeting house (see *fig. 93*). This geometric motif of active juxtaposition came to figure prominently in Kahn's work to follow immediately after. In such Roman precursors as Hadrian's Villa, such juxtapositions remained passive, for they lacked symmetrical disposition and were not planned together from the viewpoint of exterior presentation. Piranesi's reconstructed plan of the Campus Martius in Rome contained individual elements that more closely anticipate Kahn's, yet they had remained undeveloped as three-dimensional images. A closer antecedent to Kahn's design is Ledoux's first project for the Saltworks at Chaux, yet the superimposition of the two squares in that design neutralizes their visible interaction. Appropriately, Ledoux's compositions have been cited for leading the way from a classical toward a juxtapositional composition.[26] Out of such diverse sources, Kahn forged angular compositions quite unlike those of his contemporaries, for there was no longer any real resemblance to the relaxed meanderings best typified by Alvar Aalto's work, and even less to the cohesive triangular essays of Frank Lloyd Wright.

Kahn's plan for the Erdman dormitory at Bryn Mawr, with three parallel squares joined at their corners, lies at the threshold of the Dhaka proposal. Its difficult resolution in December 1961 came a few days after Kahn had defined a central and troubling issue: "The architecture of connection . . . that which connects the usable space. . . . This is the measure of the architect—the organization of the connecting spaces—that which gives the man walking through the building . . . a feeling of the entire sense of the institution."[27] During ensuing months Kahn cited his plan for Bryn Mawr as resolving the issue: "It never occurred to me that I could take the square and turn it . . . so that it made its own connection."[28] Anne Tyng's Bryn Mawr proposal had surely been the catalyst for this change; connecting its angled, central squares to surrounding rooms were linear walkways much like the angled corridors of Ledoux's plan for Chaux.

In his first scheme for Dhaka, Kahn effected a still more powerful connection than in the Erdman dormitory. By angling the mosque against the assembly building, he brought into dynamic balance places for two kinds of assembly, with the contemplative holding the active in check. In such angled geometries Kahn found a principle of broad meaning and wide applicability, for Dhaka's plan seemed to inspire other designs, like the Norman Fisher house (1960–67). The early date of the Fisher commission would suggest otherwise, but in January 1963 Kahn admitted that it was still undesigned and assigned it to his students at the university while he made his first trip to Dhaka. As documents show, it was only later in 1963 that he reached a solution. It was also after his return from Dhaka that he added similar shapes to his Levy Memorial Playground plan (1961–66). Likewise resolved were the Indian Institute of Management and the University of Virginia Chemistry Building (1960–63). Sketches for the former had included angled lines representing prevailing breezes and suggesting angled orientation, but it was only in March 1963 that Kahn resolved its plan with juxtaposed squares. It was also in March that the towered, fortresslike auditorium of the chemistry building gave way to an angled square joined at its corners to surrounding wings. During the summer of 1963 he began to incorporate similar geometries in studies for the Fort Wayne Fine Arts Center.

After his March presentation in Dhaka, Kahn reduced the size of the mosque and incorporated it more fully within the assembly building. Yet the richly curvilinear structure he ultimately designed, with cylindrical light-giving elements at the corners, was resolutely angled away from the main axis and toward Mecca (*fig. 103*), maintaining a visible presence. The Mosque of the Shah in Isfahan (1612–38) had been similarly angled away from the axis of the Royal Square but its site was constrained in a way that Dhaka's was not, and Kahn could easily have eliminated the angle through a slight realignment of the entire complex. Again it seemed a willful means of strengthening identity; as Kahn described, "I made it differently that way so that you could, in fact, express [the mosque] differently."[29]

Other, more separate elements of the program were either eliminated or brought toward the assembly, juxtaposed in a manner

102

103

104

102. Sher-e-Bangla Nagar, Dhaka, Bangladesh, 1962–83. Site model, ca. March 1963.
103. Sher-e-Bangla Nagar. Plan of National Assembly Building, 1966.
104. Sher-e-Bangla Nagar. Site model, January 1973.

Following pages
105. Sher-e-Bangla Nagar. East hostels.
106. Sher-e-Bangla Nagar. Aerial view of east hostels.

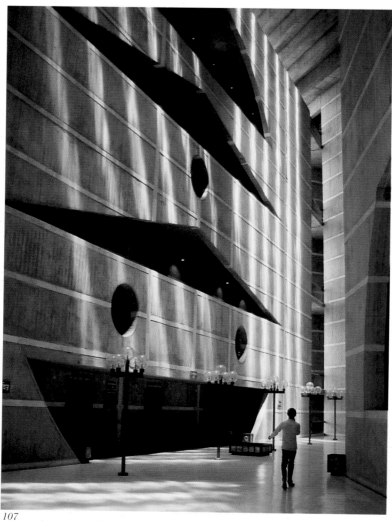

107

107. *Sher-e-Bangla Nagar. National Assembly Building ambulatory.*
108. *Sher-e-Bangla Nagar. Assembly chamber.*

Following pages
109. *Sher-e-Bangla Nagar. Ceiling of assembly Chamber.*

111

Preceding pages
110. Sher-e-Bangla Nagar. National Assembly Building,
view from east.

111. Sher-e-Bangla Nagar. North entrance staircase.
112. Sher-e-Bangla Nagar. National Assembly Building,
west detail.

emphasizing centralized focus. Hostels flanking the assembly remained at each side, visually supporting the central structure (figs. 105, 106). Their original purpose of providing places of temporary residence for the legislators was thus demonstrated. Within the assembly building itself an ambulatory of grandly sublime scale further amplified the assembly's elevated purpose while providing a less formal space for related activity (fig. 107). To bring natural light to the interiors of the vast structure, Kahn developed "hollow columns"—something akin to light wells, but in his mind having greater architectural purpose:

> In the plan of the assembly I have introduced a light giving element to the interior of the plan. Consider if you see a series of columns you can say that the choice of columns is a choice in light. The columns as solids frame the spaces of light. Now think of it just in reverse and think that the columns are hollow and much bigger and their walls can themselves give light, then the voids are rooms, and the column is the maker of light and can take on complex shapes and be the supporter of spaces and give light to spaces.[30]

In study models these "hollow columns" were given clear geometric definition; as realized, they were shaped by the volumes they adjoined, and they brought light to the outer offices rather than to the assembly itself. There Kahn struggled to find the ideal roof for this most important of spaces, a structural solution that would sustain the abstract geometry of his design and, perhaps most importantly, bring light from above. Kahn had praised the Pantheon's oculus as a source of light "that is most transcending" and "an expression of a world within a world";[31] now that ideal seemed likely to elude him. He disagreed with August Komendant, his consulting engineer, who saw no structural logic in what he sought,[32] and ultimately settled for a melon-shaped vault that lacked the visual strength of his earlier proposals (figs. 108, 109).

Elsewhere on the site Kahn's design was subject to the vicissitudes of a complicated and ever-developing program. As more components were added, the simple clarity of his early schemes gave way to greater crowding, and outside the area of governmental buildings his controlling concept became more difficult to perceive (fig. 104). Of necessity, associates assumed responsibility for much of the housing and some related structures, although Kahn oversaw even these smaller elements to the degree possible during his visits to the site.[33] Evidence suggests he was more closely involved with the design of the observatory (added to the program in September 1963) and of the higher categories of housing. But it is in the assembly and related hostels that his hand remained most sure.

During construction, views of the assembly suggested the timeless geometry of the observatories of the Maharajah Sawai Jai Singh II at Jaipur and Delhi, as do views of the members' hostels (fig. 106). Kahn would have noticed Isamu Noguchi's photographs of the observatories published in *Perspecta*,[34] and surely he visited the Jantar Mantar in Delhi. Sympathetic to those eighteenth-century observatories, Kahn's building, too, seems to chart cosmic order. In the assembly building itself the elemental forms that surround the central chamber sustain this image, as do the unglazed openings in the outer walls (see fig. 105). Echoes of antiquity—at least antiquity as it was imagined—seem to lie behind even the most abstract of these shapes. Like eyes looking in both directions toward wider realms that lie beyond, they also recall Ledoux's famous drawing of the proscenium in his Théâtre Besançon (1771–73). By limiting himself to basic Euclidian shapes, Kahn disciplined sentiment and achieved that rare level of abstraction wherein each individual could discover personal meaning. Thin lines of white marble accent the joints, ennobling the exposed concrete of the walls while marking increments of construction and also tracing an element of human scale. The red brick of adjoining terraces and of the hostels further reinforces the special nature of the assembly. Everywhere are marks of local effort in building so mighty a structure, and they enlarge its already heroic scale (*fig. 112*).

For some, the assembly building recalls such Italian fortifications as the Castel del Monte.[35] Others have likened its plan to the centralized traditions of Islamic and Buddhist architecture, believing that Kahn fused Eastern and Western traditions.[36] In 1990, observant of the building's power to generate national pride, one writer said:

> This cosmo-geographical macrocosm, whose microcosms are those of the city, the mosque, the house and the garden, distills a concept of divine essence which leads us by specific ways and paths in earth-paradise ascension. . . . This is architecture which restores something to those who have no heritage, who find in it an image their dignity, and who—for lack of anything better—see in it vision of a different life.[37]

More simply, Kahn himself said, "The image is that of a many-faceted precious stone, constructed in concrete and marble."[38] Some have criticized the building for lacking human scale,[39] yet partly this may have been Kahn's purpose, at least from distant viewpoints. By avoiding such conventions, he stressed the "transcendent nature" of assembly rather than the smaller dimension of the individual. For those who assemble within, and for the larger populace who gather peacefully on its broad terraces, the building surely fulfills its purpose.

The architectural representation of assembly must have been compelling as an idea, for it seemed to guide Kahn's parallel work in Islamabad, the new capital of West Pakistan. This was designated as the executive capital of the country, balancing the legislative capital in East Pakistan. The government selected Constantine Doxiadis to devise the master plan, which was published in May 1961, and various prominent architects were assigned major buildings, including Gio Ponti and Alberto Rosselli for a central secretariat and Arne Jacobsen for a second, supplementary assembly.[40] In July 1963, while refining his master plan for the east capital in Dhaka, Kahn was selected as the architect for the President's Estate in Islamabad, intended as a residential and administrative complex.[41] Gradually he assumed responsibility for other components of the capital as well, including the assembly when Jacobsen's design was judged unsatisfactory.

There is no evidence of any design effort on Kahn's part before December 1963, and sketches made during ensuing months show little more than preliminary effort, with juxtaposed geometries portraying an active engagement of interrelated parts. Beginning in September of the following year, while Kahn was being pressured to present some indication of his design, his sketches suggest a firmer sense of architectural composition (*fig. 113*).[42] The President's Estate, shown as a linear complex along the left, is linked by an angled square containing administrative offices to a triangular element designated as a center for Islamic studies. These three elements enclose one corner of what came to be known as Presidential Square; at the top of the drawing, Kahn, beginning to take over from Jacobsen, sketched his first diagrammatic indication of the assembly building for Islamabad, shown as a circular building much like the hollow-column study for Dhaka. By the time of his first presentation in October 1964, this had taken the form of a truncated pyramid; at its center was a circular opening, and within that, an obliquely placed cube. By January 1965 Kahn was also designing a national monument on the square, apparently developed as part of the

113

114

115

113. President's Estate, First Capital of Pakistan,
Islamabad, 1963–66. Site plan. Inscribed LIK
September 30, 64.
114. President's Estate. Site model, ca. March 1965.
115. President's Estate. Site model, September 1965.
116. President's Estate. First-floor plan of Assembly
Building, after March 1965.

116

President's Estate. Describing his initial idea to Robert Matthew, the architectural coordinator for the Administrative Sector of Islamabad, he said, "It could be a new concept of Minaret embodying a small chapel raised above the level of the square, and a special platform from where one could preach facing Mecca. . . . The square is being suggested as a roofless Hall of Meeting. . . . The Assembly Building has remained essentially the same. Its shape was praised by Noguchi."[43] By March 1965 Kahn had further refined the assembly building, shown at the left of a site model (fig. 114) as a cube atop a square platform with towerlike elements at the corners. At the bottom of the model the linear President's Estate is elaborated with monumental apses, and at the top the National Monument appears as a truncated obelisk. The triangular center for Islamic studies defines the fourth side of Presidential Square, and behind it Ponti's administrative buildings are indicated as low rectangles.

At what point Kahn was invited to design the assembly building, and how definite its commission, remain uncertain. Jacobsen's design for the assembly, with facades of anodized aluminum and glass, had been rejected sometime after its presentation in January 1964, and reports identified Kahn as its new architect.[44] Yet in Kahn's much-delayed contract of January 1965 there is no mention of any responsibility for the assembly, and following his presentation in March he was criticized for not restricting his efforts to the President's Estate and the related monument.[45] Kahn apparently began to study the problem without an official invitation, believing its sympathetic design critical to his own efforts and to the entire venture of the new capital. Kahn's own notes at the time allude to this, for he wrote, "The master plan and the spirit of its architecture are one," explaining that the "establishment of a building order" was essential to the city

as a whole and that "the buildings of the higher institutions must be the inspiration for the continuance of . . . buildings designed by many architects."[46]

After March 1965 Kahn's invitation to design the assembly must have been more legitimized, for during the summer he focused on its design without further complaint from Matthew, and a developed scheme resulted. By August it had attained a clear definition that made the rambling shapes of the President's Estate seem unplanned by comparison. In place of the generalized form of his earlier cube, Kahn now proposed a shallow dome resting on an elongated drum that rose from its base like Choisy's idealized drawings of the Pantheon (fig. 115).[47] Ambulatories enclose the central chamber, where the rotated squares, indicated as generating the plan, emphasize centrality (fig. 116). The low wings of the outer enclosure are geometrically less complicated than Dhaka's, but only slightly less protective. Government officials had stipulated "that the architecture be given an Islamic touch,"[48] and this accounts in part for both the dome and the plan; Kahn had written, "The insistence of the Islamic touch is plaguing . . . but in spite of this, it can stimulate resources not called on before."[49]

Ultimately the Pakistan government rejected Khan's designs for both the assembly and the President's Estate, diverting the commission to Edward Durell Stone.[50] He designed a predictable confection of no apparent distinction; without the guiding intellect of Dhaka's Mazharul Islam, government officials were apparently unwilling to gamble with genius. Yet however distinctive Kahn's proposals were by comparison with Stone's, they seemed to lack the conviction of his work at Dhaka. His simplified Islamabad assembly may have represented a conscious effort to distill essential components—a powerfully centralized form with the pressure

117

118

117. *Hurva Synagogue, Jerusalem, Israel,*
1967–74. Site section, ca. July 1968.
118. *Temple Beth-El Synagogue, Chappaqua,*
N.Y., 1966–72. Perspective. Inscribed Lou K '68.
119. *Hurva Synagogue. Plan, ca. July 1968.*
120. *Hurva Synagogue. Model for first scheme, ca.*
July 1968.
121. *Hurva Synagogue. Section of third scheme.*
Inscribed Lou K '72.

119

120

121

122. *Palazzo dei Congressi, Venice, Italy,*
1968–74. Elevation. Inscribed Lou K 1970.
123. *Palazzo dei Congressi. Interior perspective.*
124. *Palazzo dei Congressi. Model for Giardini*
Pubblici site, January 1969.
125. *Palazzo dei Congressi. Model for Arsenale*
site, May 1973.

of its single vaulted chamber relieved by ambulatories—yet without the firm positioning established by Dhaka's hostels and terraces, its presence was not fully appreciable. And the President's Estate seemed never to have achieved fixed location or perceivable form. Kahn had insisted on full control of the master plan at Dhaka; at Islamabad there was no such opportunity, and the results were telling.

Of Kahn's three remaining commissions focused on assembly, only the smallest and least consequential was realized: Temple Beth-El in Chappaqua, New York (1966–72). Yet even with so small a commission he conceived a strongly centralized structure symbolic of its purpose (fig. 118). Kahn was selected as architect in July 1966, but he deferred its design until after a contract was signed in March of the following year.[51] From the outset he urged that an ambulatory be added to the program, justifying it as a place for extra seating.[52] Well before he reduced Beth-El's final design to the relatively simple wood-framed structure that was built from 1970 to 1972,[53] he had initiated proposals for assemblies that were less realistic yet more stimulating: the Hurva Synagogue in Jerusalem and the Palazzo dei Congressi in Venice.

With the Hurva Synagogue, Kahn had his first opportunity to build within the archaeological boundaries of the ancient world that had so moved him during his earlier travels. In August 1967 he was asked to rebuild a smaller synagogue that had once stood on the site,[54] which he visited in December, but he did not begin concentrated effort on its design until July of the following year, a few days before returning to Jerusalem to present his proposal.[55] The rich architectural heritage of the site must have charged the commission with special meaning. As Kahn worked on the design, he spoke of the honor of expressing "the spirit of history and religion of Jerusalem,"[56] recalling his earlier statement, "The ancient building still vigor-

ous in use has the light of eternity."[57] His early studies reinforce this caring attitude, for they show a proposal that is in a sympathetic relationship with the ancient city. The broader setting of the synagogue included two of the world's most significant religious monuments, the Dome of the Rock (A.D. 688–691) and the Church of the Holy Sepulchre (ca. A.D. 326ff); Kahn conceived his design in relation to these, sensing its potential to symbolize a third religion. Drawings suggest how these buildings also related to the still more ancient terrain of their setting (fig. 117); as he had once depicted the weight of human history in his drawing of the Athenian acropolis, so Kahn also evoked it in Jerusalem, though now with the added dimension of his own creation.

Kahn's monumental vision exceeded the expectations of his patrons, who had thought of the structure in more modest terms, yet they came to support it. After the first presentation, Mayor Teddy Kollek of Jerusalem described the design as a "world synagogue," saying, "It's an idea that a beautiful synagogue should be built in Jerusalem."[58] The scheme also reinforced Kahn's ideas of assembly. Four hollow piers defined the corners of a centrally focused, square sanctuary (fig. 119). Surrounding the piers, an ambulatory separated the sanctuary from an outer enclosure of sixteen square niches. These were provided— or, more likely, were justified—as spaces for a special candle service. Stairways at the centers of the outer enclosure led to an upper gallery, and the corners were left open as entrances. The four central piers flared out near the top as a roof for the cubical space, and the niches tapered inward, rising above the roof like fortifying pylons (fig. 120). Shown unglazed and composed of simple, almost neutral elements, the building bore the air of an occupied ruin from some ancient yet unspecifiable epoch.

Kahn's primitivistic plan recalls such conjectural reconstructions of the Temple of

Solomon as in Fergusson's *History of Architecture*, a resemblance that was soon noted.[59] Seeking information on early synagogues from New York's Jewish Theological Seminary, Kahn had been sent a copy of an article which emphasized the importance of Solomon's Temple;[60] filed with slides of his first proposal was an unidentified reconstruction of its ancient precinct. The temple would have been an appropriate inspiration, for it not only marked a beginning of Jewish architecture, but also, as recounted by Wittkower, embodied cosmic ratios transmitted by God to Moses.[61]

While Kahn altered details in later variations of the Hurva Synagogue, his basic concept remained unchanged. The version he presented in July 1969 substituted a curved shell with perimetral supports for the hollow piers of his first design and moved the ark and the bema to an outer location.[62] In a final version of July 1972 the ark and the bema had regained a more central position where they might more effectively interact as a focus of participatory assembly, and four hollow piers were again located at the corners of the sanctuary, now with capitals enriched by oval openings (*fig. 121*).[63] The calm symmetry of the design contrasts with the more active shapes of Dhaka and corresponds appropriately to Kahn's later work of a more commemorative nature. Kollek remained supportive but unable to convince the congregation to build Kahn's design.[64] Thus the "light of eternity" Kahn sought remained all too elusive.

In Venice, as in Jerusalem, Kahn found a city rich in the evidence of its beginnings. The idea of a hall for meeting with which he was presented in April 1968 seemed clear enough, but its functional necessity within the Biennale and its larger purpose were both sufficiently vague to stimulate Kahn's imagination. With the Palazzo dei Congressi commission came an opportunity to shape an institution that would be experienced and judged in close proximity to examples of great architecture, and in the noted Venetian professor Giuseppe Mazzariol he again found an understanding intellect who would guide and support his proposals. Kahn offered to work without his usual fee as a gift to the city.

The Palazzo dei Congressi was less tied to ritualistic or procedural requirements than were Kahn's earlier designs for assembly, and he seemed to begin, as he had with Adath Jeshurun some fifteen years earlier, by recalling early places of meeting. At the time of his initial presentation he described his design as "a place of happening," continuing, "In the Congress Building in Venice . . . I am thinking of building a place which is the meeting of the mind and a place where expressions of the meeting of the mind can take place."[65] Its form, however, was more structured, perhaps in the way Kahn imagined the first architecturally defined places for assembly to have developed, and in it he drew a fine distinction between passive and participative assembly: "I can see the Congress Hall as if it were a theater in the round—where people look at people—it is not like a movie theater where people look at a performance. My first idea, regardless of the shape of the site, was to make so many concentric circles with a nucleus in the middle."[66]

Restrictive site conditions worked against Kahn's ideal form. To avoid existing trees while staying within the portion of the garden he was assigned, it was necessary for him to give the building a long and narrow shape, and to simplify foundation problems in the spongy soil, he elected to support the building in the manner of a bridge, with only a minimal number of supports at each end (*fig. 122*). The idea of a bridge held special meaning in Venice, and Kahn's design has been compared to the Rialto, described as "the most effective stage of the theater of Venetian life."[67] In contrast to the massive piers supporting each end of the building, the visually light suspension structure of the hall itself would have sustained the spirit of celebration he felt essential to its purpose.[68] Early sketches (probably done before his first informal presentation to Mazzariol in October 1968) suggest the design's evolution. Near both the upper and lower right, amidst hammock-like diagrams, are sections showing a theatrical cavea within a suspended frame. He further narrowed this form, explaining as he presented his design in Venice in January 1969: "Because the site is long and narrow, I simply sliced the theater in the round with two parallel cuts . . . the impression in the hall will be of people seeing people. The curve of the meeting hall is slight in order to retain the sense that it is really a street-like-piazza gently sloping. One could be reminded of the Palio Square in Siena."[69] Kahn's travel sketch of Siena had been one of his most powerful images, an agora molded advantageously for assembly.

To the ideal form of a theater in the round Kahn also added an ambulatory-like space (*fig. 123*), bringing his design more into alignment with his other designs for assembly. As he explained, "to each side . . . are two streets . . . which lead to the seating place . . . provided with niches where people can go away from the congress and discuss things separately."[70] His model (*fig. 124*) showed the sensitive positioning of the Palazzo dei Congressi on its site and its relation to the added elements, which he kept distinct: an entrance pavilion in the shape of a cube, and another cubical structure containing galleries and studios behind. In these, as in the meeting hall itself, he seemed to work mainly with simple, whole numbers, maintaining basic modular relationships.[71] Komendant again served as Kahn's consultant, insuring structural efficiency. In 1970, at his insistence, segmentally arched openings were removed from the parapet and replaced with balusters that Kahn rendered in the manner of an Archaic stoa.

In typical fashion, Kahn continued to design even when the commission was uncertain, for political debate made realization unlikely. And later, in 1972, he willingly revived his design for a new site near the Arsenale; there the building would actually bridge a canal (*fig. 125*). As with Mikveh Israel, Islamabad, and Hurva, he clung tenaciously to a concept that had assumed real existence in his mind and seemed too vitally a part of his thinking to abandon. And he remained steadfast in seeking to build his ideas, no doubt partly as proof of their validity and as a measure of his accomplishment. In his designs for assembly, he gave shape to universal qualities of meeting that enlarged individual worth.

D.D.L.

Chapter 4

The Houses of the Inspirations

Designs for Study

126

126. *Salk Institute for Biological Studies, La Jolla, Calif., 1959–65. Perspective of site, ca. January 1960.*

At the same time that Louis Kahn was devising an architecture to accommodate the human desire to assemble, he was also at work making an architecture for the complicated mixture of collective and individual activity that occurred in schools, research centers, and monasteries. These institutions were among those that he called "the houses of the inspirations"—places defined by the fundamental inspiration to learn and by the concomitant need to shelter learning within a supportive community.[1] Such idealistic clients brought him many of the commissions that poured into his office in the early 1960s, projects that seemed to bring with them the optimism and commitment that radiated from John F. Kennedy's presidency. For these institutions, Kahn created an architecture rooted in natural order and human tradition.

Learning was for Kahn an existential quest. It was at heart an exploration of life itself, as he told a medical school conference in 1964:

> I believe that the institution of learning actually stems way back from the nature of nature. Nature, physical nature, records in what it makes how it was made. Within us is the complete story of how we were made, and from this sense, which is the sense of wonder, comes a quest to know, to learn, and the entire quest, I think, will add up to only one thing: how we were made.[2]

Community making was also one of mankind's—and the architect's—chief responsibilities. Kahn proclaimed to an interviewer in 1961, "I wanted very much . . . to demonstrate to the man on the street a way of life."[3] Three years later he was even more emphatic about the task: "I don't believe that society makes the man. I believe that man makes the society."[4] The combined challenges of supporting learning and making model communities generated three of Kahn's most successful built works—the Salk Institute for Biological Studies in La Jolla, California, Erdman Hall at Bryn Mawr College, and the Indian Institute of

Management in Ahmedabad—as well as a large handful of extraordinary unbuilt projects.

Work on many of these similar problems began in a rush. Late in 1959, with the Richards Building under construction, Kahn was contacted about designing the Salk Institute and an arts center in Fort Wayne. In 1960, while the design of the Rochester church was being developed, commissions were received from Bryn Mawr College, the University of Virginia, and the Philadelphia College of Art. The following year brought Wayne State University and St. Andrew's Priory into the office—contemporaries of Mikveh Israel synagogue—and 1962 saw the start of the Indian Institute of Management, in the same year that the commission for the new capital of East Pakistan was assigned. After a lapse, three similarly motivated clients hired Kahn in 1965: St. Catherine's convent, the Maryland Institute College of Art, and Phillips Exeter Academy, followed by Rice University in 1969. Because Kahn's work defies ordinary typological classification, two of these functionally related commissions—Fort Wayne and the Philadelphia College of Art—will be treated in chapter 5 with Kahn's urban design work of this period. For the same reason, his library and dining hall for Exeter will find their place in chapter 6, with the commemorative and honorific buildings that occupied much of his time during the last years of his career. But all need to be tabulated here to portray the full impact this species of work had on his practice.

The first step of Kahn's planning, as always, was to strip clients' architectural programs down to the essence of the human activity they contained. It was thus that he established the character of a building, based more on his own feelings than the conditions stated by his employers. His consideration of these institutions devoted to study and contemplation was defined by his knowledge of education, his imaginings about monastic life, and his commitment to activist, social architecture.

Kahn's educational experience had begun with years as a commuting student, criss-crossing Philadelphia to public school, to special art classes, and finally to the University of Pennsylvania. Then, as a teacher, he had first worked informally, outside the academic establishment, and subsequently as a part-time critic who commuted to Yale and Penn. This peripatetic pattern produced an anti-establishment view of education and inspired one of his most repeated architectural fables:

> Schools began with a man under a tree, who did not know he was a teacher, discussing his realizations with a few others, who did know they were students. The students reflected on the exchange between them and on how good it was to be in the presence of man. They wished their sons, also, to listen to such a man. Soon the needed spaces were erected and the first schools came into existence. The establishment of schools was inevitable because they are part of the desires of man.[5]

In Kahn's idealization of the programs for these buildings, he combined this hazy image of the collective work of education with an even more abstract vision of monastic solitude. Like Le Corbusier before him, he revered the monastery as a model habitat, and he often spoke with admiration of the famous monastery plan of St. Gall. Although Kahn designed a number of synagogues, churches, and mosques, he was personally more inclined toward private reflection, like that of monks, than public manifestations of religion. He admired the Pantheon in part because its great circular form was "a non-directional space, where only inspired worship can take place. Ordained ritual would have no place."[6] Contemplation, it seemed to him, was of universal educational significance, and it was thus a relevant model for the complementary, independent part of learning.

The obvious pleasure that Kahn took in working on programs of this kind also derived from his long-standing interest in the making of human communities. During his early career this concern had been focused on the challenges of public housing, a field that was nourished by a national enthusiasm for social action during the Depression and then accelerated by the urgency of wartime needs. But after World War II, American public housing drifted downward, providing only minimal shelter for the poorest of the poor. Kahn himself witnessed this dispiriting spiral in working on the two phases of housing at Mill Creek in West Philadelphia (1951–63). By the time he received this new wave of commissions, he was looking for renewed inspiration.

Despite the apparent vagueness of Kahn's reinvented, composite program for these educational institutions—the sheltering tree and the monastery—his thinking rapidly assumed concrete form when it came into contact with his strong and mature visual preferences. His ideas were handily captured by his favorite shapes. In plan, the pavilions of the Richards Building and the concentric served and servant hierarchy of the Rochester Unitarian Church were useful starting points. In elevation, there continued the drama of historic rediscovery that had begun in his towered and seemingly thick-walled buildings of the late fifties, full of allusion to the power of medieval and ancient monuments. Created at the point of intersection between Kahn's poetic understanding of human life and such lively visual desiderata, these were works whose genesis was sometimes stormy. Compromise seemed impossible; it was a matter of adjusting conditions perfectly until fusion could occur. Many of the projects remained unbuilt.

Kahn's solutions for the first two of these projects—the Salk Institute and Erdman Hall, a dormitory for Bryn Mawr College—translated the abstract problem into convincingly material terms. In both cases, a powerful but sympathetic client demanded the best from Kahn and wrested an excellent design from his some-

times too reluctant fingers. He liked dealing with individuals who were intelligent and could hold up their side of the client-architect relationship. In 1963 he told a Yale audience: "It's the man, the man only, not a committee, not a mob—nothing makes anything but a man, a single, single man."[7] Naturally, he thought he was describing himself at the same time.

Jonas Salk, the inventor of the first effective polio vaccine, was the most impressive intellectual Kahn ever had as a client. Fortunately, their thinking converged on the challenge of repairing the modern schizophrenia that had divorced human intellect from spirit, and they became friends and collaborators. As no one else might have, Salk could reject Kahn's proposals without deadening the architect's interest in the project, and he did so on two significant occasions. Kahn, who met Salk in December 1959, called him "my most trusted critic."[8]

What Salk wanted was nothing less than a recombination of science and the humanities. To mend the rift that had split modern life between the "two cultures" C. P. Snow had described in 1959, Salk foresaw a facility that would both support scientific research and foster the exchange of ideas between scientists and other cultural leaders.[9] "Instead of writing a book, I decided to make the statement architecturally," he later recalled.[10] The test of this architecture, as he often said, was that it should be a place where he could entertain Pablo Picasso.[11]

Kahn translated Salk's description of the two cultures into the "measurable" and the "unmeasurable," a vocabulary that was obviously congruent with his own concept of "design" and "form," and he accepted the challenge of fulfilling Salk's holistic vision as part of his own architectural quest.[12] He was sincere, seeing to it that Snow was invited to the dinner party following Kahn's presentation of the annual discourse of the Royal Institute of British Architects in London in 1962, but, being an artist, Kahn did not always describe the two cultures in morally equal terms. "Science finds what is already there," he told an audience in 1967, "but the artist makes that which is not there."[13]

Kahn first visited Salk's spectacular site atop the Pacific cliffs at La Jolla in January 1960. His initial sketches, and the model worked up from them during the next few months, reflected his own formulation of the program (Salk had given him only the barest outline), with a tripartite division of the facility into laboratories, residences, and a meeting house for the exchange of ideas among researchers and with the wider world (figs. 126, 128). Salk accepted the three-part parti, but he immediately rejected the planned laboratories, which Kahn proposed to assemble at the inland end of the site in studio towers like those of the Richards Building. Although the Richards design was already famous, Salk insisted on the kind of practical, open-plan building that was usual for laboratories. This open planning was what Kahn himself had created in the Yale Art Gallery, but he now saw it as an old-fashioned modernist cliché. He could not, however, reject Salk's directive.

Salk also explicitly suggested to Kahn that his scientific community might be modeled on the monastery of San Francesco in Assisi. Salk had visited the monastery in 1954, and Kahn had sketched it in 1929.[14] That the architect accepted this suggestion as a friendly one does not need to be questioned, given the repeated praise for historical sources that had dotted his utterances since the 1940s and his specific interest in monasteries. But that does not mean that the Salk Institute was created as a medievalist romance. Its design was an imbricated pattern of historical and modern thinking of the kind that was now natural to Kahn.

The labs themselves were reworked during 1960–62 as four large, two-story buildings, spanned by a prodigious system of folded plates and box girders that provided a walk-through space for plumbing and ventilation (what Kahn called servant space) (fig. 127). This heroic structural honesty made amends for the cunning deceit of the Yale Art Gallery, where the elaborate ceiling pattern, so suggestive of a space frame, was actually composed of relatively simple tilted beams. Kahn, although ultimately willing to sacrifice material demands to the logic of the eye, as he had at Yale, always tried to avoid doing so. In the Salk solution, he proudly confided, "I thought I had something pretty hot."[15]

While the laboratory spaces were very flexible, in keeping with Salk's directive, they were not designed to contain all of the research activity of the building. Kahn also proposed small studies for each of the principal scientists, which were attached to the sides of their open-plan laboratories. These studies were grouped into towers that rose in the two courtyards between the paired laboratory blocks, and they thus re-created some of the studio-like environment of the Richards Building. The researchers at first professed no desire for these refuges from the noise of the lab; they were willing to remain all day beside their apparatus, even eating lunch on a work bench "after a few microbes were swept away." But Kahn seduced them and Salk with the image of "an architecture of the oak table and the rug," separated from the hard, "clean architecture" of the laboratory.[16] This divided organization permitted him to create the functional individuation of space that had become a central theme in his work of the fifties, and the type of environment created by the studies—solitary retreats overlooking the gardens—was very like the monastic setting that had interested Salk and him from the start.

The broader division of the Salk Institute program into three buildings was a more general indication of Kahn's desire to mark each function with a specific architectural character. Utterly unlike the laboratories, the residences and the meeting house, although never

127

128

129

127. *Salk Institute for Biological Studies, La Jolla,*
Calif. 1959–65. Model, ca. March 1961.
128. *Salk Institute for Biological Studies. Model of*
master plan, ca. March 1960.
129. *Salk Institute for Biological Studies.*
Perspective of meeting house from residences, ca.
1962.

built, were provocative expansions of his new, allusion-rich vocabulary.

Kahn planned a meandering "little village" of houses for the visiting fellows on the south brink of the ravine that cut into the site from the sea *(fig. 129)*.[17] The residences must be seen in the context of the medieval-inspired urbanism that had won a broad following in America during the late fifties and sixties. Among its most familiar monuments were Stiles and Morse Colleges (1958–62), the pair of craggy dormitories that Eero Saarinen built on either side of a curving pathway at Yale shortly after Kahn had shifted his teaching to Philadelphia. Saarinen's colleges rejected the orthogonal rationalism and the sleekness of the modern movement in favor of sentimental associations and varied texture, and Kahn's design showed that he, too, was intrigued by this alternative view of urban development. He had, of course, enthusiastically recorded the hill and coastal towns of Italy in his youth, and the towered skyline of his Richards Building already suggested the endurance of his memories of those places. But while the Salk village was an accomplished design, its sweet neopicturesqueness, so different from the crisp rectilinearity of Richards, stood out as an exception among his works. Kahn's larger urban designs, with which it might properly be compared, had advanced since the forties from the heroic ambitions of the Triangle redevelopment to the visionary monumentalism of his later plans for central Philadelphia and Dhaka *(figs. 31, 63, 102)*. These all possessed a more profound sense of geometric order than his La Jolla design. His remarks regarding another project, recorded after he had worked for Salk for a year, might be taken as the summation of his more usual, tougher attitude: "I didn't want anything pretty; I wanted to have a clear statement of a way of life."[18]

Kahn came closer to attaining this objective in the meeting house planned for the promontory north of the ravine. It was here that Salk hoped to accomplish the remarriage of the two cultures: the extraordinary setting where Picasso and the rest of the nonscientific world would encounter the community of science, in spaces to which Kahn refused to assign conventional labels. He described the cloistered garden of the meeting house, for instance, as "a religious place—a place which has no other meaning but is just a good place to go."[19]

The meeting house program was expanded to contain everything that Salk and Kahn could imagine would be useful, including a large library, quarters for unmarried scientists, an auditorium, and all sorts of facilities for casual mingling and talk. Kahn elaborated:

> It was a place where one had his meal, because I don't know of any greater seminar than the dining room. There was a gymnasium. There was a place for the fellows who were not in science. There was a place for the director. There were rooms that had no names, like the entrance hall, which had no name. It was the biggest room, but it was not designated in any way. People could go around it, too; they didn't have to go *through* it. But the entrance hall was a place where you could have a banquet if you wanted to.[20]

The architectural vocabulary of the meeting house was as unusual as the agenda mapped out for it *(fig. 130)*. Kahn adopted an additive plan of strongly individualized units that was consonant with the building's use for conferences and entertainment at a variety of scales and in differing formats. The layout bore more than a passing resemblance to the great suburban villas of imperial Rome and to the haunting geometries of Piranesi's imaginary reconstructed plan of the Campus Martius, which hung over Kahn's desk.[21] Moreover, the elevations, with glare walls pierced by giant openings encircling the meeting and dining rooms, looked like nothing so much as the masonry carcass of a Roman ruin. This was not by chance. The ancient ruin, Kahn reasoned, was a symbol of the enduring values upon which art was founded, but it was a symbol that had been cleansed of the specific meanings brought to it by prior occupation. It was thus ready to serve the new purposes that a Jonas Salk might invent in order to heal the world. As Kahn said in 1963, "A building that has become a ruin is again free of the bondage of use."[22]

Of course, neither the residences nor the meeting house were constructed, and only the laboratories, designed from the start to be unlike the other two parts, stand today to represent Salk and Kahn's grandiose vision. Before they were completed, Salk once again rerouted Kahn's design, shifting it to a trajectory that converged with the architect's Beaux-Arts training.

It was in the spring of 1962, with construction of the labs about to start, that Salk had a swift change of heart. He and Kahn were flying back to San Francisco after signing the construction contract when he told the architect that he had suddenly realized that the four-laboratory solution, with the buildings organized in pairs around two courtyards, did not represent the wholeness that he desired for his institution.[23] Two buildings, facing each other across a single common space, would be better, and he paced off the dimensions of such a layout in a park when he reached his destination. Kahn was not at first sympathetic. He was especially pleased with the integrated structural truss and servant space system of the four-lab design, and he called the new solution "much dumber than the building I originally conceived."[24] But, never one to shy away from last-minute changes himself, he came to appreciate the logic of Salk's point of view. In this, his classical sense may have been decisive, for it naturally predisposed him to favor a single axis. Later he explained: "I realized that two gardens did not combine in the intended meaning. One garden is greater than two because it becomes a place in relation to the laboratories and their studies. Two gardens were just a convenience. But one is really a place; you put

meaning in it; you feel loyalty to it."[25] The design was reworked very quickly, and construction began that summer *(figs. 131, 132)*.

As built, the taller, three-story laboratory buildings preserved much of the structural and functional logic of the earlier, two-story version. Although the trusses were less elaborate, they still created a walk-through space for tending mechanical services. And the separate studies were still clearly delineated, grouped in towers that rose on either side of the courtyard and only connected to the laboratories by bridges *(fig. 133)*. Beneath the towers, a sheltered walkway circled the courtyard.

The airy study towers, consisting of concrete frames with teak cubicles inserted on two of their four floors, were the subject of much loving attention. Here, in monastic cells overlooking a cloistered court, Kahn was able to bring his own feelings to bear on the design with a directness that was not possible in those parts of the building that were saddled with complex technical specifications. Seemingly animated by the innate "existence will" that he always postulated for his designs, each little cabin craned its neck to catch a glimpse of the Pacific *(fig. 134)*. This required a slight staggering of the paired studies and interrupted the apparent regularity of the facades with an idiosyncrasy born of need. The interiors were plainly finished with unstained teak, and their rustic air intensified the distinction between this territory of "the oak table and the rug" and the sterile laboratories. There was inevitably something of the simple air of a beach house in these domestic-scale units, perched on their sun-washed clifftop above the sea.

Because the lowest laboratories were at the level of a conventional basement, Kahn provided long, sunken courtyards on either side of the main plaza to bring them light. Generously scaled and bridged by the study towers, these were more like streets than light wells. Similar streetlike courts ran along the outer facades of

130. *Salk Institute for Biological Studies, La Jolla, Calif., 1959–65. Perspective of meeting house, 1961.*
131. *Salk Institute for Biological Studies. Model, Summer 1962.*
132. *Salk Institute for Biological Studies. Laboratories, seen from west.*

Following pages
133. *Salk Institute for Biological Studies. Study towers.*
134. *Salk Institute for Biological Studies. Courtyard, looking east.*
135. *Salk Institute for Biological Studies. South facade.*

130

131

132

the laboratories, spanned by the sober service blocks that carried the mechanical systems up into the buildings *(fig. 135)*. The severe, repetitive vocabulary of the towers was like that being adopted at the same time by minimalist sculptors, but although Kahn shared their interest in reinvesting modern art with dignity and meaning, there is no evidence that he was aware of their work.

At the Salk Institute, Kahn's lifelong care for construction materials flowered into an absolute passion for scrupulous detailing and excellent finish. The standards that were set there for poured-in-place concrete have never been surpassed and have rarely been equaled. Transformed into an elegant material, the concrete overshadowed even the beauties of the travertine paving. To attain this high state of finish, Kahn established a branch office in San Diego. His resident staff inspected the concrete as it was colored, mixed, compacted, and cured, insuring that it received an unusually hard surface and that it was patterned exactly as intended, with formwork edge markings laid out with thoroughgoing calculation. Kahn, indeed, saw concrete as the near equivalent of ashlar masonry, observing in 1972 that "Concrete really wants to be granite." But he also recognized its own unique qualities: "Reinforcing rods are the play of a marvelous secret worker that makes this so-called molten stone appear wonderfully capable—a product of the mind."[26]

It was also at the Salk Institute that Kahn designed extensive woodwork for the first time since building houses in the late 1940s. He adopted a new vocabulary for the occasion, with doors and shutters of timeless paneled construction, assembled out of teak, a wood that needed only to be cleaned and oiled regularly to resist deterioration. It is perhaps the greatest tribute to Kahn's comprehensive design sense that concrete and wood, often conceived as materials of opposite character, complemented each other at the Salk Institute.

Both were provocatively detailed in a way that moved back and forth between abstraction and structural description; neither was allowed to stand in the background.

Most of the laboratory construction had been completed when Kahn made his final, long-postponed decision about landscaping the courtyard. This central space, the axis of his quasi-classical plan, demanded special attention, but, like the best Beaux-Arts work, this apparently straightforward demand was complicated by an underlying ambiguity. Here the peculiarity stemmed from the absence of any architectural feature on axis, such as the stereotypical domed pavilion.

Guided by the monastic imagery that both he and Salk associated with the project, he had initially imagined this central courtyard as a verdant garden, a thing apart from the arid surrounding landscape. He had experimented with various plantings, coming in the end to favor an allée of poplar trees, although never fully accepting this solution *(fig. 136;* see *fig. 131)*. The somewhat contrived appearance of these possible configurations was weighing on Kahn's mind when he visited Mexico City in December 1965 and saw the house and garden of Luis Barragan. Kahn was impressed by Barragan's austere vocabulary, with its strong connections to vernacular patterns, and he invited the Mexican architect to come to La Jolla and offer advice about the courtyard. Barragan's famous suggestion was often recounted by Kahn:

When he entered the space he went to the concrete walls and touched them and expressed his love for them, and then he said as he looked across the space and towards the sea, "I would not put a tree or blade of grass in this space. This should be a plaza of stone, not a garden." I looked at Dr. Salk and he at me and we both felt this was deeply right. Feeling our approval, he added joyously, "If you make this a plaza, you will gain a facade— a facade to the sky."[27]

Kahn ultimately designed the courtyard

136

136. *Salk Institute for Biological Studies, La Jolla, Calif., 1959–65. Perspective of courtyard with poplars, before December 1965.*

Following pages
137. *Salk Institute for Biological Studies. Courtyard, looking west.*

with a central channel through which water flowed, beneath the axis of the sun, toward an artificial cascade at the seaward end. This was a conceit certainly borrowed from the Mughal gardens with which he had become familiar through his work in India. But more than any particularity of inspiration, the hard-surfaced courtyard was a general statement about the essential distance an artist had to establish between his work and nature *(fig. 137)*. "Architecture is what nature cannot make," Kahn preached to a Yale audience in 1963.

"Nature cannot make anything that man makes. Man takes nature—the means of making a thing—and isolates its laws."[28] Beginning in 1961 and continuing throughout the period that Kahn was isolating the laws of nature for the Salk Institute, he was also occupied with a dormitory for Bryn Mawr College, a women's school in the western suburbs of Philadelphia. Eleanor Donnelley Erdman Hall was a project with a more conventional program, but its design was not easy for Kahn. It became a battleground between what had been the twin objectives of his architecture throughout the fifties: clearly expressed structure and geometric order. These had gradually come to resemble antagonists. Although he had found that structure could generate pleasantly simple geometry at a small scale, like that of the Trenton Bathhouse, the necessarily complex structural systems of larger works, like the City Tower project, seemed to demand formal solutions of equal complexity *(see figs. 53, 59)*. Kahn was never entirely happy with such visual complication, and at Bryn Mawr he sublimated his interest in heroically expressed structure to allow geometric order to win a decisive victory.

His patron at Bryn Mawr was another formidable personality, college president Katharine McBride. She was not one to accept lame excuses, as Kahn apparently learned the hard way; he observed, "If you took a position that someone else was responsible for what went wrong, her whole point of view changes."[29] Indeed, he gave McBride every reason to doubt his sense of responsibility, making little effort to conceal the fact that he was torn between two design solutions and carrying out their testing before her eyes.

Kahn had reformulated the Bryn Mawr program in his usual way, replacing the particulars provided by the college with his own perception that a women's dormitory needed to evoke "the presence of a house."[30] He interpreted this to require the familiar domestic separation of public areas (living room, dining room, and entrance hall) from sleeping quarters, just as in his binuclear house plans of the forties, albeit at a larger scale. In order to achieve a sense of domestic completeness within this all-female environment he placed fireplaces in the major rooms to give "the feeling that a man is present, because somehow you associate the fireplace with a man."[31]

As envisioned by Kahn as a giant house, the Bryn Mawr dormitory posed two great problems of organization—problems in what he called "the architecture of connection," a phrase reminiscent of his training in plan composition under Paul Cret. In question were the connections between the three large public spaces and between those spaces and the much smaller bedrooms.

For these problems, Anne Tyng was eager to put forward a structural solution: a concrete honeycomb that could enfold spaces of all sizes and wrap them in aggregated polyhedra (fig. 138). The design was the sophisticated outgrowth of her continuing exploration of the relationship between architectural structure and visual order, an exploration that was now shaped by her newly gained insights into the Jungian interpretation of human creativity and the collective unconscious. But the animated elevations generated by such systems had lost much of the appeal they had had for Kahn, who increasingly preferred an ancient kind of monumentality. He and Tyng debated

openly about the Erdman design throughout 1961, bringing forward their alternative proposals in a succession of meetings with McBride. She allowed the competition to take its natural course. At the end of the year Kahn established the final *parti* of three concatenated diamonds, each with a central public room (living room, dining room, or entrance hall) enveloped by bedrooms (fig. 139). This echoed the visual pattern but not the functional logic of a concentric served-servant hierarchy, and its majestic orderliness marked a turning point in Kahn's career. It was not that he subsequently ignored matters of construction and structure, but composition in plan—the centerpiece of his Beaux-Arts training—was never again challenged as the foremost of his priorities.

Although Erdman's three diamonds at first appear to be willfully unconventional, Kahn developed them at the end of a long line of compositional experiments with pavilion plans that stretched back into the 1950s. For years he had explored an architecture of connected pavilions, alternately testing picturesque groupings, like those of the Richards Building and the Adler and DeVore houses, and seeking to assert an axial order over the composition, as seen most dramatically in the Trenton Bathhouse (see *figs. 50, 51, 52, 69*). Despite its apparently arcane geometry, Erdman Hall falls in the latter group, disciplined by the underlying classicism of Kahn's compositional sense.

The diagonality of the Erdman design allowed Kahn to achieve classical balance without the artificiality inherent in conventional axial planning, in which useless elements were retained and held in position for the sake of symmetry. By rotating the three squares, he converted their otherwise dead corners into connectors, making each square "its own connection" with an unorthodox logic that would be impossible in an orthogonal arrangement.[32] In part, this was the same

138

139

138. *Erdman Hall, Bryn Mawr College, Bryn Mawr, Pa., 1960–65. Model, 1960.*
139. *Erdman Hall. Aerial view.*

Following pages
140. *Erdman Hall. Rear facade.*
141. *Erdman Hall. Entrance.*

kind of ad hoc, "circumstantial" diagonal that he had discovered to be useful in the Goldenberg house (see *fig. 78*).[33] Kahn was delighted to find a solution emerging in this way: "It is always the hope on the part of the designer that the building in a way makes itself rather than be composed with devices that tend to please the eye. It is a happy moment when a geometry is found which tends to make spaces naturally, so that the composition of geometry in the plan serves to construct, to give light, and to make spaces."[34] Once the entire system of planning had been realigned along the diagonals, however, the ad hoc quality of the design vanished, and a majestic sense of classical order settled over the composition. This order was celebrated by the great stairways of the central hall, accenting the new axis that skewered the squares through their corners.

Although it was important to him, Kahn did not feel that the powerful planning logic of Erdman Hall's three great diamonds had to be revealed to average visitors. Their experience of the building was not confined to the two dimensions of plan; it was strongly shaped by Kahn's other, seemingly contradictory interest in monumental massing and ancient resonances. At Bryn Mawr, this produced an active, towered skyline—without apparent symmetry—that echoed the silhouettes of the Middle Ages and the college's own historic neo-Tudor campus *(fig. 140)*. On the uphill, entrance front, the clear plan was so obscured by this picturesque impression that even the central door was hard to find *(fig. 141)*. The historical allusion was furthered by the cladding of slate panels (the material Kahn would have used for the Salk Institute if travertine had not been cheaper), whose color closely matched the masonry of Bryn Mawr's older buildings. It was also to be seen in the cavernous living and dining rooms, lit from above and hung with tapestries *(fig. 142)*.

Kahn admitted that his perennial interest

in medieval architecture could be detected in the Bryn Mawr dormitory, whose plan might be "compared to that of a Scottish castle." [35] But, wary of being branded a historicist, he was always a little sheepish about allowing this connection to be drawn. "I have a book on castles and I try to pretend that I did not look at this book," he confessed in 1962, "but everybody reminds me of it and I have to admit that I looked very thoroughly at this book."[36] He did make a flying visit to Scotland to see castles in March 1961, when he was called to London by another job while in the midst of the Erdman design.[37]

Kahn often defended his enthusiasm for castles by claiming that it stemmed strictly from the fact that castles demonstrated served-servant planning, with great central living halls and auxiliary spaces nestled into thick outside walls. It is true that this arrangement was successfully adapted in Erdman Hall (as it was earlier in the Rochester Unitarian Church), but Kahn's fascination with castles was not limited to their interesting plan typology. A lover of fairy tales, he was not immune to the broader power of these—and all—historical monuments, and he very movingly explained to several audiences in the mid-sixties how art outlived the particular circumstances of its making and exerted an enduring influence over human experience. In response to the question "What is tradition?" he began his answer with an imagined visit to Elizabethan England:

"My mind goes back to the Globe Theatre in London." Shakespeare had just written "Much Ado About Nothing" which was to be performed there. I imagined myself looking at the play through a hole in the wall of the structure, and was surprised to see that the first actor attempting his part fell as a heap of dust and bones under his costume. To the second actor the same thing happened, and so to the third and fourth, and the audience reacting also fell as a heap of dust. I realized that circumstance can never be recalled,

that what I was seeing then was what I could not see now. And I realized that an old Etruscan mirror out of the sea, in which once a beautiful head was reflected had still with all its encrustation the strength to evoke the image of that beauty. It's what man makes, what he writes, his painting, his music, that remains indestructible. The circumstances of their making is but the mould for casting. This led me to realize what may be Tradition. Whatever happens in the circumstantial course of man's life, he leaves as the most valuable, a golden dust which is the essence of his nature. This dust, if you know this dust, and trust in it, and not in circumstance, then you are really in touch with the spirit of tradition. May be then one can say that tradition is what gives you the powers of anticipation from which you know what will last when you create.[38]

It was with such an eye to future appreciation that Kahn argued in 1964 for the creation of "very archaic looking buildings, buildings that will be considered archaic in the future."[39]

Of course, not every client agreed with Jonas Salk and Katharine McBride that Kahn's ancient imagery was appropriate. In 1961–62, while at work for them, he lost or failed to win three commissions for university research buildings because his designs differed so radically from the expected architecture of modern science. The Chemistry Building for the University of Virginia was much studied and restudied, with the auditorium successively conceived as an antique semicircular theater and a towered, irregular hexagon.[40] The latter design was flatly rejected as "rather cold and forbidding" by the university president, who added, "I am reminded of a Norman castle with its formidable towers."[41] Shapero Hall of Pharmacy at Wayne State University, which Kahn proposed to wrap in a circular "ruin" like the Salk meeting house, met with a similar reaction.[42] It was said that donors were "accustomed to more conventional buildings."[43] And Kahn was also undone by the unorthodoxy of the earthwork-encircled citadel which he pro-

142. Erdman Hall, Bryn Mawr College,
Bryn Mawr, Pa., 1960–65. Living room.

posed for the Lawrence Memorial Hall of Science at the University of California, Berkeley.[44] It was sometimes difficult for patrons to believe that Kahn's ancient-looking monuments could represent the future of their institutions.

There was no such lack of understanding on the part of those who called Kahn to India in 1962 to design—and build—the Indian Institute of Management in Ahmedabad. Here, in a graduate school of business administration, he was able to create a complete environment for learning—the type of ideal campus of which Erdman Hall and the Salk laboratory were only fragments. This was the environment he had described in 1959: "It is . . . a realm of spaces which may be connected by ways of walking, and the walking is a protected kind of walking. . . . You consider it as high spaces together with low spaces, and various spaces where people can sort of find the places where they can do what they want to do."[45] With the commencement of the Ahmedabad project, the subcontinent became the most receptive testing ground for Kahn's art, as reinforced by the even more far-reaching commission for the new capital at Dhaka that arrived in his office at almost the same time.

The Indian Institute of Management was created with the support of the state and national governments and under the sponsorship of the Sarabhai family, who had earlier brought Le Corbusier to their city to build houses, a museum, and a grandiose clubhouse for themselves and the other prosperous leaders of the textile industry. Kahn threw himself into the project with enormous energy, making the long, uncomfortable journey to India for the first time in November 1962 and returning on more than a score of occasions.

In mystical, timeless India, Kahn discovered that the unchanging essence he sought in all things seemed to lie closer to the surface, and he was in turn discovered by Indian admirers who were immediately receptive to his way of looking at the world. For the rest of his life, Indian students flocked to the University of Pennsylvania to study in his master's studio. His great friend and the engineer of his appointment, the Ahmedabad architect Balkrishna Doshi, spoke for many of them when he said, "Lou appeared to me a Yogin [yogi] because of his 'Samadhi' [heightened consciousness] to discover the value of the eternal—the Truth—the Atman—the Soul."[46]

India was also full of rich architectural experiences, from the powerful medieval buildings of her Mughal rulers to the twentieth-century work of Lutyens in New Delhi and Le Corbusier in Chandigarh and Ahmedabad. Kahn drank in all of this from the past, enjoying, too, the energy of Ahmedabad's contemporary artists and architects. Most of all, in Ahmedabad (as in Dhaka), he found ambitions that were large enough and support that was deep enough to build on a scale nearly equal to his vision, despite the limited resources of his clients.

As usual for Kahn, his thinking about the Indian Institute of Management began with its overall plan, one that could unite the required classrooms, offices, library, dining hall, dormitories, faculty residences, workers' housing, and market. The recently finalized design for Erdman Hall apparently inspired him to base his plan on diagonals, with long, interconnected dormitory blocks stretching outward like fingers from the main instructional building, ending at the edge of a lake *(fig. 143)*. Across the lake, houses for faculty were arranged in chevrons. As at Bryn Mawr, Kahn found this diagonal system to be a powerful "architecture of connection." It could cope with the exigencies of the program and at the same time impose his sense of order over the multipart plan, doing both far better than an orthogonal scheme in which "everything is . . . answerable to a square."[47]

The diagonal layout had the particular

143

144

143. *Indian Institute of Management, Ahmedabad, India, 1962–74. Model, ca. 1963.*
144. *Indian Institute of Management. Model, ca. November 1964.*

Following pages
145. *Indian Institute of Management. Classroom building, courtyard.*

advantage of responding well to the requirement that the buildings be oriented toward the southwesterly breezes, a matter that required several readjustments and Doshi's assistance before Kahn got it right. In the course of this revision he also subdivided the dormitories into twenty-bedroom units *(fig. 144)*. As in the Richards Building, the importance of air circulation was probably overstated, and in the end it was clearly abstract pattern that governed the placement of units. But, for a time at least, Kahn saw proper orientation to the wind as the key to building in the tropics. This had been brought home to him by a magical but uncomfortable experience:

> I was impressed with the need for air when I happened, with twenty other people, in the palace in Lahore, where the guide showed us the ingenuity of craftsmen who had covered an entire room with multi-colored mirrored mosaics. To demonstrate the mystery of the reflections, he closed all the doors and lit a match. The light of the single match gave multiple and unpredictable effects but two people fainted for lack of air in the short moment that the room was shut off from the breeze. In that time, in that room, you felt that nothing is more interesting than air.[48]

Ultimately, Kahn's scrupulous attention to the use of local brick, the material prescribed to him by the client because of its economy, was more effective in attaching the school design to its Indian environment than his concern for ventilation *(fig. 145)*. In brick Kahn seemed to have discovered a friend, a simple and robust building system that invited honest exposure without the distracting visual complications that came with more sophisticated technology. Although he had frequently employed brick veneer before, in Ahmedabad he was committed to using brick as a structural material, and he gave himself over completely to a study of its properties. The almost painful straightforwardness of his arched forms bore witness to the sincerity of this investigation. Kahn often dramatized the earnest dialogue with brick that he claimed lay at the heart of his use of the material: "You say to brick, 'What do you want, brick?' And brick says to you, 'I like an arch.' And you say to brick, 'Look, I want one too, but arches are expensive and I can use a concrete lintel over you, over an opening.' And then you say, 'What do you think of that, brick?' Brick says, 'I like an arch.' "[49]

Kahn himself pointed out that arcuated brick construction made his buildings look "old-fashioned," by now a highly complimentary description.[50] His point of comparison was probably utilitarian Roman brickwork, like that which mounted skyward in the Basilica of Constantine or on the rear slope of the Palatine Hill, but Doshi also saw references to the medieval architecture of India in Kahn's design, specifically the thickset twelfth-century monuments of Mandu.[51] He had succeeded in creating forms of such elemental authority that they resisted any single identification.

Brimming with primitive tectonic energy, the Indian Institute of Management derived another kind of power from the academic life that it so effectively promoted. "When one walks around the complex silently," Doshi reported, "either in cool winter or hot and stark summer, one gets the vibrations of conversations, dialogues, meetings and activities. The spaces that are created for these activities link the entire complex."[52] That is exactly how Kahn had hoped the school would work, for even before receiving the commission, he had maintained that the best education was informal, like the gathering of students under his proverbial tree. He argued eloquently against the arrangement of classrooms along ordinary hallways—what he called "sneak passage[s]"—and in favor of substituting places for impromptu gathering-spaces of no obligation."[53] He explained this ideal school in some detail in 1960:

The corridors, by the provision of greater width and alcoves overlooking gardens, would be transformed into classrooms for the exclusive use of the students. These would become the places where boy meets girl, where student discusses the work of the professor with fellow student. If classroom time were allotted to these spaces instead of only the passage of time from class to class, they would become not merely corridors but meeting places—places offering possibilities in self learning. In this sense they would become classrooms belonging to the students.[54]

This accurately forecast the shape taken by the main building at Ahmedabad, in which freestanding lecture rooms and blocks of faculty offices stood on opposite sides of a great central courtyard, linked not by corridors but by shady walkways that offered many places to stop and talk (figs. 145–148). Presiding over the courtyard at one end was the austere face of the library, illuminated by two vast glazed circles set within a shady recess. At the other end Kahn planned to build the dining hall, its attached kitchen set within a smell-confining truncated cone, and for the center of the courtyard he designed an amphitheater. Reflecting on the usefulness of this kind of plan for schools in general, Kahn said, "The court is the meeting place of the mind, as well as the physical meeting place."[55]

The life of learning and self-instruction was also integral to the design of the residential part of the complex, which was closely linked to the main building. This pattern, Kahn believed, was demanded by the particular mode of teaching at the institute, the "case study" method borrowed from the Harvard Business School, with its emphasis on the analysis of sample business cases by teams of students, under faculty guidance. As Kahn somewhat incorrectly explained it: "[There are] no lectures, the lectures are just inspired out of case studies. All the dormitories are also places where people can meet. So the dormitories and the school are really one; they

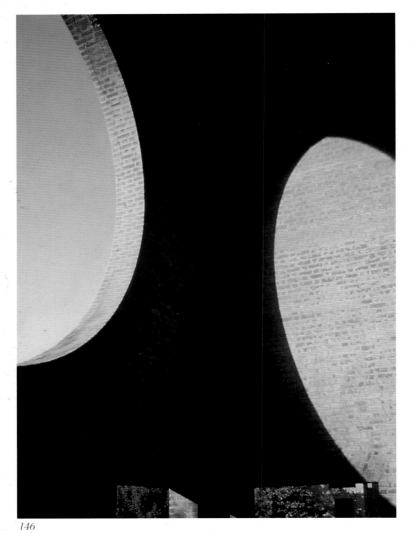

146

146. *Indian Institute of Management,
Ahmedabad, India, 1962–74.
Classroom building, loggia.*

147. *Indian Institute of
Management. Classroom building,
classrooms.*

148

149

148. Indian Institute of Management, Ahmedabad, India, 1962–74. Courtyard of classroom building, seen from corridor.
149. Indian Institute of Management. Dormitories with classroom and administration building foundations in foreground, ca. 1969.

Following pages
150. Indian Institute of Management. Dormitories.

are not separated."[56] Such an integrated environment suggested an obvious and familiar model; in explaining the Indian Institute of Management, Kahn declared, "The plan comes from my feelings of monastery."[57]

This thinking generated a wonderfully rich arrangement of public, semiprivate, and private spaces in and around the eighteen dormitory units that grouped themselves on two sides of the main building (*figs. 149, 150, 151, 153*). Each four-story block accommodated twenty private rooms, arranged on the two upper floors around triangular lounges or "tea rooms" that opened to the outside through gigantic circular perforations. Serving kitchens and toilets were contained within a square tower attached to the long face of the overall triangular plan. The lower floors were entirely devoted to communal space, intended to serve as meeting rooms for student organizations and for the kind of unchoreographed interaction that Kahn wished to promote. Among the dormitories was woven a network of small courtyards, interconnected by partially unenclosed ground floors. While these spaces read in plan as an orderly grid, Kahn's activating diagonality and the rapid and continuous transition from sunny exterior to shady interior would quickly disorient the casual visitor. For the resident, however, the environment was a private realm of special personality and charm, like the medieval colleges of Oxford and Cambridge.

Kahn planned for the dormitories to be surrounded on two sides by a shallow lake, with more elaborate classrooms in the strongly buttressed ground floors of the buildings adjacent to the water (*fig. 150*). The lake would separate the dormitories from the houses of the faculty and staff, providing privacy for the older members of the community without moving them very far from the students. Although concern about malarial mosquitoes kept the lake from being filled, Kahn insisted to the end that it was an essential part of the plan.

The simple faculty housing that lay to the south and east contrasted sharply with the robust and sculptural dormitories *(fig. 152)*. The fifty-three houses were articulated by little more than Kahn's "composite order"— the system of shallow brick arches and concrete tie beams that he invented for Ahmedabad—and, indeed, Kahn said that "houses should be dumb looking so that the families and children can have their own say."[58] But for all their simplicity, the houses possessed a variety of wonderful amenities, including enclosed upper floor terraces (really outdoor rooms) and a staggered siting scheme that secluded each house from its neighbors. The even plainer one-story houses for the school's workers were joined together in straight blocks at the southern edge of the site.

Construction in Ahmedabad proceeded with excruciating slowness, due in part to a shortage of funds and in part to Kahn's penchant for procrastination and reconsideration. Responsibility was increasingly shifted to Doshi and Anant Raje, a younger architect who worked on the project for a time in Kahn's Philadelphia office. Upon Kahn's death, Raje assumed responsibility for designing the dining hall, as well as the executive education center and married-student housing, which had been later additions to the program. Despite this, the Indian Institute of Management possesses a completeness and a unity of vision that is rare for works of this scale. It is the nearest the twentieth century has come to creating a successor to Thomas Jefferson's great academic village at the University of Virginia. There, as in Ahmedabad, the essential elements are an integrated environment for faculty and student life, interwoven by covered walkways and dominated by a great library.

In Ahmedabad and La Jolla monastic images had inflected Kahn's thinking, and in 1966 he finally got to design two real religious communities: a monastery in California and a convent in Pennsylvania. This must have seemed like the fulfillment of a dream, for he had long challenged himself and his students to consider the monastery as the model for communal life. He had also frequently described the invention of the primordial monastery as an example of the kind of fundamental searching on which all institutional architecture should be based: "Why must we assume that there cannot be other things so marvelous as the emergence of the first monastery, for which there was no precedence whatsoever? It was simply that some man realized that a certain realm of spaces represents a deep desire on the part of man to express the inexpressible in a certain activity of man called a monastery."[59] As it happened, neither of these actual commissions lived up to his expectations about the cloistered life, although, as planning exercises, they gave him an opportunity to test some of his more radical ideas about juxtapositional composition to their maximum.

Kahn's first, tentative contact with Saint Andrew's Priory in Valyermo, California, had been in 1961, when he visited its extraordinary hilltop site in the high desert north of Los Angeles.[60] He was impressed by the arid vastness of the place and intrigued by the remarkable prior, Father Raphael Vinciarelli, who had founded Saint Andrew's and made it a center for the arts and ecumenicalism after his monastery in China was closed by the Communists.[61] Kahn sketched out for Vinciarelli a poetic design that would begin with the building of a fountain at the place where precious water had been discovered, because "something must be done to show your appreciation." Next would come a system of aqueducts, and "only then should you think in terms of placing your buildings, your chapel and your church and the place of meditation and rest."[62] These were never more than word pictures, however, for the abbey had already retained another architect and

151

151. Indian Institute of Management, Ahmedabad,
India, 1962–74. Dormitory walkways.
152. Indian Institute of Management. Faculty
houses.

Following pages
153. Indian Institute of Management. Dormitories.

152

Kahn was prevented by his scruples (and the strict professional code of the American Institute of Architects) from accepting the monks' invitation to go further.[63]

Late in 1965, with the other architect long out of the picture, Vinciarelli's successor inquired if Kahn would now consider taking up the commission. He replied with delight, "It is rare that the client of an architect feels the inspiration to express in the realm of architecture," and he waived his usual fee.[64] Kahn returned to Valyermo in March 1966 and developed the design over the summer, in time to unveil a model to the tens of thousands who came to the monastery's annual fall festival in late September *(fig. 154)*. The gathering was described by the *Los Angeles Times* as "a true fiesta of art, music and spiritual excitement."[65]

The collagelike monastery plan reflected the continuing evolution of Kahn's thinking about juxtapositional, diagonal composition. Whereas at Bryn Mawr and Ahmedabad he had used a diagonal armature to reaffirm the authority of Beaux-Arts plan-making (purging it in the process of some of its artificiality), the more varied diagonals of the Valyermo design were related to another line of development, in the direction adumbrated by his energetic World War II community buildings (see *fig. 11*). This avenue toward freer composition had been followed in his mature period by the day camp for the Trenton Jewish Community Center and, most recently, by the mosque/assembly complex at Dhaka and the 1964 redesign of the Fisher house (see *figs. 73, 103, 179*). Nominally dependent on the imagined programmatic demands of adjacency between units, these designs were defined in the final analysis by Kahn's visual sensitivity—a kind of modern baroque that, like David Smith's "Cubi" sculptural series, broke down static paradigms with an affection for gestural placement. The independent units of the monastery plan seemed to come together of their own free will, creating the democratic plan type that Kahn would call "a society of rooms."[66]

To describe the dynamic equipoise of part to part in this kind of planning, Kahn employed eloquence that he ascribed to the students in his master's studio at the University of Pennsylvania. He had assigned them the Valyermo monastery as a project, and he recounted that they had spent the first two weeks, without a program, discussing "nature". Then, he said,

> An Indian girl gave the first remark of significance. She said, "I believe that this place should be so that everything stems from the cell. From the cell would come the right for the chapel to exist. From the cell would come the right for the retreat, and for the workshops to exist." Another Indian student (their minds work in most transcendent ways) said, "I very much agree, but I would like to add that the refectory must be equal to the chapel, and the chapel must be equal to the cell, and the retreat must be equal to the refectory. None is greater than the other."[67]

Working thus, without programmatic constraints, it is not surprising that the students confounded a "merry monk" from Pittsburgh who came to the studio to advise them about monastic life. An artist himself and a modern, worldly man, he preferred a big studio to a cell, and, when some of the students proposed placing the refectory a half-mile away in order to create a proper sense of ceremony, he horrified them by saying that he would rather have his meals in bed. "We were dejected when he left," Kahn recalled. But he was used to clients who failed to appreciate the new directions that he mapped out for them, and he added, "But then we thought, '*Well, he's only a monk—He doesn't know any better.*' "[68]

The lively public life of the monks at Saint Andrew's must have disappointed Kahn in similar ways, but it was their lack of resources that halted his work. Before the end of their relationship early in 1967, he had, however, sketched elevations for the priory. The attached chapel and refectory were lit through huge circular openings like those he was using in south Asia, and at the center of the composition rose a faceted reception tower, containing the administrative offices and library and topped by the symbolically and functionally important water tank.

Shortly after he began work on the Valyermo project in 1966, Kahn undertook a very similar commission for the Dominican Motherhouse of St. Catherine de Ricci at Media in the southwestern suburbs of Philadelphia. At a slightly slower pace it followed the same route that had been charted by St. Andrew's toward eventual disillusionment and disappointment, owing to the worldliness and poverty of the sisters. But along the way Kahn created for the convent an even more incandescent realization of the planning principles that he had adopted for the monastery.

Those principles were emblematized by a design method adopted by Kahn's office early in the fall of 1966, when they were at work on the convent. His staff decided to study the design by cutting up an existing drawing so that the component parts of the program could be shifted and reassembled like a real collage. Kahn could thus experiment with relationships while preserving the integrity of the separate elements each of which was really a room, for him the infrangible unit of architectural design. It may have been this method that Kahn had in mind in 1972 when he said "The rooms talk to each other and they make up their minds where their positions are."[69] On another occasion he offered a variant wording: "I think architects should be composers and not designers. They should be composers of elements. The elements are things that are entities in themselves."[70]

The resulting plan, a model of which was ready for presentation on October 10, 1966, had a wiry energy even greater than that of the just-complete scheme for St. Andrew's (fig. 155). This strong vision was expensive to realize, however, and Mother Mary Emmanuel asked Kahn to reduce the size of the building,

reminding him that he had to deal with the contemporary realities of an outward oriented church, not some gentle fantasy of Trappist spirituality in the Middle Ages.[71] During the first months of 1967 he made sharp reductions, and economizing continued into 1968, when working drawings were prepared. The more compact plan compressed most of the energy of its predecessor into a smaller space (fig. 156). In the end, however, no common meeting ground could be found for the convent's budget and Kahn's architecture.

The consideration of these projects for communities devoted to education and contemplation can properly conclude with two further academic commissions that Kahn received toward the end of this period. His proposals for the Maryland Institute College of Art, in Baltimore and the Art Center for Rice University in Houston, were both defined by his vision of a life of learning, and both were undermined by his rewriting of the programs at a scale beyond the means of his clients.

In Baltimore the assignment was to accommodate studios, an artists'-supply store, and an auditorium on a narrow site that lay across the railroad tracks from the old Mt. Royal railroad station (1896) recently occupied by the school.[72] Kahn proposed a very slender building whose plan was driven by diagonals and whose austere facades were punctuated by circular and triangular openings. He planned to cover the tracks and connect the new and old buildings with a pedestrian mall. There was some uncertainty on the part of the College of Art about the extent of its needs and during the first design phase in 1966–67 the program was adjusted upward from roughly 22,000 to 39,000 square feet. But they expressed no uncertainty when Kahn presented a model for a 100,000-square-foot building in March 1967. College president Eugene Leake wrote that the "model presentation did nothing but put everybody in deep shock for, I guess, at least five or ten years."[73]

154

155

156

154. St. Andrew's Priory, Valyermo, Calif.,
1961–67. Model, September 1966.
155. Dominican Motherhouse, Media, Pa.,
1965–69. Model, ca. October 1966.
156. Dominican Motherhouse. Plan, ca. April
1968.

Over the next months Kahn's office struggled to reduce the size of the building while retaining, as they explained, "a long 'wall' shape very much in the spirit of our first studies."[74] Despite these problems, relations remained cordial. Kahn was awarded an honorary doctorate by the college in 1968, and Leake seemed to be genuinely grateful that he was still interested in working for them after his dream of a gigantic building was dashed. "Thanks for your continued interest—we're *lucky*," he wrote. "We believe that a Kahn building is a must and that it would make us the best art school in the country."[75] The project was finally killed by cutbacks in federal education support made during the Nixon administration.

Kahn's proposal for the Art Center at Rice University encompassed the programs in architecture, theater, art history, music, and fine arts, as well as a large performance hall and a new gallery for the Institute of Art (to be relocated from the University of St. Thomas by its director Dominique de Menil).[76] He was asked to prepare only a preliminary report, and his site plan and model were readied during the late spring of 1970 and presented to the university on June 29 and 30. West of the main library Kahn created a large courtyard, nearly equal in size to the handsome main quadrangle that lay to the east, a truncated version of the one planned by Ralph Adams Cram and Bertram Grosvenor Goodhue in 1909–10. Because construction of the Art Center would necessitate the demolition of the existing student center, a replacement facility was also part of the program. Kahn showed it standing within the new courtyard, surrounded by buildings for the various art departments. None of this was worked out in detail, and the university never called on Kahn to go further, but his image of the ensemble, functioning as a school, was strong. In a discussion with Rice students, he explained how he had chosen between two possible planning approaches, rejecting a linear arrangement and choosing a courtyard, like that at Ahmedabad:

> Suppose you had a great kind of alley, or gallery, and walked through this gallery, and connected to this gallery are the schools which are associated in the fine arts, be it history, sculpture, architecture, or painting, and you saw people at work, in all these classes. It was designed so that you felt always as though you were walking through a place where people are at work.
>
> Then I present another way of looking at it, say as a court, and you enter this court. You see buildings in this court, and one is designated as painting, one as sculpture, another as architecture, as history. In one, you rub against the presence of the classes. In the other, you can choose to go in if you want to.
>
> I think the latter is the greater by far.
>
> There is something that has to do with the feeling of association which is remote, rather than direct, and more remote association has a longer life and love.[77]

This diffidence toward involuntary contact with the resources of education seemed to preserve a memory of Kahn's own early experience as a commuting student, choosing carefully among the many opportunities offered by his urban boyhood. For him the perfect school was a courtyard of institutional opportunities—or "availabilities," as he called them late in his career—combined with monastic cells for individual contemplation. Students were free in such a setting to establish their own relationships with each other and with the available resources, creating a human collage, just as the architectural elements in Kahn's "society of rooms" found their own points of contact and established their own equilibriums. Design was the overlaying of these human and architectural patterns, whether at the scale of a house, a public institution, or a city.

D.B.B

Chapter 5

The Forum of the Availabilities

Designs for Choice

157

157. *Philadelphia College of Art, Philadelphia, Pa., 1960–66. Model, ca. December 1964.*

When Louis Kahn spoke of "architecture and human agreement,"[1] he expressed a belief in the social nature of humanity. He viewed architecture as supportive of this nature and strove to provide a framework for human interaction within which each individual could realize a greater degree of worth. For Kahn, a sense of self-determination through choice was essential to such realization, and thus he maintained a certain degree of neutrality in his designs, feeling that the architect's imposition of rigid patterns could suppress spontaneity. Balancing structured order with provisions for individual choice seemed to incline him toward complex geometric patterns that could demonstrate opportunities for varied use. Instead of being formally aligned, his shapes were more often joined in complicated ways to suggest what he began to call "availabilities." This term he favored in alluding to his objectives: "The architect's job, in my opinion . . . is to find those spaces . . . where the availabilities, not yet here, and those that are already here, can have better environments for their maturing into."[2] He found effective vehicles in a broad range of commissions that were not dedicated to a single purpose of study or assembly, but were more inclusive of varied pursuits. Most of these were institutional complexes within cities, or speculative urban complexes, which Kahn studied to discover some deeper purpose. But they could also include more remotely located complexes and even individual houses wherein a "society of rooms"[3] provided diverse yet mutually supportive activities, like those of a small city.

Kahn continued to speak about cities even as he became less involved in their overall design; in one of his last public lectures he spoke of their potential: "Probably the measure of a city is the degree or the quality of the availabilities. . . . If I were to make a city plan, I think I would say, 'In what way can I make the architecture of connection which would enliven the mind as to how the availabilities can be even more enriched than they are?' "[4] He came to distrust conventional urban planning as superficial in its consideration of human aspiration, once saying, "If I had to give lectures on town planning I should not want to call them that, but rather 'architecture of high intention.' "[5] He particularly disliked popular jargon, for him a substitute for thought. He once said, "'Urbanism' immediately makes all minds as heavy as lead. You don't think anymore because it's all finished."[6]

During his mature years of practice, Kahn tended to define the city as "the place of the assembled institutions" and as something "measured by the character of its institutions."[7] An institution he described as "that which can be called availability. You might say the city street is actually an institution because it is an *availability*."[8] Institutions were brought into being by "inspirational sources" that he came to define as "the inspiration to learn, the inspiration to meet, and the inspiration to express."[9] The first led to places of study and the second to places of assembly. The third was both more general and more profound: "The reason for man's living is to express. . . . The inspiration to express is that which sets up man's urge to seek shapes and forms which are not in nature."[10] He had movingly described this inspiration as "a revolt against that approximation of nature which makes us live for only a short time. It is the most numbing revolt we have."[11] Its architectural embodiment assumed special significance.

Of Kahn's commissions in the 1960s, none seemed more dedicated to the "inspiration to express" than those complexes he designed for performing and visual arts, perhaps most effectively envisioned in the Philadelphia College of Art (1960–66, unbuilt; *fig. 157*). Unlike some of his other academic architecture, these complexes dealt less with independent studies tied to libraries or cloistered spaces and more with the interaction associated with theaters and galleries. His first opportunity came with the Fine Arts Center for Fort Wayne, Indiana (partly built) which had been formally commissioned in 1961 but on which he delayed work until the following year, when he advised the city in its selection of an appropriate site. Early studies show parking structures related to an existing viaduct, recalling the viaduct studies for Philadelphia that he had completed the month before (see *fig. 158*). Only after the site was selected in April 1963, following his second presentation in Dhaka, did Kahn begin to plan more intensively. The means to urban expression that he had initiated at that remote site he now exploited more fully in his proposals for Fort Wayne.

Less hierarchically bound than the elements at Dhaka, the component parts of the Fine Arts Center were also less defined in terms of functional relationships. This is clear in Kahn's sketches of mid-1963 *(fig. 159)*: actively juxtaposed shapes engage to define variously bounded courts, and conventional, orthogonal relationships seem avoided with purpose, almost as if the unresolved geometries symbolize the activity of ideas within. By the fall of 1963 the philharmonic hall, the theater, the art school, the art alliance, and the historical museum had assumed positions that would remain basically unchanged. Even after the historical society withdrew from the proposed complex in early 1964, Kahn managed to retain essential features of connection *(fig. 160)*. An entrance garden would serve as a gateway linking the center with the city beyond, and within, a Court of Entrances would provide the sense of choice so essential to Kahn's concept *(fig. 161)*. Like the shapes of the buildings themselves, it encouraged spontaneity rather than formal movement. Within such complexes, as the Fine Arts Center illustrates, Kahn's avoidance of rigid patterns was intentional. In criticizing a stu-

158

159

160

161

158. *Fine Arts Center, School, and
Performing Arts Theater, Fort Wayne, Ind.
1959–73. South elevation of arts center,
showing viaduct system, ca. April 1962.*
159. *Fine Arts Center, School, and
Performing Arts Theater. Site plan
diagrams, ca. October 1963.*
160. *Fine Arts Center, School, and Performing
Arts Theater. Site plan. Inscribed January 2
1965 Louis I. Kahn.*
161. *Fine Arts Center, School, and
Performing Arts Center. Bird's-eye
perspective, ca. 1966.*
162. *Performing Arts Theater. Front facade.*

162

dent's proposal to link similar elements with a hall-like bridge rather than a court, he later said:

> In [the bridge] you rub against the presence of the classes. In [the court], you can choose to go in if you want to. . . . If you can choose to go there, even if you never do, you can get more out of that arrangement than you can of the other. There is something that has to do with the feeling of association which is remote, rather than direct, and the remote association has a longer life and love.[12]

At Fort Wayne, as at Dhaka, Kahn argued passionately for the entirety of the complex, believing that wholeness was essential to its meaning. Yet as proposed the center was vastly more expensive than its backers had expected; confidence in Kahn's ideas and in the ability to raise the needed funds waned, and elements began to drop away. By October 1966 only the theater, expanded to accommodate the philharmonic, remained as an immediate reality. From the beginning Kahn had conceived both the philharmonic hall and the theater as essentially rectangular volumes, for unlike places of interactive assembly each was frontally rather than centrally focused, and each conformed to Kahn's earlier description of an ideal theater as "something which presents a building in which people gather to see something which has an inevitable kind of nature."[13] In appearance the theater was very much the incomplete fragment that one would expect, designed no doubt with little spirit. Construction began in 1970 and was completed in 1973 (fig. 162).

Kahn's suggestion of spontaneity by means of unconventional geometric arrangements came into stronger focus with the Levy Memorial Playground (1961–66, unbuilt), which in turn led to the Philadelphia College of Art. Both, like Fort Wayne, seemed driven by an urge to stimulate creative energy, thus honoring Kahn's "inspiration to express." With the Levy Playground such effort was

directed toward children, but it was no less seriously considered. Designed for a New York City site along Riverside Drive between 102nd and 105th streets, it was supported by the estate of Adele Levy, who had been active in funding earlier playgrounds.[14] Isamu Noguchi was commissioned to begin its design in 1961, and he sought the collaboration of Kahn in August of that year.[15]

Kahn worked intermittently on the Levy project, producing that fall a preliminary scheme of discrete circular elements that lacked strong form, but he did little more during the following year, and in January 1963, sponsors complained that proposals were insufficiently developed for presentation to the mayor.[16] By late February matters had changed. Within three weeks of Kahn's return from Dhaka he presented a design rigorously shaped by monumental steps and broad terraces; these gave position to play mounds and other elements. Recalling in its geometry his design for Dhaka, an obliquely turned square at one end was developed as a skylight for a grottolike enclosure below. Kahn lessened the severity of this scheme in a third version, designed by October 1963 (fig. 163),[17] and in a final version, completed by January 1964, he created an archaic landscape of ramped and staired elements that recalled Minoan ruins (fig. 164).[18] Noguchi complained that "the architecture is now in ascendancy over the playground. I had hoped it might be the other way around."[19] Kahn, in turn, seemed dismayed by the overly particularized elements contributed by Noguchi: "The spontaneity of participation . . . if you sense this, you also sense that a thing is *made* to be incomplete for play. This sense of incompleteness has to be affirmed. I'll have to speak to Noguchi; there are many things that need tremendously harsh criticism."[20] By then local opposition to the project had grown, for the playground would have taken part of the open space of Riverside Park, and by October 1966 the mayor's office had withdrawn the necessary support, dooming the proposal.[21]

In April 1964, while refining proposals for Fort Wayne and the Levy Playground, Kahn received a commission from the Philadelphia College of Art to design a major addition adjoining their existing buildings on Broad Street. The design evolved through several phases. His final scheme was publicized by university officials in March 1966 (see *fig. 157*); it gave tangible form to Kahn's belief in the inspiration to express within the supporting framework of an urban matrix. How sad that the university president—appointed in 1965, after Kahn had begun to work—lacked the courage to realize Kahn's vision.

The complex program of related parts, including a theater, a library, an exhibition hall, and studios as well as other elements, was not unlike Fort Wayne's, yet it focused on visual arts rather than performance and was closely contained within the dense center of the city. Again Kahn resisted demands that it be built in phases, believing the totality of parts essential to its very being. Its entrance courts opened more fully to the city than the entrance at Fort Wayne, and they led as well to interior courts and gardens within the complex, so that compelling unity was achieved. As Kahn said, "The campus is interwoven into the building. . . . The roof is a landscape, too."[22] Adjoining the entrance court, the multistory library and exhibition hall, in plan a square turned like the assembly building in Dhaka, served as both gateway and citadel of precious objects, linked at the back to the more actively shaped studios *(fig. 165)*. Their outer, north facing walls, dramatically battered, were stepped to create skylights *(fig. 166)*, and inside, connecting passages were varied in dimension and direction, reflecting Kahn's dislike of monotonous corridors and avoiding what he now characterized as the "bondage of use."[23]

Rarely had Kahn's designs offered greater promise of new urban form. A massive composition of juxtaposed shapes and layered enclosures, with spaces differentiated according to use and structural definition, the design sustained those departures from convention that he had earlier initiated. Yet individual shapes were more obviously distorted by extrinsic demands of connection and approach, rendering the geometry more rational and less Euclidian than such earlier work as the capitol at Dhaka. By these means Kahn provided protectively framed openings to the wider availabilities of the city itself, for which the Philadelphia College of Art was a microcosm.

Like Dhaka, so large a complex as the Philadelphia College of Art lacks an exact historical parallel in its cohesive unity. It departs more radically than Dhaka from the carefully balanced manner advocated for such complexes by followers of the École des Beaux-Arts, an approach Kahn never fully endorsed in his mature work. With few exceptions the achievement of such compositional unity eluded modern practitioners of the twentieth century, for, as exemplified in Mies van der Rohe's campus for the Illinois Institute of Technology (begun 1939), isolated elements were rarely joined to form some greater whole. Le Corbusier's proposal for the Palace of the League of Nations, Geneva, 1927–28, was among his designs offering an exception; in light of Kahn's intense admiration for that architect, it might be regarded as a point of departure, but its more neutral, orthogonal elements speak of an earlier phase of the twentieth century. Closer in spirit to Kahn's designs of the mid-1960s are two unbuilt examples by Frank Lloyd Wright that Kahn must have noticed: Florida Southern College in Lakeland (begun 1938) and the Crystal Heights hotel, shops, and theater complex in Washington, D.C. (1940). As published they were readily accessible and reflected Wright's more rational side, which Kahn favored. Both contain complexly angled ele-

163

164

*163. Levy Memorial Playground, New York, N.Y.,
1961–66. Model, October 1963.
164. Levy Memorial Playground. Bird's-eye
perspective, ca. January 1965.
165. Philadelphia College of Art, Philadelphia,
Pa., 1960–66. Plan, final version, January 19,
1966.
166. Philadelphia College of Art. Section facing
west. Inscribed January 19, 1966.*

165

166

ments that are architecturally unified without recourse to conventional symmetries, and the former approximates Kahn's plan for the Dominican Motherhouse at Media (1965–69, unbuilt), but both also answer to underlying systems of triangular geometry that isolate them from Kahn's freer approach. Yet until Kahn, Wright's achievement of monumental unity had not been surpassed, and however much Kahn may have favored Le Corbusier, it was Wright who more fully prepared the way. As noted in chapter 4, only certain contemporary examples of painting and sculpture—works by Franz Kline or David Smith, for example—seemed to express a comparable spirit. From Kahn's beginning stem major works of late-twentieth-century architecture.

Researchers examining office documents have found it difficult to identify the intended materials of the Philadelphia College of Art, for its structural concrete walls and extensive areas of glazing, while mentioned in newspaper accounts, were not a matter of obvious record. By this stage Kahn had evolved his own approach to structural design, employing concrete slabs, walls, and columns in a manner derived largely from Le Corbusier. Specific representation of structural devices or materials was unnecessary unless some special condition governed, as in the Palazzo dei Congressi. He seemed past the more dramatic but complicated structural displays of the Yale Art Gallery or the City Tower, and he disdained Wrightian essays shaped by new or unusual materials. Particular shapes and exact dimensions came later, guided by Komendant or other engineers with whom he consulted. Yet what seemed obvious and easily attainable to Kahn and efficient to Komendant did not always satisfy the more restricted criteria of clients, especially those engaged in speculation.

Kahn was ill-attuned to the pragmatic demands of developers, yet on several occasions he strove to supply proposals that met

their needs, no doubt spurred by the chance to contribute to the urban fabric he found so enthralling. His ventures also revealed an interest in skyscrapers that would otherwise have gone largely unfulfilled. The first of three such commissions for which designs were prepared—each for speculative office buildings incorporating elements that were calculated to enhance their civic appeal—was for the Broadway United Church of Christ and Office Building in New York (1966–68, unbuilt), and it was followed within only a few days by the second, an office building in Kansas City (1966–73, unbuilt). The two were intertwined in terms of their design, and while still working on the latter Kahn was commissioned to design the third, the Inner Harbor development in Baltimore (1969–73, unbuilt). Yet however drawn he might have been to these opportunities to express new ideas about urban space, in the end his efforts came to nothing.

The Broadway Church and Office Building was an early example of collaboration between a tax-exempt institution—the Broadway United Church of Christ—and a developer, the Carlyle Construction Company, represented by its own architect, Emery Roth & Sons.[24] Kahn had been contacted by the church in late June of 1966, and by mid-July he was charged as its representative in the venture and expected to coordinate design for the development as a whole.[25] The site, occupying much of the block bounded by Broadway, Seventh Avenue, 56th Street, and 57th Street, was well placed in relation to a developing area of the city.

The prospect of incorporating a church and various commercial functions within an office tower must have stimulated Kahn's imagination, for preliminary sketches show a skyscraper unlike any of its time. Closely resembling the Philadelphia College of Art, on which Kahn had ceased work only a few months before, its plaza was depicted as a landscape of actively juxtaposed shapes; the tower above, rising like an all-encompassing master roof, tapered inward and was enriched by a similarly complicated geometry *(figs. 167, 168).*[26] The tower itself, like the plaza level, was envisioned as a series of interrelated segments defined by giant "notches" (as termed on the drawing) that opened to a central court within. Receiving the light below was the church, nestled beneath the tower like some ancient foundation of another age. Instead of a single, sharply defined building, Kahn had proposed a complex of parts; lacking a clear line of boundary, they could open more freely to the city they served, and their "availabilities" would be more inviting.

The battered walls of the Broadway project, in form so like those of the Philadelphia College of Art, seemed in New York to be generated first by zoning, and second by Kahn's belief in legible structure. As office drawings record, Kahn had studied New York's building regulations governing site coverage and wall planes, and the receding plane they dictated for upper floors—conventionally realized as stepped setbacks—Kahn adapted without modification. Hugh Ferriss had long before rendered similar profiles to illustrate these same regulations, but surely not with the expectation of such literal interpretation. No doubt the battering also reflected Kahn's concern with structural clarity; he had criticized architects such as Mies van der Rohe for failing (as in the celebrated Seagram Building, 1956–58) to express the different structural requirements of a tall building's lower floors, where both wind bracing and concentrated loads made added structure necessary.[27]

Representatives of the church supported Kahn's proposal, but the developers were uneasy and urged a more routine solution.[28] Market forces were not yet supportive of such architectural complication: John Portman's profitable, self-financed Atlanta Hyatt Regency was completed only in 1967, and such later examples as New York's Citicorp Building,

167

168

167. *Broadway United Church of Christ and Office Building, New York, N.Y., 1966–68. Sections, August–September 1966.*
168. *Broadway United Church of Christ and Office Building. Plan, August–September 1966.*

which also incorporated a church within its base and for which Kahn was briefly considered as architect, were not yet conceived.[29]

Before returning with a second proposal for the Broadway Church and Office Building, Kahn turned his attention to the Kansas City office building. A more typical commission of the time, it was to include underground parking, street level shopping, a health club and a restaurant on the upper floors, and, for a while, even a heliport. It had been under discussion since July 1966, when its developers, Richard Altman and Arnold Garfinkel, visited Kahn in Philadelphia to engage him in what they hoped would be a building of special quality for their city.[30] It was not until January 1967 that Kahn presented his preliminary sketches, and only in May that his first model followed.[31] Again Kahn began by reexamining the very nature of the problem, and his unexpected proposal reflected structural determinism: at each corner, four hollow, room-sized columns were to support a multistory truss at the top of the building, and from this height intermediate floors would he suspended *(fig. 169)*. Komendant, working with Kahn, devised an elaborately choreographed operation for the building's construction; using slip forms, the corner columns and the truss were to be erected first, followed by the pouring of the individual floor slabs, beginning at the top. Kahn embellished the hollow columns with round openings to light the corner offices, and segmental arches defining the top truss lit the restaurant and club contained within. Distinctive form was thus achieved through rational means, at least as Kahn defined it. As an associate said, "It was a wonderful project to work on because he was thinking of new ways of building and expressing the nature of the elements of a skyscraper."[32]

Within the next year both the Broadway and Kansas City projects were redesigned, and clearer statements of slip-form construction emerged. Giving in to client pressure for a less complicated floor plan and a single elevator core—both considered essential to profitability—Kahn first revised his proposal for New York, presenting his second scheme for that commission in September 1967.[33] Gone were the richly complicated profile and the elaborate plan, which were replaced by a simple structure of rectangular floors supported by hollow cylindrical columns *(figs. 170, 171)*. Only the church, partly projecting beyond the overhanging slabs, escaped rigid discipline.[34] Kevin Roche's Knights of Columbus Headquarters in New Haven (1965–69), then under construction, seems to have inspired its structural form,[35] yet Kahn's earlier travel sketches of Albi are also similar. The Broadway tower's slip-form construction still alarmed New York developers, and the project languished.[36] Work on the Kansas City project, however, continued. By the fall of 1968 a revised model had been completed, and it, too, had been greatly simplified, though without a sacrifice of unusual construction *(fig. 172)*. The roof truss was now reduced to an elegant inverted arch, and the corner columns, no longer hollow, had become fluted stems. Kahn's proposal was well received, but before financial arrangements could be completed a new, more advantageous site became available, and he again revised his design.[37] In March 1972 Kahn depicted the final version of his building as it would appear during construction; it had been extended by more than ten floors, resting on a square plinth that held related facilities, and its corner columns were made square *(fig. 173)*. But however compelling the image and however supportive the clients, its unusual structure proved impossible to finance. Komendant then produced a version of his own, but it, too, went unrealized.[38]

The 1971 commission for the Baltimore Inner Harbor development provided Kahn with an opportunity of greater scale, for the expansive site overlooking the waterfront was

169

170

171

173

172

169. *Kansas City Office Building, Kansas City, Mo., 1966–73. Model of first version, April–May 1967.*
170. *Broadway United Church of Christ and Office Building, New York, N.Y., 1966–68. Elevation. Inscribed Louis I. Kahn '67.*
171. *Broadway United Church of Christ and Office Building. Plan. Inscribed November 13, 1967.*
172. *Kansas City Office Building. Perspective of third version. Inscribed Lou K '72.*
173. *Kansas City Office Building. Model of second version, September 1968.*

to contain an urban nucleus of office buildings, apartments, a hotel, and a broad range of
shops.[39] The progress of the complex, part of
Baltimore's ambitious, comprehensive plan,
was closely monitored; developers were
expected to select distinguished architects in
return for receiving the city's permission to
build on newly assembled sites, and strict
guidelines, including a seventy-five-foot
height limit, were imposed. Kahn's first ideas
for its plan brought to the project an active
play of juxtaposed shapes corresponding to his
proposals elsewhere. By the time of his first
presentation in November 1971, these shapes
were further sharpened without an apparent
loss of spontaneity *(fig. 174)*. Rather than
recreating the experimental structures of his
earlier skyscrapers, Kahn worked pragmati-
cally with conventionally framed yet still distinctively shaped buildings, expressing the
diagonal lines of their wind bracing and
adding pyramidal tops to gain additional
rentable area while still honoring the spirit of
the height limit. He joined the individual
structures with monumental stairways and
broad bridges in a manner gauged to generate
a sense of urban vitality, exploiting the master
plan's requirement that upper-level walkways
be incorporated and the developer's demand
that a high podium be provided to minimize
problems created by the harbor site's high
water table *(fig. 175)*. As Kahn explained,
"The main idea was to develop a richness of
place, full of availabilities. . . . We wanted an
interlocking relationship between buildings so
the view would not he obstructed. In turn, that
caused the buildings to be multi-faced instead
of four sided: the hotel, the apartment and
office buildings respect each other."[40] As was
typical of such complicated enterprises and
even more to be expected of Kahn, many variations were explored. By the summer of 1972,
although the major elements had retained
their positions, the parts were reduced in
number and the shapes were somewhat sim-

plified. By then office associates were discour-
aged about the prospects of the development
and felt Kahn's talent was being unfairly
exploited by the developer.[41]

In March 1973 Kahn's contract for the
Inner Harbor was terminated.[42] In Paris two
months later he seemed to air his displeasure
with developers when he characterized speculative office towers like the Tour
Montparnasse as "related only to money,"
continuing, "ours [in the United States] seem
high in a financial sense. The latter [in
Europe] are 'anarchitectural,' they are just
heaps of masonry."[43] Yet at the time of his
death Kahn was again engaged in a speculative venture, this time in Iran, where in association with Kenzo Tange he was to devise the
master plan for Abbasabad, an extensive commercial and residential development on the
northern outskirts of Tehran (1973–74,
unbuilt).[44] Perhaps, to judge by a letter of
appreciation to the shah's wife, Kahn felt royal
patronage would assure a better outcome, and,
inspired by the "strength and beckoning of
this ancient land,"[45] he tried to find meaning
when apparently little was expected.
Following his first visit to the site in
November 1973 he began to plan, but his
drawings of the next few months fell short of
his words. Lacking a detailed program, he
incorporated a broad range of governmental
and cultural institutions, even including a
"Palazzo dei Congressi" *(fig. 176)*. Among
images filed with Kahn's project papers are
plans for Persepolis, Isfahan, Vatican City,
and several chessboards—the latter perhaps
the inspiration for the lower portion of his preliminary scheme for Abbasabad.[46]

During the years of demanding involvement
with projects of almost unchartable complexity, the design of private dwellings may
have offered Kahn some sense of relief. With
these Kahn related to people he knew as
friends, fewer pressures for production were
imposed, and there was greater likelihood of

174. Inner Harbor, Baltimore, Md.,
1969–73. Site plan, November 1971.
175. Inner Harbor. Perspective from
east, 1971.
176. Abbasabad Development, Tehran,
Iran, 1973–74. Site plan diagram (with
later annotations), February 1974.

174

175

176

178

Preceding pages
*177. Fisher house, Hatboro, Pa., 1960–67. Rear
facade.*

178. Fisher house. Side facade.
179. Fisher house. First-floor plan, redrawn 1990.
180. Fisher house. Living room.

182

Preceding pages
181. Korman house, Fort Washington, Pa.,
1971–73. Side facade at dusk.

182. Korman house. First-floor plan. Inscribed
Louis I. Kahn Architect August 10, 1971.
183. Korman house. Living room.

realization. Yet the houses carried their own frustrations; in 1963 Kahn expressed dissatisfaction with his ability to design houses and admitted being unable to conceive a suitable design for the Norman Fisher house (1960–67), commissioned by a physician and his wife some three years before for a suburban site near Philadelphia.[47] As noted in chapter 3, its solution a few months later *(figs. 177–180)* recalls in its geometry the first plan he proposed for Dhaka and later exploited more fully in proposals for urban complexes.[48] Some twenty years earlier Kahn had characterized houses as each being a "society of rooms," parallel to the city;[49] now, it seems, he sought to provide a parallel sense of "availabilities." In his later designs for houses, of which the Fisher was the first, there was a similar lack of symmetrical balance, and separately articulated elements were actively juxtaposed so that no single one dominated. A framework more supportive of

individual choice would result from this obscuring of conventional hierarchies and the invitation of personal selectivity. These designs for actual houses differed from the idealized domesticity of such designs as the Kimbell Art Museum (1966–72), where a calmer order prevailed.

Kahn tried to resist imposing his own choices in the houses he designed. Neutral finishes—most typically vertical wood siding—clarified volumetric definition, and details were restrained. The detailing attests to his care with even the smallest of parts, and it possesses an elegant spareness that can only be imagined in the larger, unbuilt projects. Kahn's first plans for the Steven Korman house (1971–73), designed near the end of his life for a young developer and his family in suburban Philadelphia, contain angled elements like those of the Fisher house *(fig. 182)*.[50] By August 1972 Kahn had simplified the design, yet he retained the clear definition of rooms for individual family members *(figs. 181, 183)*. As realized, the Korman house, too, reflected Kahn's sensitivity to detail.[51] The Korman house stands as Kahn's last realized design in the Philadelphia area or even in his home state of Pennsylvania; other, more ambitious designs—the Pocono Arts Center (1972–74) and the Philadelphia Bicentennial Exposition (1971–73)—remained unbuilt.

Like the Fort Wayne project begun more than a decade earlier, the Pocono Arts Center was intended as a center for visual and performing arts, and it was also to be supported by public funds, in this instance provided by the Commonwealth of Pennsylvania. To be located in the foothills of the Pocono Mountains about five miles from Whitehaven, it was meant to include both indoor and outdoor theaters, art galleries, and artists' studios, for in addition to housing the Philadelphia and Pittsburgh orchestras during the summer, it was seen as providing year-round facilities for artists. Rich in promise and loosely programmed, it was the

184

185

184. *Pocono Arts Center, Luzerne County, Pa.,*
1972–74. Model, April 1974.
185. *Bicentennial Exposition, Philadelphia, Pa.,*
1971–73. Site plan, February–March 1972.

sort of challenge that stimulated Kahn. He began designing in July 1972 well before his appointment was confirmed in November.[52] By the time a formal agreement was signed in January of the following year, Kahn had submitted a model of his first design. His image of monumental terraces remained essentially unchanged during the months that followed (fig. 184).

While Governor Milton Shapp struggled to convince the state legislature of the project's value, Kahn said, "Some of our institutions may have lost their inspiration but their potentials—what I would call their 'availabilities'—remain. The Art Center in the Poconos would be a jewel of availabilities in the arts."[53] At the top of the complex Kahn located the major concert hall, roofed but left open at the sides and approached by a gracefully curved entrance arcade. Along the axis below lay two smaller theaters, enclosed for year-round use. An open-air theater flanked by enclosed studios and related facilities terminated the axis below.

Within the arts center's pastoral setting, the active, unresolved geometries that Kahn had favored for urban complexes gave way to balanced order, and like other examples of his late work it seemed to assume an almost honorific aspect. In its monumental embankment of the landscape it recalls some late Hellenistic acropolis, or more closely the great Roman complexes erected during the last years of the Republic, like the Sanctuary of Fortuna at Praeneste.[54] Whether or not Kahn was aware of this prototype seems of less consequence than what the physical resemblance alone reveals: his continued sympathy with the spirit of the ancient world and with the timeless principles that underlie its noble monuments.

Perhaps no design better reflects Kahn's belief in architecture as a social art than one that may be his least architectural: the Philadelphia Bicentennial Exposition (1971–73), in which he still held hope of participation at time of his death. Although Kahn's formal involvement with the bicentennial started only in 1971, he had begun to consider its possibilities by 1968, when he was asked to contribute ideas for publication.[55] He urged that the bicentennial's qualities as an event be emphasized rather than the creation of permanent, monumental buildings: "This will not be an exposition of accomplished work. It will be the wonder of the yet unmade thing . . . the meeting [of] people [in] the realm of its spaces which offer all communication means, all meeting places, the places of expression."[56] When he was later asked to provide an actual design, it was just such a place of unstructured meeting he seemed to seek. The design was conceived as a loosely defined street linking buildings of unspecified shapes, and he called it the Forum of the Availabilities (fig. 185). Urged by Harriet Pattison, he incorporated a canal as a mode of transportation appropriate to the event and provided gardens as a matrix for the individual pavilions that participating nations would erect.[57] To sponsors both the drawing and the model that followed must have lacked the architectural bombast they sought. But ultimately his design had effect, for no special structures were erected to commemorate the bicentennial, and Kahn's ideas, uncontaminated by material limitations, retain their presence. Yet he did not claim these ideas as his personal inventions any more than he did the others of his all too brief career; as he said only a few months before his death, "I believe that a man's greatest worth is in the area where he can claim no ownership."[58] This may have been his great accomplishment: not the specific shapes, which have inspired an entire generation of architects, but the ideas that knew no shape and would endure.

D.D.L.

Chapter 6

Light, the Giver of All Presences

Designs to Honor Human Endeavor

Architecture comes from The Making of a Room.
The Plan - A society of rooms is a place good to learn, work, learn.

A great American Poet once asked me, the Architect, "What is the sun does your building in a Room as if to say the sun never knew how great its world it shone on. The side of a building."

The Room

is The place of the mind. In a small room one does not say what one would in a large room. In a room with only one other person could be generative. The vectors of each meet. A room is not a room without natural light.

186

186. "The Room." Inscribed Lou K '71.

By the middle of the 1960s, Louis Kahn had taught for nearly twenty years, and his buildings were being built around the world. He had made modern architecture seem morally important and artistically challenging again, at a time when many had come to regard it as a simple utilitarian device.

In the last decade of Kahn's life, the importance and difficulty of all creative work seemed to become even greater. America staggered under the burden of its power, divided by racial strife and sapped by the ethical and material losses of Vietnam. Kahn, who had long argued that architecture was the servant of human institutions, recognized that his country was in crisis, and in November 1967 he lamented that "all our institutions are on trial."[1] However, in this time of frightening ambiguities, he created the simplest and strongest architecture of his career: the library for Phillips Exeter Academy, the Kimbell Art Museum, the Yale Center for British Art, the Memorial for the Six Million Jewish Martyrs, and the Franklin D. Roosevelt Memorial.

The power of most of these last buildings derived from their almost alchemical integration of mass and space—Kahn's long-sought wedding of the fundamental and apparently antithetical elements out of which architecture was made. For Kahn, mass was always analyzed rationally as a question of structure—the substance of building—while space was defined more mystically in terms of natural light—the energy that brought space to life. The manipulation of both structure and light was essential in making "the room," which Kahn had long maintained was the basic compositional element of architecture, and he believed that they could be made to work together. He loved to say that architecture itself had begun "when the walls parted and the columns became," admitting light and creating a system of support at the same time.[2] It was thus that the earliest Greek temples had come into being, and in 1971 he summed up: "The room is the beginning of architecture. It is the place of the mind. You in the room with its dimensions, its structure, its light respond to its character, its spiritual aura, recognizing that whatever the human proposes and makes becomes a life. The structure of the room must be evident in the room itself. Structure, I believe, is the giver of light."[3] This was a concept that he frequently discussed with his students and tried to draw (fig. 186).

At a tiny scale and without having to worry about glazing, Kahn had been able to achieve the room-making integration of structure and light in the Trenton Bathhouse, where the wooden pyramidal roofs were carried by load-bearing concrete-block walls in such a way that light washed into the building through the construction (see fig. 53). Since then, he had experimented with systems that could work in larger, more complex buildings, like the great perforated screen walls he devised for use in tropical countries and the towering light rooms he created for Mikveh Israel synagogue and the mosque at Dhaka. By the late sixties he was able put forward several extraordinary solutions to this vexing problem almost simultaneously. His success is to be seen in the silver-lit barrel vaults of the Kimbell Museum, the interfingering light patterns that reach through the grid exterior of the Exeter library, the luminous coffers of the Yale Center for British Art, and the glowing glass pylons of the monument for the Jewish martyrs.

Not coincidentally, the achievement of a space-defining alliance between structure and light quieted Kahn's planning. The dynamic asymmetries of the monastery plans and the baroque diagonals of his buildings in Asia dropped out of his latest works, which recentered themselves around strong interior spaces and in compact, symmetrical arrangements. In this way, the original decorum of the Beaux-Arts plan was restored after decades of Kahn's strenuous testing, and the attention to structural truth and lighting that effected this restoration was, of course, also part of his Beaux-Arts heritage. He became fond of saying about architecture that "what will be has always been," words that applied to his own recursive habits as well.[4]

The serenity of this last group of designs depended on what was even for Kahn a low level of programmatic specificity. The museums for the Kimbell collection in Fort Worth and Paul Mellon's collection at Yale were similarly and simply imagined as large houses filled with art, or, alternatively, as monuments to human creativity with few ordinary functional responsibilities. "A museum," Kahn said in 1972, "seems like a secondary thing, unless it is a great treasury."[5] Much of the same mixture of domestic and honorific imagery pervaded the Exeter Academy library; and, of course, memorials like those for victims of the Holocaust and for Franklin Roosevelt were truly "free of the bondage of use," like the ruins of antiquity Kahn most admired.[6] Uncomplicated by the demanding program considerations that had inflected his plans for the big institutions of the early sixties, these buildings were free to be simple.

This evolution toward an almost classical coherence was not readily apparent to those who were looking at Kahn's work at the time. For one thing, the visible fruits were slow to ripen. Although the commissions in which this process occurred had begun to occupy Kahn's office fully in 1967–68, the first of these last great projects to be completed, the Exeter library and the Kimbell Museum, were dedicated only in October 1972, less than a year and a half before Kahn died. The Yale Center was finished posthumously, and the Jewish martyrs' and Roosevelt monuments were never built.

What observers had to go on suggested that a very different evolution was under way, for in the long, rambling speeches that Kahn was now invited to give ever more often, he rarely talked about his most recent work. Revisiting instead the commissions of the fifties and early sixties, he veiled his methods with increasingly inscrutable vocabulary. Those who liked him best were alarmed by this tendency. Vincent Scully recalled:

> Sometimes even I and the people who loved him most found it hard to let him do it, to listen to him talking this terribly vague stuff and even slightly sort of false stuff. Then, to hear so many people pick it up as gospel, the sort of philosophical gospel of Lou, was distressful because in his later years it had become more of a smoke screen around his actual methods than anything else.[7]

Even someone who first met Kahn during this time, like Jules Prown, who represented Yale's client interests in building the Center for British Art, could detect the disjunction between the "very factual, very direct" man he dealt with on the job and the man who spoke "more abstractly, more poetically" when he was nervous and trying to impress. When Kahn and he met with Paul Mellon or Yale president Kingman Brewster, Prown found himself "acting as a kind of intermediary between him and them, trying to convince them that this guy wasn't some kind of mad poet."[8] Kahn's longtime assistant Marshall Meyers, who returned to the office in 1967 when work on these commissions was beginning, dealt with this behavior on a day-to-day basis. He complained, "In the later years, one of the difficulties was that he seemed to have too many people in his office who almost deified him."[9]

In fact, little had changed in what Kahn thought. He continued to believe in an idealist architecture, oriented toward the durable essence of things, and what he said was still informed by the fundamental Platonic distinction between "form" and "design," worked out with care and expressed with simple power in

the much-reprinted Voice of America broadcast of 1960. What had changed, however, was the vocabulary with which he expressed this versatile idealism, and the increasing allusiveness of his words led some to believe that he was saying something different.

Having successively rechristened underlying "form" and pragmatic "design" as "law and rule" (1961),[10] "belief and means (1963),[11] and "existence and presence" (1967),[12] by the late sixties Kahn had come upon a favorite formulation that was more mysterious: silence and light. In November 1967, in what may have been his first public explanation of these newest terms, he told a Boston audience that architecture was created at a point that lay between a silent ideal and the illumination of the real, a place that he called "the threshold where Silence and Light meet, Silence with its desire to be, and Light, the giver of all presences." This artistic workplace was also "the sanctuary of all expression, which I like to call the Treasury of the Shadows."[13] A year later, at the Guggenheim Museum, Kahn elaborated on this theme. Silence was the realm of ideal truth which had existed even before the pyramids had been built—"before the first stone was laid." Light, on the other hand, was the energy of the real: "I sense Light as the giver of all presences, and material as spent Light. What is made by Light casts a shadow, and the shadow belongs to Light. I sense a Threshold: Light to Silence, Silence to Light—an ambiance of inspiration, in which the desire to be, to express crosses with the possible."[14] In preparing the Guggenheim lecture for publication, Kahn drew a series of illustrations of this architectural universe. The reflexive discourse between silence and light was expressed in mirror writing and presided over by a pyramid *(fig. 187)*.

Although few observers seem to have noticed, even this most poetic rendering of "form" and "design" was strongly grounded in the vocabulary that Kahn had used ever since the fifties. He had long assigned light a key role in the making of architecture, maintaining that "no space is really an architectural space unless it has natural light."[15] The notion that art was created at a "threshold" between real and ideal had also been expressed earlier, in simpler terms. "A great building must, in my opinion, begin with the unmeasurable and go through the measurable in the process of design," Kahn wrote in introducing a publication of his drawings in 1962, "but [it] must in the end be unmeasurable."[16] Largely unrecognized, too, was the degree to which this new vocabulary was fortified by allusions to respected authority. Most fundamentally, the role played by light and shadow in differentiating the ideal world from the world of daily experience was an echo of the famous discussion of the same subject in Plato's *Republic*: the parable of the prisoners whose only glimpse of the outside was the shadow it projected on the wall of their cave. And Kahn's seemingly eccentric identification of ideal architecture with silence depended, as he said, on one of the most widely read postwar analyses of visual culture, André Malraux's *Voices of Silence* (1953).[17]

In the end, however, Kahn's poetry was his own. He toiled over the making of words with the same indefatigable energy that he devoted to architecture, crossing out and rubbing out and remaking a phrase or a plan. If, after all this labor, his words had failed to elevate and illuminate his subject, he might have been justly accused of succumbing to a cantankerous mysticism. And if his architectural creativity had faltered in his last years, it could have been said that he was preaching what he could not perform. But his words were eloquent, and his architecture was ever more profound.

The first building in which the traits of Kahn's final style could be clearly seen was the library for Phillips Exeter Academy,

187

187. *Page from sketchbook, ca. 1969.*

188

188. *Phillips Exeter Academy Library, Exeter, N.H., 1965–72. Section, facing south, ca. May 1966.*

designed in 1966–68. There, upon a simple plan, he erected a great room filled with light. Functionally a library, it was spiritually a sanctuary. Kahn had always loved books, browsing in bookshops, paging through volumes, and buying books with unaffected reverence, but, as he freely admitted, rarely reading more than the first pages of anything. A book was therefore not an ordinary useful object. "A book is tremendously important," he told a design conference at Aspen in 1972. "Nobody ever paid for the price of a book, they pay only for the printing. But a book is actually an offering and must be regarded as such. If you give honor to the man who writes it, there is something in that which further induces the expressive powers of writing."[18] A library was therefore a place of piety.

So powerful was Kahn's vision of books as objects of reverence that he felt it was appropriate to adapt the terraced, closely planted mausoleums of the Roman emperors in his later, unbuilt design for the Graduate Theological Union Library at Berkeley (1971–74).[19] For Exeter, however, no such monumentalism was ever contemplated; the program called instead for an almost domestic environment that would "encourage and insure the pleasure of reading and study."[20] That, perhaps, was all the reverence that books required.

Kahn's first thinking about the Exeter library showed the influence of his contemporary monastery projects, wrapped in allusions to the Middle Ages in general and monasteries in particular. Corner towers and interior and exterior arcades imparted a castellar feeling to the first design of May 1966, and Kahn explained that his work had been influenced by the example of monastic libraries *(fig. 188).*[21] When the Exeter commission was expanded early in the design development phase to include an adjacent dining hall, he established their relationship with the kind of casual, conversational angularity that he was employing in the Valyermo monastery and the Media convent at the same time.

However, as work continued into 1967, the towers and arcades of Kahn's personal kind of medievalism disappeared, and they were replaced by a contained, regular, and symmetrical vocabulary. The result was a much more classical design that faced inward to one of Kahn's primordial rooms *(fig. 189)*. Here, one level above the ground, the reader was introduced to the building by a square space, confidently defined by structure and light: circles of concrete framed each interior elevation, bracing the main piers at the corners, and the sun entered from above to bathe the whole in quiet brightness. Still and balanced, the central hall took the circle-in-square as its leitmotif—an inversion of the venerable square-in-circle paradigm of natural order cited by the Roman architect Vitruvius and echoed before in Kahn's plan for the Salk meeting house.

Arrayed around the central space on all sides were the book stacks, their floors suspended like the shelves of a giant bookcase between the corner piers. Although the bold display of shelving within the circular openings accomplished Kahn's desired "invitation of books," the books themselves were kept in relative darkness.[22] Only beyond the stacks, at the perimeter of the building, did the walls part to admit natural light to the double-height reading areas. In each, a mezzanine balcony created an upper work level next to the stacks, and a row of wooden carrels, each with its own shuttered, desk-level window, lined the exterior wall *(fig. 190)*. This environment responded to what Kahn considered the instinctive behavior of the reader: "A man with a book goes to the light./A library begins that way."[23] The carrels, which gave students the ability to let in the view or close it out, also afforded them an essential autonomy. Kahn said about schools

in general, "The windows should be made particular to suit a student who wants to be alone even when he is with others."[24]

In plan, the concentric arrangement of great hall, book stacks, and reading areas seemed to echo the earlier served/servant hierarchies of the Richards Building and the Rochester Unitarian Church. This time, as in Erdman Hall, the authentic service functions (elevators, secondary stairs, toilets, photocopying, etc.) were concentrated in the corners, and Kahn quite forthrightly adopted the concentric pattern for the sake of its visual clarity. His pursuit of order was even more obvious in the bilateral symmetry of the Exeter dining hall, with each elevation rising to a central chimney.

The rectilinear brick elevations of the library paid homage to the surrounding neo-Georgian architecture of the campus, for Kahn said that he "didn't try to make something that stands out" *(fig. 191)*.[25] But the load-bearing exterior walls also reflected his continuing love affair with honest brick construction, which he had originally hoped to use both inside and out. Openings were spanned by versatile jack arches, and Kahn thickened the walls as they reached downward and narrowed the piers between the windows as they rose, clearly portraying the varying loads carried at different levels of the facade. In typical language, he explained that he had reached his construction decisions after consulting the material: "The brick was always talking to me, saying you're missing an opportunity. . . . The weight of the brick makes it dance like a fairy above and groan below."[26]

The truth telling of the facade included the external expression of the wooden carrel units, but there was nothing to signal other functional elements, most notably the location of the entrance. This was to be found within the low, covered passage that circled the building, and Kahn made a rather lame effort

190

189. *Phillips Exeter Academy Library, Exeter, N.H.*
1965–72. Central hall.
190. *Phillips Exeter Academy Library. Carrels.*

Following pages
191. Phillips Exeter Adademy Library. View from
northwest.

to describe its ambiguity as an advantage: "From all sides there is an entrance. If you are scurrying in a rain to get to a building, you can come in at any point and find your entrance. It's a continuous campus-type entrance."[27] It was plain that he simply declined to interrupt the taut, repetitive rhythms of his facades with a monumental entrance. Rather than compromise, he banished the problematic element.

In a similar way, Kahn cropped off the corners of the library instead of papering over the collision of adjacent elevation systems or finding another compromise solution to the age-old, classical problem of "turning a corner." He had solved this dilemma at Bryn Mawr with similar radicalism, tucking the corners of the three dormitory units into each other, and he was forthright about his return to this contentious arena of Beaux-Arts debate at Exeter: "It's always a problem to know how to treat a corner. Do you suddenly introduce diagonal members, or make some kind of exceptional rectangular structure at this point? So I thought why eliminate the problem?"[28] Such iconoclasm preserved the purity of the design.

The final design of the Exeter library was taking shape in 1967 when Kahn began to turn his attention to what was to become his most universally admired and loved building, the Kimbell Art Museum in Fort Worth, Texas. His client was the museum's first director, Richard Brown, who was entrusted with comprehensive responsibility for the project by an unusually tolerant board of directors. Kahn was already on the short list of architects Brown recommended at his own job interview.[29]

Brown conducted himself like an ideal client within Kahn's system of "form" and "design," beginning, before Kahn was hired, by composing a conceptual, "Pre-Architectural Program." This defined the spirit of the institution as much as it detailed

its functioning, and in its call for natural light in the galleries and a comfortable, human scale, it was already steering the commission in a direction that Kahn was eager to pursue.[30]

In large measure, the Kimbell design was Kahn's reconsideration of the open planning of his own Yale Gallery. There, the flexible plan had allowed for such freedom that a subsequent director of the museum had been able to denature Kahn's interiors. Moreover, Kahn's commitment to open planning had declined as he came to see the discrete "room" as the basic architectural unit. By 1959, when the Yale Art Gallery had been open for only a few years, he was already announcing that his next museum would be divided into spaces with "certain inherent characteristics."[31] One of those characteristics would be natural light.

Kahn's conception of an architecture of skylit rooms accorded well with Brown's intentions for the new museum, and together they produced a building of domestic scale that was closely attuned to Kay and Velma Kimbell's collection of moderate-size paintings. They shared a distaste for gigantic exhibitions and tiresome didacticism, and they banished both. Echoing Brown's worries about the fatigue induced by the usual, bombastic displays, Kahn admitted, "The first thing you want in most museums is a cup of coffee. You feel so tired immediately."[32]

From the start, Kahn conceived of the basic unit (or room) of the design as a barrel-vaulted space—an idea that Brown remembered "was already in Lou Kahn's mind and had been for a long time."[33] Although he first experimented with polygonal vaulting of folded plate construction, most of the design development concentrated on segmental vaults, for which Marshall Meyers, Kahn's project captain for the museum, invented a cycloidal section *(fig. 192)*. It may have been the example of ancient Roman warehouses like the Porticus Aemilia, with their concatenated barrel vaults, that had implanted this

192

193

194

195

196

192. Kimbell Art Museum, Fort Worth, Tex., 1966–72. Sketch
section. Inscribed September 22, 1967.
193. Kimbell Art Museum. Site model, also showing Amon
Carter Museum, May 1967.
194. Kimbell Art Museum. Model, September–November 1967.
195. Kimbell Art Museum. Model, September 1968.
196. Kimbell Art Museum. West facade, 1989.

Following pages
197. Kimbell Art Museum. South garden with sculpture by
Isamu Noguchi.

form in Kahn's imagination, but Le Corbusier had also regularly employed shallow vaulting in his domestic architecture of the fifties, most notably the villa of Manorama Sarabhai at Ahmedabad (1951–55). Kahn was often entertained by the Sarabhais while working on the Indian Institute of Management. Moreover, Kahn's assembly of many such independently roofed elements to create a large building had been proposed by Le Corbusier at an even greater scale in projects like his Usine Verte (1944), published in the fourth volume of the *Oeuvre complète*. A few months before his death, Kahn spoke candidly of the lasting impression of such designs: "Somebody asked me, *Hasn't the image of Le Corbusier faded in your mind?* I said, *No, it hasn't faded, but I don't turn the pages of his work any more.*"[34] He did not need to turn the pages to remember.

Composing the Kimbell Museum out of independently vaulted units was not unrelated to the assembly of elements that Kahn had practiced in most of his major projects, from the Richards Building and Erdman Hall to the monasteries. But in contrast to those earlier exercises in the picturesque or diagonal grouping of pavilions, the Kimbell was an orthogonal project from the start, even in the grandiose early version that Brown had to reject as too large for the intimate museum that he wanted *(fig. 193)*. Shorn of the round-arched portico that had encircled that first developed design, the modular vaulting system of Kahn's second, smaller proposal was exposed on all elevations and allowed to assert an increasing measure of classical control *(fig. 194)*. This authority increased when the smaller plan was in turn abandoned in the fall of 1968, after Brown realized that its layout would compel visitors to pass the often-empty temporary exhibition gallery as they entered the building. Starting almost from scratch, Kahn created a C-shaped, forecourt-centered design that was even more inherently classical, although he avoided the clichéd accentuation of the central axis *(fig. 195)*. Before construction, one bay was eliminated from the plan to save costs, and this strengthened the clarity with which the parts announced their presence and interrelationships *(figs. 196, 197)*. Here was a crystalline composition quite unlike the rough-hewn Le Corbusian designs to which it was most closely related.

Small in size and breathtakingly straightforward in the organization of its public spaces, the Kimbell achieved the domestic spirit that Brown had wanted. Like the entrance hall of a rich collector's house, the lobby afforded views of virtually all of the public parts of the building: the café where Kahn's sleepy visitor could find a cup of coffee (analogous to the dining room of the house); the bookstore (akin to the library); and, on both sides, the galleries (surrogates for the picture-filled entertaining rooms) *(figs. 198, 200, 201)*. Kahn called the museum "a friendly home."[35]

In part to lessen the fatigue of the museum-goer, Kahn planted the forecourt with a regimented grove of miniature Yaopon holly trees, centered between two reflecting pools that spilled continuously over their curbing. This setting was needed, he explained shortly before the Kimbell opened, because "a museum needs a garden. You walk in a garden and you can either come in or not. This large garden tells you you may walk in to see the things or you may walk out. Completely free."[36] But the forecourt planting also represented the orderly natural world within which Kahn imagined that all human labor was accomplished, most especially the making of idealist architecture such as his own. The visitor was to be physically oriented to this view of nature before the building itself, hidden by the trees, was easily visible. (Kahn, who did not drive, never accepted the fact that Texans would arrive by car, crossing the parking lot to

198

198. Kimbell Art Museum, Fort Worth, Tex.,
1966–72. Café.

Following pages
199. Kimbell Art Museum. North portico.
200. Kimbell Art Museum. Gallery.
201. Kimbell Art Museum. Gallery.

the back door of the museum.) Like most of his landscape and site-planning work during the sixties and seventies, this carefully articulated procession through a landscape was created in consultation with Harriet Pattison, who delighted in making calculated juxtapositions of environmental effects. She was then working for George Patton, Kahn's landscape architect for the project.

Inside, the Kimbell Museum was conceived as a succession of rooms defined by an integrated system of structure and lighting. Nowhere did Kahn better achieve his intentions in this respect. The supporting system was guilelessly explained to the visitor by the three unwalled front bays of the building, which formed a generous portico that echoed the familiar colonnades of classical museums (fig. 199). Here, Kahn said, "how the building is made is completely clear before you go into it," and everything could be inspected: four concrete piers supported an exquisitely elongated concrete shell, whose shape was that of a cycloidal vault.[37] Comparison with the adjacent, enclosed bays revealed that the travertine walling was non-load-bearing, its role carefully choreographed in relation to the concrete. As at the Salk Institute, where travertine was also used, the detailing of the poured concrete resulted from a combination of painstaking formwork design and the unpredictable (but expected) accidents of coloration and texture.

Thus announced on the outside, the same structural system continued within. Kahn's dictum that "space is not a space unless you can see the evidence of how it was made" was obeyed, rejecting the infinitely divisible open planning of the Yale Art Gallery, a system now epitomized for him by the work of Mies van der Rohe.[38] From the entrance, the 100-by-23-foot vaults swept away in all directions, each exposing its four supporting piers and each cupping beneath it a spatial unit that had a "room-like quality" and "the character

of completeness," despite the fact that the overall plan was quite open and capable of subdivision with movable panels (fig. 200).[39] Even the library and the auditorium were adjusted for enclosure under single vaults, while the lower, flat-ceilinged spaces between the vaults were rather vaguely assigned to servant duty within Kahn's served/servant hierarchy (fig. 202).

Reinforcing the sense of totality possessed by each gallery room was its integral natural lighting. In Fort Worth, Kahn created a skylight system without peer in the history of architecture, opening the building to the sun in just the way that he had long recommended—by parting the structure and thus weaving support and illumination together. As he explained in 1972, "structure is the maker of light, because structure releases the spaces between and that is light giving."[40] But whereas Kahn believed that the first architecture had been made when the opaque, primordial walls were broken apart to make columns, at the Kimbell it was not the walls but the roofs that were parted, each vault split along the full length of its crown. Of course, the positioning of this skylight where the keystone should have been demonstrated that the structures were not true vaults, but curved poured-in-place, post-tensioned concrete beams, each 100 feet long. As had often been the case, Kahn was willing to obscure the real complexity of a structure for the sake of visual clarity.

The splinters of sun that penetrated the concrete of the Kimbell danced as images through many of Kahn's later lectures, as he tried to explain the ability of natural light to imbue space with meaning—to make rooms. He often misquoted a scrap of uncannily apposite poetry that Harriet Pattison had shown him:

The great American poet Wallace Stevens prodded the architect asking, "What slice of the sun does your building have?" To paraphrase: What slice of the sun enters your room? What range of

202

202. *Kimbell Art Museum, Fort Worth, Tex.,*
1966–72. Auditorium.
203. *Kimbell Art Museum. North courtyard.*

204

Palazzo Melloni

205

204. Olivetti-Underwood Factory, Harrisburg, Pa., 1966–70. Aerial view, 1970.
205. Yale Center for British Art, New Haven, Conn., 1969–74. North elevation, June 1970. Inscribed Palazzo Melloni.
206. Yale Center for British Art. Library court with semi-circular stair, December 1970.

206

mood does the light offer from morning to night, from day to day, from season to season and all through the years?

Gratifying and unpredictable are the permissions that the architect has given to the chosen opening on which patches of sunlight play on the jamb and sill and that enter, move, and disappear.

Stevens seems to tell us that the sun was not aware of its wonder until it struck the side of a building.[41]

In the spirit of this exposition, Kahn predicted that the skylighting of the Kimbell galleries would "give the comforting feeling of knowing the time of day."[42] This was diminished, however, by the diffusers that Kahn called "natural light fixture[s],"[43] employed to reduce the damaging intensity of the Texas sun. These transformed all daylight into an even, silvery luminosity that washed the undersurfaces of the vaults. More successful in conveying the natural variety of light were the tiny, glass-walled courtyards with which Kahn brought the outside world directly into the galleries (fig. 203). He spoke of "a counterpoint of courts, open to the sky, of calculated dimensions and character, marking them Green Court, Yellow Court, Blue Court, named for the kind of light that I anticipate their proportions, their foliation, or their sky reflections on surfaces, or on water will give."[44]

So successful were most of these lighting devices that the Kimbell Museum disarmed virtually every potential critic and Kahn told those closest to him that it was his favorite building.[45] The cycloidal vaults fulfilled his greatest dream, defining spaces through the unification of light and structure (albeit with some deceit about the nature of the structure), and he found it hard to resist copying his success. He proposed variations on the same kind of vaulting for the galleries of the Yale Center for British Art (1970), the laboratories of the Wolfson Center for Engineering at the University of Tel Aviv (1971), and the De Menil Foundation in Houston (1973); the formula was later rejected at Yale and the De Menil project was unbuilt, but part of the Wolfson Center was completed after Kahn's death, without supervision from America.

Despite the celebrity of the Kimbell vaulting formula, it was not Kahn's only successful space-making combination of light and structure. In 1967, at the same time that he was developing the Kimbell design, he created another solution based on entirely different principles for the Olivetti-Underwood business machine factory near Harrisburg, Pennsylvania. Here the problem was again to give spatial texture to an interior without losing the practical advantages of an open plan, for the building had to be "ready to jump and change, overnight."[46] After considering a grid of pyramidal roofs, skylit at their apexes, Kahn worked out a solution with his engineering consultant, August Komendant, that consisted of self-supporting concrete roof sections, each balanced on a single pier in a manner reminiscent of his own Parasol Houses and Wright's Johnson Wax Administration Building. The meeting of the cropped corners of the roof units defined diamond-shaped skylights that were integral to the overall system. Kahn explained this in now familiar terms: "We wanted to achieve a structure that was the giver of light. Normally the column is dark. But we made it, in this case, the Maker of Light. It embraced the clearstories, which are really our windows."[47]

The spatial control exerted by this roof system was strong, even though it left the work floor almost entirely unobstructed. Rather than follow the orthogonal grid established by the placement of the piers, the space was reoriented obliquely, in obedience to the diagonal pattern established by the clerestories and reinforced by the suspended lighting (fig. 204). The Olivetti factory thus retained some of the baroque planning energy of Kahn's mid-sixties work, although here it was contained within a calm, rectangular envelope.

A third system for modulating spaces with a structural roofing system and natural light was developed for the Yale Center for British Art, a building that was nearing completion when Kahn died. This commission presented another, even more poignant opportunity for Kahn to reconsider the design of the Yale Art Gallery, which faced the site of the new building from across Chapel Street.

Like the Kimbell Museum, the Yale Center was created under the leadership of a powerful director, Jules Prown, who envisioned a naturally lit, houselike setting for a private collection. However, unlike the Kimbell, the site was decidedly urban, and the program was complicated by the nature of the collection (that of Paul Mellon) and the educational mission of the center. The building was to include large facilities for the study of prints and drawings, painting galleries, and a library—for a time expanded to include the main art library of the university. Moreover, in a deal with the city of New Haven, it was agreed to insert retail space on the ground floor to provide the city with tax income.

These conditions suggested a *parti* for the building, which Kahn began to sketch early in 1970: a block with skylit galleries on top, commercial space on the bottom, and everything else in between arranged around two courtyards. An obvious historical analogy for this kind of building could be found in the great town houses of the Italian Renaissance, courtyard-centered palaces whose ground floors were rented out to shopkeepers. Kahn acknowledged this allusion, labeling an early facade study "Palazzo Melloni" *(fig. 205)*.

The same elevation showed his powerful first proposal for a integrative system of structure and light, with two long, low arches leapfrogging the entire length of the building and turning clerestory windows to the north. Prown was worried, however, that this mighty architecture would overwhelm the small works of the Mellon collection—just what Brown had also feared when contemplating Kahn's huge first proposal for the Kimbell. Prown recalled, "We finally just had to say, 'No.' "[48]

Kahn's second design, worked out in the winter of 1970–71 adopted a variant of the Kimbell barrel vaults, this time glazed on their north-facing surfaces rather than split along their crowns. Mechanical services were to be contained within four semicircular corner towers, clad in steel to symbolize their contents, and in the entrance courtyard (now also covered with barrel vaults) Kahn placed a great curved stairway *(fig. 206)*. This design was far advanced in April 1971 when it, too, was abandoned—a victim of inflation at a time when Mellon was also paying for I.M. Pei's vastly more expensive East Building of the National Gallery in Washington, D.C.

After the Yale program was reduced by about one third, work on the realized design began. Based on the same *parti*, this revolved around two covered courtyards. The first, with its floor at ground level, served as the lobby (see *fig. 209*). The second, one floor up at the level of the library, was connected to the first court by the main stairway, and the circular stair in turn rose through the volume of this "library court" to serve the upper floors *(figs. 210, 211)*. These courtyard spaces, encircled by the galleries that looked out into them through large windows, were transformed by paneling and paintings into something approximating the receiving rooms of a country house. Shifting now from an Italian metaphor to one in keeping with the British art that was to hang on the walls, Kahn explained: "I think of the Mellon Gallery as an English hall. When you walk into the hall, you're introduced to the whole house. You can see how the interior is laid out, how the spaces are used. It's as though you can walk into the house and meet the whole house and say, 'Gee whiz, I think you're great.'"[49] In fact, the planning clarity that was apparent on paper was obscured in reality by one major barrier, the impossibility of looking directly from one courtyard into the other and thus understanding the armature of the design.

In the small upper-floor galleries, the domestic imagery was continued in a series of twenty-by-twenty-foot "rooms" that were defined by the strong concrete framing of the square skylights *(fig. 212)*. Here the challenge of providing a naturally lit environment for art, nestled within a clearly expressed structural system, was met again. As at the Kimbell, it was necessary to accommodate a fundamental dichotomy: "Of course," Kahn said, "there are some spaces which should be flexible, but there are also some which should be completely inflexible."[50] The result was a strongly figured ceiling beneath which neutral wall panels could be placed with some freedom. The system of diffusers in the skylights, although long studied before Kahn died, was not worked out until afterward by Marshall Meyers.

The exterior of the Yale Center, shorn of the service towers that were part of the earlier design, became a mute prism, inherently classical in its containment and modularity, yet clearly inflected by complex meanings *(fig. 208)*. The concrete skeleton was revealed in the facades, the piers narrowing floor by floor as they rose and as the superincumbent weight of the building decreased, like the piers at Exeter. The infill walling— the selection of which, like most details of the exterior, was delayed by Kahn until the last possible moment—was dark, unpolished stainless steel. Kahn chose this material over the objections of Jules Prown, perhaps influenced by Paul Mellon's stated preference for

gray granite and by the prevailing gray tonalities of Yale's nearby neo-Gothic buildings.[51] Kahn had become familiar with the properties of stainless steel while working on earlier projects, where it was used as trim, and from the start it had been his chosen material for the ultimately abandoned service towers of the Yale Center. He liked the fact that its textures and coloration varied perceptibly, admiring, too, the way its slight reflectivity mirrored the variety of the environment. To Prown he predicted, "On a grey day it will look like a moth; on a sunny day like a butterfly."[52] He sought to ennoble steel (perhaps for Prown's benefit) by likening it to lead and pewter.

Windows replaced the steel panels on the facades where interior usage called for daylight, and two-story spaces on the inside were represented by two uninterrupted stories of steel and glass on the outside. By no means, however, did this modest external expression make the Yale Center seem extroverted, and although the first-floor shops did bring the life of the street to the building, it replied only with reserved urban mannerliness. Like Exeter, the final design did little to reveal its entrance, which was tucked under a corner *(fig. 207)*. Nothing was allowed to disturb the prismatic completeness of the building. Vincent Scully, who had thought that Robert Venturi or another younger architect should have been given the commission in preference to his now well-established friend, was delighted by this final effect. "I think it is wonderful," he said in 1982, "so quiet, so soundless, so timeless. It is really silence and light and that is what Lou was always talking about."[53]

Construction of the Yale Center was beginning in 1973 when Kahn undertook preliminary studies for a third museum designed for a private collection—or, more properly, the several collections (including surrealist painting, Greek antiquities, and African sculpture) of John and Dominique de Menil. He had

208

Preceding pages
207. *Yale Center for British Art. North facade.*

208. *Yale Center for British Art, New Haven,*
Conn., 1969–74. Exterior from northwest.
209. *Yale Center for British Art. Entrance court,*
looking up.

211

210. Yale Center for British Art, New Haven,
Conn., 1969–74. Library court.
211. Yale Center for British Art. Stair in
library court.

Following pages
212. Yale Center for British Art. Upper gallery,
looking into court.

come to know them in 1967 when Dominique de Menil organized the "Visionary Architects" exhibition at the University of St. Thomas in Houston, for which Kahn contributed a poetic catalogue introduction. She had also had a hand in the abortive Art Center project for Rice University on which he worked in 1969–70.

The program for the De Menil Foundation was complicated and loosely stated, including not only a museum (designed to allow easy, informal access to works in storage) but also a conference center and housing. All was to be located adjacent to the Rothko Chapel and close to Philip Johnson's campus for the University of St. Thomas. For Kahn, this kind of comprehensive project was hugely exciting, and he proceeded with a site plan that showed his proposed museum, with parallel vaulted galleries, and the Rothko Chapel occupying opposite sides of a central lawn. The new residential buildings and meeting halls were located to the west, while existing St. Thomas dormitories occupied the eastern part of the master plan. The death of John de Menil in March 1973 slowed the project, and it was halted by Kahn's death a year later. After several years of delay, the museum was built to the design of Renzo Piano.

Among the most powerful works that Kahn created during this period were a pair of memorials in New York City—both as yet unbuilt. They were to commemorate the victims of the Holocaust and Franklin Delano Roosevelt. Kahn was thus occupied with representing both the tragedy and the aspirations of twentieth-century life in the last years of his own life.

Although both projects were compromised by the addition of descriptive or pictorial elements, they started by affording Kahn the chance to create something almost purely architectural, unfettered by ordinary and practical restrictions. Kahn described this precious field of opportunity in Platonic terms:

> Architecture has little to do with solving problems. Problems are run-of-the-mill. To be able to solve a problem is almost a drudgery of architecture. Though it is tremendously delightful, there is nothing equal to the delight of coming to realizations about architecture itself. There's something that pulls on you as though you were reaching out to something primordial, something that existed before yourself. You realize when you are in the realm of architecture that you are touching the basic feelings of man and that architecture would never have been part of humanity if it weren't the truth to begin with.[54]

He could also explain this with vivid concreteness: "In the mind . . . is the temple, yet not made. A manifestation of desire, not need. Need is so many bananas. Need is a ham sandwich."[55]

The Memorial to the Six Million Jewish Martyrs was a project defined by human feelings of such magnitude and complexity that they resisted expression. Indeed, several designs had been proposed and abandoned before 1966, when Kahn was asked to join a new memorial advisory committee by its energetic chairman, David Kreeger, a philanthropist and collector. A few months later Kahn was awarded the commission, and over the winter of 1967–68 he did his best to create an architectural solution for the spectacular site in Battery Park at the southernmost extremity of Manhattan.

Kahn decided almost at the start that the memorial should be a group of pylons formed out of clear glass, a material of great purity. Lighting was a vital part of this design, just as it was in the contemporary vaults of the Kimbell Museum, and he explained its effect on the memorial in similar words: "Changes of light, the seasons of the year, the play of weather, and the drama of movement on the river will transmit their life to the monument."[56] Even more than the concrete vaults of the Kimbell, however, a glass structure could literally be "the maker of light," a phrase he began to use at exactly this time.[57] Here at last was an effective expression of "the spiritual quality inherent in a structure" that he had spoken of in defining "monumentality" in 1944.[58]

The first plan for the memorial, developed in the fall of 1967, was the least compromised: a three-by-three matrix of pylons standing on a pedestal *(figs. 213, 214)*. The gridded arrangement bespoke the classical discipline that prevailed in Kahn's late work, but, as usual, this was a discipline that his Beaux-Arts sophistication prevented from descending into banal predictability. Thus the central axes were occupied by pylons rather than the expected circulation passages, and the spacing between the pylons equaled the dimensions of the pylons themselves. The latter established a disconcerting equality of solid and void, like that sometimes seen in contemporary Op Art and also seen in early Doric temples, where the intercolumnar spacing nearly matched the diameter of the columns.

Transmitting light by day and radiating light by night, the memorial seemed to afford a glimpse into the usually invisible order of pure architecture. It was an ineffably poignant symbol of the human idealism exterminated by the Nazis' terrible reality. But it was too abstract for those members of the committee who had witnessed the grisly particulars of the Holocaust, and in response to their suggestions, Kahn revised the design in December 1967. He replaced the nine identical piers with a more complicated pattern of seven: six around the edge of the platform to symbolize the six million dead and a seventh at the center, bearing an explanatory inscription. This arrangement set forth the meaning of the monument without ambiguity. Several variations

213

214

213. Memorial to the Six Million Jewish Martyrs, New York, N.Y., 1966–72. Model, Fall 1967.
214. Memorial to the Six Million Jewish Martyrs. Model, Fall 1967.

215

215. *Memorial to the Six Million Jewish Martyrs, New York, N.Y., 1966–72. Model showing chapel, Fall 1968.*

were tested with models, with the central pylon evolving into a chapel-like structure. At the end of this development, the chapel had a circular interior, as shown in a large and elaborate model that was assembled out of miniature plexiglass bricks and mounted on a lead-sheathed plinth *(fig. 215)*. This was exhibited at the Museum of Modern Art in November 1968, but the project failed to kindle enthusiastic support in the Jewish community. Although Kahn revised his design again in 1972, substituting a cheaper construction method, the memorial was not built.

By chance, the end of the project for the Holocaust memorial preceded by only a few months the commission for another monument on another breathtaking waterfront site in New York City. This was a memorial to Franklin Delano Roosevelt, and the location was the southern tip of Welfare Island (renamed Roosevelt Island) in the East River. The United Nations Building was only a few hundred yards away across the water. The commission came from the New York State Urban Development Corporation, which was then demolishing Welfare Island's public hospitals and launching a new urban community, the master plan for which had been drawn by Philip Johnson and John Burgee in 1968–69.

Kahn worked on the Roosevelt Memorial throughout 1973, returning to a subject that had occupied him once before, when, in 1960, he had submitted an unsuccessful entry in the first stage of the competition for a Roosevelt monument in Washington, D.C.[59] That monument was to be located in West Potomac Park, a peninsula lying between the Potomac River and the cherry tree-encircled Tidal Basin. As demanded by the instructions, Kahn's design deferred in site and spirit to the nearby Lincoln and Jefferson Memorials *(fig. 216)*. Rather than a building, it consisted of sixty traditional-looking fountain basins—each sending a jet of water fifty feet into the air and arranged in a giant arc, nearly half a mile long. The result would have been a curved screen of water, abstract in effect yet conservative in architectural detail.

For Roosevelt Island thirteen years later, Kahn strove to solve the problem on his own architectural terms.[60] It was an important commission for him, for he had been an ardent supporter of the New Deal who "loved Roosevelt and knew much more about him than most of us," according to Theodore Liebman, director of design for the Development Corporation.[61] Kahn conceived of the memorial as a combination of two suitably archetypal forms: "I had this thought that a memorial should be a room and a garden. That's all I had. Why did I want a room and a garden? I just chose it to be the point of departure. The garden is somehow a personal nature, a personal kind of control of nature, a gathering of nature. And the room was the beginning of architecture."[62] Again collaborating closely with Harriet Pattison, Kahn placed this ideal room at the tip of the island, to be approached across a controlled landscape of lawn framed by closely planted trees. At first he imagined the room defined by huge slabs, at a relative scale worthy of Ledoux or Boullée, but by the time a model was presented on April 26, 1973, it had been reduced to a paved platform with shelters on two sides.[63] This, in turn, yielded by the end of the summer to an outdoor room with two simple ashlar walls, in which the required statues of Roosevelt were to stand in company with two rows of four pillars, representing the "Four Freedoms" (of speech and worship, and from fear and want) that Roosevelt had proclaimed as the bases of American life in January 1941 (fig. 217). The walls were to be constructed out of the largest possible blocks, through which precisely aligned slits would admit sunlight at dawn on the anniversary of Roosevelt's birth and at sundown on the anniversary of his death.[64] This alluded unmistakably to Kahn's description of the beginning of architecture as the parting of walls.

The final design, worked out in the months immediately before Kahn's death, was a further simplification. The markers of the Four Freedoms were removed, and after traversing Pattison's successive funnel-shaped gardens, the visitor entered Kahn's room: his architecture reduced to a primitive quintessence that he called a "pre-Grecian temple space."[65] Walled by masonry of unquestionable tectonic honesty and ceiled by the light of the sky itself, the memorial room allowed outward views only to the south, down the river and past the UN toward the Williamsburg Bridge. The nearby tumult of Manhattan and its spiky midtown skyline were screened from sight. Here was quiet at the end of a journey.

The last years of Louis Kahn's life were especially full of accomplishment and honor. Temple Beth-El, the Kimbell Museum, and the Exeter library were dedicated in 1972, followed by the theater at Fort Wayne in 1973. The museum and the library were among his greatest works and among the greatest buildings of the twentieth century. Kahn's architecture was the subject of retrospective exhibitions at the Museum of Modern Art in New York (1966) and the Eidgenössische Technische Hochschule in Zurich (1969), and it was comprehensively surveyed in special issues of L'architecture d'aujourd'hui (1969), Architectural Forum (1972), and Architecture + Urbanism (1973). In the year before he died, two teams of authors were preparing books about him, completed as Romaldo Giurgola and Jaimini Mehta's Louis I. Kahn (1975) and Heinz Ronner, Sharad Jhaveri, and Alessandro Vasella's Louis I. Kahn: Complete Work, 1935–1974 (1977).

216

217

216. *Roosevelt Memorial, Washington, D.C., 1960.*
Section (detail of sheet), Summer 1960.
217. *Roosevelt Memorial, New York, N.Y., 1973–74.*
Perspective, ca. August 1973.

All of the highest awards of Kahn's profession also arrived in a rush during these years: the gold medals of the Philadelphia and New York chapters of the American Institute of Architects in 1969 and 1970, the AIA's national gold medal in 1970, and the gold medal of the Royal Institute of British Architects in 1971. Not to be overshadowed by this architectural recognition was the 1971 Philadelphia Award, called the "Bok Award" for its donor, Edward W. Bok. This was usually seen as the highest honor accorded to a citizen of Kahn's native city.

The architectural work, of course, continued, and much of it was exhaustingly far away. The school in Ahmedabad and a family planning center in Kathmandu required supervision. Construction in Dhaka resumed with a revised program after the war for Bangladesh independence, and new commissions arrived from Morocco, Israel, and Iran. Closer to home, Kahn taught as much as ever at the University of Pennsylvania, although he was now technically an emeritus professor. And the invitations to lecture poured in.

With his eyesight saved by a cataract operation in 1966 and a hernia repaired in 1972, Kahn entered his seventies in apparent good health. Indeed, he usually seemed to be energetic and robust, even on the grueling trips that took him across Europe to Asia, often with several lecture or business stops along the way, and returned him to Philadelphia just in time to teach a class or meet an American client in a far-off city. He had, however, begun to consult a doctor about a worrisome heart condition, and friends and family noted that he occasionally looked gray and tired.

There was, amidst all of this honor and tiring activity, some disappointment, too. While Kahn was honored as an "architect's architect" by his colleagues and adored by many students, his influence remained rather narrow. He had difficulty winning the type of support he wanted most, from the large, often public institutions that controlled what he thought was the architect's most important work. Although he had been respected by discerning individuals like Jonas Salk, Richard Brown, and Jules Prown, this kind of personal backing could not secure the success of his largest plans. Numerous ambitious projects were thus abandoned: the President's Estate in Islamabad, the new city of Gandhinagar, the Hill Area Redevelopment in New Haven, the convention hall in Venice, the Art Center for Rice University, and (except for a fragment) the arts complex at Fort Wayne. In the year before he died, he faced increasing frustration in elevating Philadelphia's planned celebration of the bicentennial of American independence to an appropriate level, and two large commercial developments in which he had invested much energy went abandoned: the Inner Harbor in Baltimore and the skyscraper in Kansas City. Only in India and Bangladesh was he able to complete large projects, and there the work was forcefully advanced by local representatives to whom Kahn was compelled to grant much discretion.

Even among the colleagues and students who admired Kahn, few recognized that his philosophy demanded that each architect seek his own understanding of human institution and then test for himself the natural laws that established the limits of design. What they could see clearly was only the example of Kahn's own powerful architecture, and it was this that they emulated. The results were often unhappy, for no one could equal his ability to infuse hard materials with humanity or to lift complex planning above formalist pattern making. Only in south Asia (again an exception) and in some other parts of the developing world did Kahn's work seem to inspire a vibrant brick vernacular style; elsewhere the architecture that was most obviously indebted to his example frequently looked derivative or worse: brutal in elevation and artificial in plan. It was thus with many unfulfilled dreams—as well as the knowledge of his great success—that Kahn made his final trip to India in March 1974.

In retrospect, many thought that the time before his departure had been full of signs. Esther Kahn remembered that his chronic indigestion had gotten worse, and his daughter Sue Ann had remarked on his tiredness.[66] On the evening before his trip there had at last been time to look through the photographs of a big family party held in his honor several months earlier, and just a few days before that he and Esther had had dinner with Steven and Toby Korman in the sumptuous, recently completed house that Kahn had designed for them (see *fig. 181*). The Kormans recalled that their guests had stayed late, talking in the end as though they were alone.[67]

Kahn flew to India for a week to lecture under the auspices of the Ford Foundation and to inspect the Indian Institute of Management and see his friend Balkrishna Doshi in Ahmedabad. At the end of the visit Doshi put Kahn on the 1:15 A.M. flight from Ahmedabad to Bombay on Saturday March 16.[68] In Bombay, Kahn boarded an Air India plane en route to London via Kuwait, Rome, and Paris, expecting to connect with TWA in London and fly on to Philadelphia Sunday afternoon. He was scheduled to teach on Monday. In the event, he missed the TWA flight and had to rebook Air India into New York.

This had turned into a very long journey, and Kahn had reason to be weary. He had flown out and back to Teheran in February, to Dhaka in January, to Tel Aviv in December, and in the previous twelve months he had made four other long trips abroad, visiting Dhaka, Brussels, Paris, Tel Aviv, Rabat, and Kathmandu one or more times. Doshi remembered him being lively and full of fun during his stay in Ahmedabad, but by the time he reached Heathrow Airport in London on Sunday he was evidently in distress. Stanley Tigerman, a pupil from Kahn's last years at Yale, was traveling to inspect his own work in Bangladesh. Tigerman encountered him in the waiting room at Heathrow:

> I'm at the airport and I see this old man, who looks like he has detached retinas, is really raggy and looks like a bum. It was Lou. . . . We had two hours together. We talked mostly about this friend of mine who got me into Bangladesh, Muzharul Islam, who later gave up architecture. He was the one responsible for Lou getting the capital [project]. . . . Lou and I were sitting talking and he couldn't figure out why Islam had given up architecture. We were reminiscing. We had a nice talk. He seemed exhausted, depressed. He looked like hell. . . . He talked mostly about the state of Muzharul Islam, that he had done such a wonderful thing for Lou and then how he gave up architecture because of politics. Lou said, *There's so few things I know in life. I could never do anything but be an architect because that's all I know how to do.*[69]

After talking with Tigerman, Kahn boarded an Air India jet bound for New York. He passed through customs at Kennedy Airport at 6:20 P.M., and made his way to Pennsylvania Station to catch a train to Philadelphia. There, in the station men's room, Louis I. Kahn died of a heart attack at about 7:30 on Sunday, March 17, 1974.

The New York police advised Philadelphia authorities of Kahn's death by teletype almost immediately, but they supplied only his business address, and no further effort was made to locate his family when, on that Sunday evening, no one was found at the office.[70] On Monday concern deepened into alarm among his staff and family when he failed to arrive, and they began to retrace his itinerary. His changed routing and the lack of some passenger manifests made this inquiry difficult, but on Tuesday they at last learned from U.S. Customs that he had reached New York City on Sunday evening. Their attention now shifted to hospitals and morgues in New York. Kahn was at Missing Persons in Manhattan, and it was there that his widow identified the body.

Funeral services were conducted in Philadelphia on Friday, March 22, followed that day by a memorial meeting for students and office staff in his studio at the University of Pennsylvania. On April 2 there was a more public service for the university community. A recurrent theme in all that was said of him was that he was a very young man of seventy-three. Because the start of his career had been slowed by the Depression and the war, Kahn's most memorable architecture had been done rather recently and in an enormous rush of creative energy. Moreover, he had always seemed like a boyish enthusiast who had newly fallen in love with his life-work. Jonas Salk said, "For five decades he prepared himself and did in two what others wish they could do in five."[71] Peter Shepheard, Holmes Perkins's successor as dean of fine arts, recounted simply, "After that dry period when so many of us thought the fun had gone out of architecture, Lou brought it back."[72]

Along with the pleasure of making architecture, Kahn had also restored its importance. He rescued modernism from the banality induced by its commercial success and reattached it to serious themes: the sheltering of human institutions and the definition of space by structure, mass, and light. It was not, of course, that these fundamental matters had been ignored in the earlier years of the twentieth century. In the work of Gropius and those first Americans who had fought for public housing, Kahn had seen and known social activism in architecture. And he had recognized Le Corbusier as a sculptor of powerful structures and a magician of light. In a sense, Kahn had restored the moral and artistic importance that the modern movement had embraced at its start.

But Kahn could also do what those of an earlier generation could not. No longer fearful that creativity would be frozen by anything more than an occasional backward glance into the past, he could freely enrich his architecture by drawing on history's artistic and philosophical treasury. This had two important consequences. He was able to increase the visual range of twentieth-century architecture just as it was teetering into self-parody, and he could broaden and ennoble the sometimes arcane rhetoric of abstract art by explicitly connecting it to its neo-Platonic and classical roots.

Louis Kahn thus reassigned modern architects the most difficult work in the world, but he also opened up to them all the world's resources. He offered them daunting responsibility and terrifying liberty. As Vincent Scully said, "He broke the models and set his strongest students free."[73]

D.B.B.

Notes

Introduction

1. As in my introduction to the exhibition of Kahn's work at the Pennsylvania Academy of the Fine Arts in 1978 (*The Travel Sketches of Louis I. Kahn* [Philadelphia: Pennsylvania Academy of the Fine Arts, 1978]), to the Garland edition of Kahn's drawings (*The Louis I. Kahn Archive: Personal Drawings*, 7 vols. [New York: Garland Publishing, 1987]), and to Jan Hochstim, *The Paintings and Sketches of Louis I. Kahn* (New York: Rizzoli, 1991). These articles touch on the Roman relationships as well.

2. As in his *Antichità Romane*, vol. 4, in H. Volkmann, *G. B. Piranesi* (Berlin, 1965), pl. 37.

3. Reproduced at about the same time, along with Piranesi's *Carceri* and a number of nineteenth- and twentieth-century derivatives, in my *Modern Architecture* (New York: George Braziller, 1961), figs. 3–14.

Chapter 1
Adventures of Unexplored Places

1. Details of Kahn's early life recounted by Esther I. Kahn, interview with Alessandra Latour, May 5, 1982, in *Louis I. Kahn: L'uomo, il maestro*, ed. Latour (Rome: Edizioni Kappa, 1986), 15–28; and interview with David B. Brownlee, April 27, 1990.

2. James Liberty Tadd, *New Methods in Education: Art, Real Manual Training, Nature Study* (Springfield, Mass., and New York: Orange Judd Company, 1898); Public Industrial Art School, *Statement of the Object of the School by the Director* (Philadelphia: Devine Publishing Company, 1904).

3. E. Kahn, interview with Brownlee. Kahn's text for Fleisher Memorial annual report, December 4, 1973, "Samuel S. Fleisher Art Memorial," Box LIK 45, Louis I. Kahn Collection, University of Pennsylvania and Pennsylvania Historical and Museum Commission, Philadelphia (hereafter cited as Kahn Collection).

4. Patricia McLaughlin, "'How'm I Doing, Corbusier?' An Interview with Louis Kahn," *Pennsylvania Gazette* 71 (December 1972): 19.

5. Quoted in, e.g., Vincent J. Scully, *Louis I. Kahn* (New York: George Braziller, 1962), 12.

6. Cret, "Modern Architecture," lecture presented to the T-Square Club, Philadelphia, October 25, 1923, Box 16, Cret Papers, Special Collections, Van Pelt Library, University of Pennsylvania. See also David B. Brownlee, *Building the City Beautiful: The Benjamin Franklin Parkway and the Philadelphia Museum of Art* (Philadelphia: Philadelphia Museum of Art, 1989), 8–12.

7. Ann L. Strong and George E. Thomas, *The Book of the School: 100 Years* (Philadelphia: Graduate School of Fine Arts, University of Pennsylvania, 1990), 34–36.

8. Kahn's college transcript, "Passport," Box LIK 57, Kahn Collection.

9. "Beaux-Arts Institute of Design," *American Architect* 125 (February 27, 1924): 207–10; 125 (April 9, 1924): 363–68; 125 (May 7, 1924): 443–46; 126 (September 24, 1924): 295–98.

10. Cret, "Modernists and Conservatives," lecture presented to the T-Square Club, Philadelphia, November 19, 1927, Box 16, Cret Papers, Special Collections, Van

Pelt Library, University of Pennsylvania.

11. "Kahn on Beaux-Arts Training," ed. William Jordy, *Architectural Review* 155 (June 1974): 332.

12. Ibid.

13. John W. Skinner, "The Sesqui-Centennial Exposition, Philadelphia," *Architectural Record* 60 (July 1926): 1–17; John Molitor, "How the Sesqui-Centennial was Designed," *American Architect* 130 (November 5, 1926): 377–82.

14. "News of the World Told in Pictures," *Philadelphia Inquirer*, October 19, 1925, 15. For the doubts, see William H. Laird, "Records of Consulting Practice," vol. 12, Perkins Library, Fine Arts Library, University of Pennsylvania.

15. Passport, unmarked file, Box LIK 63, Kahn Collection.

16. Kahn, interview with Jaimini Mehta, October 22, 1973, in *What Will Be Has Always Been: The Words of Louis I. Kahn*, ed. Richard Saul Wurman (New York: Access Press and Rizzoli, 1986), 225.

17. Job application questionnaire, December 30, 1949, "Housing Projects—Requests for Job," Box LIK 62, Kahn Collection.

18. Kahn's Italian itinerary may be reconstructed on the basis of his travel sketches. See: Kahn, "Pencil Drawings," *Architecture* 63 (January 1931): 15–17; Kahn, "The Value and Aim in Sketching," *T-Square Club Journal* 1 (May 1931): 18–21; Pennsylvania Academy of the Fine Arts, *The Travel Sketches of Louis I. Kahn* (Philadelphia: Pennsylvania Academy of the Fine Arts, 1978); and Jan Hochstim, *The Paintings and Sketches of Louis I. Kahn* (New York: Rizzoli, 1991).

19. Kahn, "Value and Aim," 21.

20. Scully, *Kahn*, 13.

21. Letter, Kahn to architectural fellows, American Academy in Rome, March 1, 1951, "Rome 1951," Box LIK 61, Kahn Collection.

22. Courtship recounted by E. Kahn, interview with Latour, 19–23; and interview with Brownlee.

23. The journal changed its name twice: to *T-Square* in January 1932, and to *Shelter* in April 1932. *Shelter* was briefly revived in New York, March 1938–April 1939.

24. Wisdom, interview with David B. Brownlee, David G. De Long, and Peter S. Reed, July 5, 1990.

25. Scully, *Kahn*, 15.

26. Piero Santostefano, *Le Mackley Houses di Kastner e Stonorov a Philadelphia, 1931–1935* (Rome: Officina Edizioni, 1982); Richard Pommer, "The Architecture of Urban Housing in the United States during the Early 1930s," *Journal of the Society of Architectural Historians* 37 (December 1978): 235–64.

27. "Slum Elimination Project on Display," *Philadelphia Record*, April 23, 1933, F3; "Prepare Plan for Slum Modernizing," *Philadelphia Inquirer*, April 23, 1933, W9; "Slum Modernizing Plan Unique Here," *Philadelphia Inquirer*, April 30, 1933, W11; "Air Castles Rise in 'Clinic,'" *Philadelphia Record*, May 14, 1934, 1.

28. Bernard J. Newman, "Northeast Philadelphia Housing Corporation," in *Housing in Philadelphia, 1933* (Philadelphia: Philadelphia Housing Association, 1934), 22–23; Pommer, "Urban Housing," 244–45.

29. St. Katherine's Village report, typescript, unmarked file, Box LIK 68, Kahn Collection; site plan (dated December 12, 1935), partial site plan (dated November 22, 1935), and first-floor plan for house type 2A, Magaziner Papers, Athenaeum of Philadelphia.

30. Ralph H. Danhof, "Jersey Homesteads," in *A Place on Earth: A Critical Appraisal of Subsistence Homesteads*, ed. Russell Lord and Paul H. Johnstone (Washington, D.C.: United States Department of Agriculture, Bureau of Agricultural Economics, 1942), 136–61; Paul Conkin, *Tomorrow a New World: The New Deal Community Program* (Ithaca, N.Y.: Cornell University Press, 1959), 256–76; Edwin Rosskam, *Roosevelt, New Jersey: Big Dreams in a Small Town and What Time Did to Them* (New York: Grossman Publishers, 1972); Gail Hunton, "National Register of Historic Places Inventory Nomination Form . . . Jersey Homesteads," February 1983.

31. Drawings of the original designs, February–May 1935, by Lawrence and Callander, architects, "Hightstown N.J.," Box 35, Kastner Papers, American Heritage Center, University of Wyoming, Laramie (hereafter cited as Kastner Papers).

32. Noble autobiography, August 15, 1960, "Fellowships Jury of Fellows," Box LIK 57, Kahn Collection.

33. Weekly drafting room reports, December 21, 1935–May 23, 1936, notebook "11.(1938)," Box 45, Kastner Papers; personal history statement, January 9, 1939, "Housing," Box LIK 62, Kahn Collection.

34. Credit was assigned to H.D.M. [Michaelson or Martin?] for type A, to C.F.W[agner] for type B, to S.A.K[aufman] for type C, to L.H.M. [Michaelson or Martin?] for type E; photographs of lost drawings, "Hightstown, N.J.," Box 26, Kastner Papers.

35. Lewis Mumford, "The Sky Line: Houses and Fairs," *New Yorker*, June 20, 1936, 31.

36. "Tugwell Hands Out $1,800,000 for N.J. 'Commune,'" *Philadelphia Inquirer*, May 7, 1936, 1, 38.

37. Other designs, drawings 70.1, 70.3–7, "Hightstown School," Box LIK 62, Kahn Collection.

38. Blueprints of school as built, May 21–September 11, 1937, Box 25, Kastner Papers; "Schools: Community Building, Jersey Homesteads, Hightstown, N.J., Alfred Kastner, Architect," *Architectural Forum* 68 (March 1938): 227–30.

39. "Steelox Details," "Misc II," "Philadelphia Housing Authority," Box LIK 68, Kahn Collection.

40. Timothy L. McDonnell, *The Wagner Housing Act: A Case Study of the Legislative Process* (Chicago: Loyola University Press, 1957).

41. For the story of twentieth-century housing in Philadelphia, see John F. Bauman, *Public Housing, Race and Renewal: Urban Planning in Philadelphia, 1920–1974* (Philadelphia: Temple University Press, 1987).

42. Elizabeth Mock, "What About Competitions," *Shelter* 3 (November 1938): 26–29.

43. "Housing Work of Kenneth Day," typescript, "Misc," Box LIK 63, Kahn Collection; "Lost: $19,000,000 for 3451 Dwellings," *Building Homes in*

Philadelphia: Report of the Philadelphia Housing Authority (July 1, 1939–June 30, 1941), 36–37.

44. Bauman, *Public Housing*, 46.

45. Ibid.

46. "U.S.H.A. City of Tomorrow: Exhibit for New York World's Fair. Museum of Modern Art," Box LIK 68, Kahn Collection; Peter S. Reed, "Toward Form: Louis I. Kahn's Urban Designs for Philadelphia, 1939–1962" (Ph.D. diss., University of Pennsylvania, 1989), 13–35.

47. "City Wide Meeting," Box LIK 34, Kahn Collection.

48. Andrew Weinstein, "Americanizing Modernism: Housing by Louis I. Kahn during the Great Depression and World War Two" (M.A. paper, University of Pennsylvania, 1988).

49. Robert A. M. Stern, *George Howe: Toward a Modern American Architecture* (New Haven and London: Yale University Press, 1975).

50. Frederick Gutheim, ed., "Numero speciale dedicato all'opera di Oskar Stonorov (1905–1970)," *Architettura: Cronache e storia* 18 (June 1972).

51. McDonnell, *Wagner Housing Act*, 58–59.

52. Wisdom, interview with Brownlee, De Long, and Reed.

53. Howe, Stonorov, and Kahn, "'Standards' versus Essential Space: Comments on Unit Plans for War Housing," *Architectural Forum* 76 (May 1942): 308–11.

54. Letter, Stonorov to Arthur Johnson (president, United Steel Workers of America, Coatesville), August 19, 1942, "Correspondence—July—September, 1942," Box 49, Stonorov Papers, American Heritage Center, University of Wyoming, Laramie (hereafter cited as Stonorov Papers).

55. "What Housing for Willow Run?" *Architectural Record* 92 (September 1942): 51–54; Hermann H. Field, "The Lesson of Willow Run," *Task*, no. 4 (1943): 9–21.

56. Extensive correspondence, Box 48, Stonorov Papers.

57. Illustrated in Field, "Lesson," 21; and Howe, "The Meaning of the Arts Today," *Magazine of Art* 35 (May 1942): 165.

58. Letter, Saarinen to Stonorov, December 8, 1941, "Correspondence—October—December, 1941," Box 48, Stonorov Papers; letter, Stonorov to Saarinen, February 14, 1942, "Correspondence—January—March, 1942," Box 48, Stonorov Papers.

59. Letter, F. Charles Starr (National Housing Agency) to Stonorov and Kahn, August 5, 1942, "Correspondence—July—September, 1942," Box 49, Stonorov Papers.

60. "The Town of Willow Run: Neighborhood Unit 3," *Architectural Forum* 78 (March 1943): 52–54.

61. Letter, Stonorov to George Addes (UAW-CIO International secretary-treasurer), Walter Reuther, and William Nicholas (UAW), September 3, 1942, "Correspondence—July—September, 1942," Box 49, Stonorov Papers.

62. Addes to Stonorov, September 9, 1942, ibid.

63. Letter, Howe to Kahn, September 4, 1944, "Correspondence—July—September 1944," Box 50, Stonorov Papers.

64. Stonorov tried repeatedly to enlist during this period, citing the lack of architectural work. But his request to be commissioned as an officer directly from civilian life was denied.

65. Letter, Stonorov to Maubert St. Georges (president, St. Georges and Keyes advertising agency), April 5, 1943, "Correspondence—April—June, 1943," Box 49, Stonorov Papers.

66. Letter, Stonorov to Richard K. Snively (St. Georges and Keyes), April 15, 1943, ibid.

67. Stonorov and Kahn, *Why City Planning Is Your Responsibility* (New York: Revere Copper and Brass, [1943]), 14, 5.

68. Letter, Donald F. Haggerty (Revere) to Stonorov and Kahn, August 10, 1943, "Correspondence—July—September, 1943," Box 49, Stonorov Papers.

69. Letter, St. Georges to Stonorov, February 11, 1944, "Correspondence—January—March 1944," Box 50, Stonorov Papers.

70. He repeated the house/city analogy in Kahn, "Architecture and Human Agreement" (lecture, University of Virginia, April 18, 1972), *Modulus*, no. 11 (1975): n.p.

71. Letter, Stonorov to Howard Myers, February 2, 1944, "Correspondence—January—March 1944," Box 50, Stonorov Papers.

72. Kahn, "Can Neighborhoods Exist?" Box 33, Stonorov Papers; letter, Elizabeth Mock (Museum of Modern Art) to Kahn, December 5, 1944, "Correspondence—October—December, 1944," Box 50, Stonorov Papers; letter, Stonorov to Richard Abbott (Museum of Modern Art), December 7, 1944, ibid.; letter, Mock to Stonorov, December 12, 1944, ibid.

73. "ICC," Box LIK 62, Kahn Collection.

74. "National Jewish Welfare Board," Box LIK 61, Kahn Collection.

75. "Seminar—Arch. Adv. Committee," "Architectural Advisory Com. Federal Public Housing Authority Louis I. Kahn," "Arch Adv. #2," Box LIK 63, Kahn Collection.

76. "PHA Advisory Committee Wash D.C.," Box LIK 61, Kahn Collection.

77. "Committee on Urban Planning A.I.A.," Box LIK 63, Kahn Collection.

78. "A.S.P.A.," "U.N.O.," Box LIK 63, Kahn Collection.

79. Howe, "Master Plans for Master Politicians," *Magazine of Art* 39 (February 1946): 66–68.

80. Victoria Newhouse, *Wallace K. Harrison, Architect* (New York: Rizzoli, 1989), 104–43.

81. Letter, Kahn to Phil Klutznick (Palestine Economic Corporation), March 13, 1949, "Correspondence Palestine Economic Corp," Box LIK 61, Kahn Collection.

82. Letter, George Shoemaker (secretary, Philadelphia Society for the Employment and Instruction of the Poor) to Kahn, February 18, 1947, "Correspondence—January—March, 1947," Box 51, Stonorov Papers.

83. Letter, Ruth Goodhue (*Architectural Forum*) to Kahn, July 1, 1942, "Correspondence—July—September, 1942," Box 49, Stonorov Papers; telegram, Kahn to Goodhue, July 3, 1942, ibid.; letter, Stonorov to Goodhue, July 31, 1942, ibid.

84. "New Buildings for 194X: Hotel," *Architectural Forum* 78 (May 1943): 74–79.

85. Pittsburgh Plate Glass Company, *There Is a New Trend in Store Design* [Pittsburgh: Pittsburgh Plate Glass Company, 1945]. Also related was the "Business 'Neighborhood' in 194X" that Kahn sketched for a Barrett roofing ad in 1945: *Pencil Points* 26 (May 1945): 160; *Architectural Forum* 82 (June 1945): 179. Their postwar practice included some of exactly this kind of commercial work: the planned renovation of a Thom McAn shoe store in Upper Darby, the Coward shoe store in Philadelphia, and alterations to a Buten paint store in Camden.

86. Letter, Stonorov to *California Arts and Architecture*, May 19, 1943, "Correspondence—April—June, 1943," Box 49, Stonorov Papers; letter, John Entenza (California Arts and Architecture) to Stonorov and Kahn, September 7, 1943, "Correspondence—July—September, 1943," Box 49, Stonorov Papers. First- and second-floor plans in Kahn's hand, drawing 130.1, Kahn Collection.

87. "H. G. Knoll Assoc. Planning Unit," Box LIK 60, Kahn Collection; "Parasol House," Box LIK 33, Kahn Collection. The other architects were Serge Chermayeff, Charles Eames, Antonin and Charlotta Heythum, Joe Johannson, Ralph Rapson, and Eero Saarinen.

88. Letter, Stonorov to David Aarons (Gimbel Brothers), January 7, 1943, "Correspondence—January—March 1943," Box 49, Stonorov Papers.

89. Letter, G. P. MacNichol (Libbey-Owens-Ford) to Stonorov, August 25, 1945, "Correspondence—July—September, 1945," Box 50, Stonorov Papers.

90. Tyng, interview with David B. Brownlee, July 20, 1990.

91. Telegram, Earl Aiken (press relations manager, Libbey-Owens-Ford) to Stonorov, January 10, 1947, "Correspondence—January—March, 1947," Box 51, Stonorov Papers; telegram, Stonorov to Aiken, January 17, 1947, ibid.; telegram, Kahn to Aiken, January 17, 1947, ibid.

92. Maron Simon, ed., *Your Solar House* (New York: Simon and Schuster, 1947), 42–43.

93. Bill, Victory Storage Company to Stonorov and Kahn, March 4, 1947, "Veterans Administration," Box LIK 63, Kahn Collection.

94. Research assistance for the Oser house was provided by Marcia Fae Feuerstein.

95. Specifications, "Broudo Residence," Box LIK 61, Kahn Collection.

96. Chronology established from dated drawings in the Kahn Collection.

97. Research assistance for the Roche house was provided by David Roxburgh.

98. Tyng, interview with Brownlee, July 20, 1990.

99. Research assistance for the Weiss house was provided by David Roxburgh.

100. Kahn, quoted in Barbara Barnes, "Architects' Prize-winning Houses Combine Best Features of Old and New," *Evening Bulletin*, May 20, 1950.

101. Chronology established from dated drawings 305.1, 305.3, and office drawings, Kahn Collection.

102. Research assistance for the Genel house was provided by Marcia Fae Feuerstein.

103. Undated drawings 315.1–5, Kahn Collection, seem to belong to this phase.

104. Research assistance for the Philadelphia Psychiatric Hospital was provided by Peter S. Reed.

105. "Hospital to Cure the Mentally Ill," *Architectural Record* 90 (August 1941): 87–89.

106. Letter, Kahn to Rosenfield, August 2, 1945, "Correspondence—July—September, 1945," Box 50, Stonorov Papers.

107. Letter, Rosenfield to Stonorov and Kahn, February 13, 1946, "Correspondence—January—March, 1946," Box 51, Stonorov Papers.

108. In response, Kahn protested, "I am sorry for the remarks you made about me personally. I hope I shall not have to reassure you of the earnestness of my intentions and efforts"; letter, Kahn to Radbill, September 11, 1945, "Correspondence—July—September, 1945," Box 50, Stonorov Papers.

109. Tyng, interview with Brownlee, June 5, 1990.

110. Sigfried Giedion, *Architecture You and Me: The Diary of a Development* (Cambridge, Mass.: Harvard University Press, 1958), 22–24, 48–51.

111. "In Search of a New Monumentality," *Architectural Review* 104 (September 1948): 117–28.

112. Sigfried Giedion, "The Need for a New Monumentality," in *New Architecture and City Planning*, ed. Paul Zucker (New York: Philosophical Library, 1944), 549, 551; Kahn, "Monumentality," ibid., 577.

113. Kahn, "Monumentality," 578.

114. Ibid., 578–79.

115. Ibid., 581, 580.

116. Ibid., 581.

117. Ibid., 587.

118. Letter, Kahn to Joseph Hudnut, May 15, 1946, "U.N.O.," Box LIK 63, Kahn Collection.

119. Robert A. M. Stern, "Yale 1950–1965," *Oppositions*, no. 4 (October 1974): 35–62; Stern, *Howe*, 210–25; William S. Huff, "Kahn and Yale," *Journal of Architectural Education* 35 (Spring 1982): 22–31.

120. Letter, Sawyer to Stern, February 9, 1974, Box VI, George Howe Papers, Avery Library, Columbia University, New York.

121. Program for "Suburban Shopping Center," "Yale University 1948–1949," Box LIK 60, Kahn Collection.

122. Program for "The National Center of UNESCO," "Yale—Professor 1950," Box LIK 61, Kahn Collection.

123. Program for "A Suburban Residence," "Yale University 1948–1949," Box LIK 60, Kahn Collection.

124. "3 Arts Combine in Architecture Project at Yale," *New York Herald Tribune*, February 27, 1949, 44; "Student Architects, Painters, Sculptors Design Together," *Progressive Architecture* 30 (April 1949): 14, 16, 18.

125. Draft of letter, Kahn to Howe [ca. July 1949], "Yale University 1948–1949," Box LIK 60, Kahn Collection.

126. Sawyer, draft program for collaborative project, "Yale—Professor 1950," Box LIK 61, Kahn Collection.

127. Albers, quoted in François Bucher, *Josef Albers:*

Despite Straight Lines (New Haven and London: Yale University Press, 1961), 75.

128. Nalle, untitled text, *Perspecta*, no. 1 (Summer 1952): 6.

129. Letter, Scully to Kahn, February 15, 1956, "The Yale University, Correspondence," Box LIK 60, Kahn Collection; Scully, interview with Alessandra Latour, September 15, 1982, in Latour, *Kahn*, 151; Scully, conversation with David B. Brownlee and David G. De Long, August 16, 1990.

Chapter 2
The Mind Opens to Realizations

1. Kahn, "Address by Louis I. Kahn, April 5, 1966," *Boston Society of Architects Journal*, no. 1 (1967): 5–20; quoted from typescript, "Boston Society of Architects," Box LIK 57, Louis I. Kahn Collection, University of Pennsylvania and Pennsylvania Historical and Museum Commission, Philadelphia (hereafter cited as Kahn Collection).

2. Letter, Kahn to Dave [Wisdom], Anne [Tyng], and others, December 6, 1950, "Rome 1951," Box LIK 61, Kahn Collection.

3. He wrote, "I now know that Greece and Egypt are musts"; card, Kahn to office, n.d., "Letters to L.I. Kahn," Box LIK 60, Kahn Collection.

4. "Training the Artist-Architect for Industry," in *Impressions* (proceedings of the Design Conference, Aspen, Colorado, June 28–July 1, 1951), ed. R. Hunter Middleton and Alexander Ebin, Box LIK 63, Kahn Collection.

5. Kahn, notebook (K12.22), ca. 1966–72, Kahn Collection.

6. Among early references to the Pantheon in Kahn's writings is a mention in Kahn, "Law and Rule in Architecture" (lecture, Princeton University, November 29, 1961), typed transcript, "LIK Lectures 1969," Box LIK 53, Kahn Collection.

7. Kahn, quoted in Ada Louise Huxtable, "What Is Your Favorite Building," *New York Times Magazine*, May 21, 1961; filed in "Misc.," Box LIK 64, Kahn Collection.

8. Vincent J. Scully, *Louis I. Kahn* (New York: George Braziller, 1962), 10, 12–13, 37.

9. For example, after recommending D'Arcy Wentworth Thompson's *On Growth and Form* to his nephew Alan Kahn as the single book that would explain architecture, he later admitted that he had never read it; Alan Kahn, "'Conversation about Lou Kahn,' Los Angeles, California, June 20, 1981," in *Louis I. Kahn: L'uomo, il maestro*, ed. Alessandra Latour (Rome: Edizioni Kappa, 1986), 65. Also, to a former student and office colleague he wrote in reference to an article he had been sent, "without reading a word I can feel its significance"; letter, Kahn to William S. Huff, November 4, 1965, "Huff, William, Correspondence," Box LIK 57, Kahn Collection.

10. Kahn, "Space-Order in Architecture" (lecture, Pratt Institute, November 10, 1959), transcript. The transcript was mailed to Kahn on March 28, 1960; letter, Olindo Grossi (Pratt Institute) to Kahn, March 28, 1960, "LIK Lectures 1960," Box LIK 54, Kahn Collection.

11. Scully, interview with Alessandra Latour, in Latour, *Kahn*, 155. Among Brown's publications is Frank E. Brown, *Roman Architecture* (New York: George Braziller, 1961).

12. Kahn, "The Value and Aim in Sketching," *T-Square Club Journal* 1 (Philadelphia, May 1931): 18–21.

13. Reyner Banham, "New Brutalism," *Architectural Review* 118 (December 1955): 357.

14. Letter, Goodwin to Kahn, May 13, 1954, "Personal," Box LIK 66, Kahn Collection.

15. As recounted in William Huff, "Louis Kahn: Sorted Recollections and Lapses in Familiarities," interview with Jason Aronoff, *Little Journal* 5 (September 1981), reprinted in Latour, *Kahn*, 407.

16. For a general description, see David G. De Long, "Eliel Saarinen and the Cranbrook Tradition in Architecture and Urban Design," in *Design in America: The Cranbrook Vision, 1925–1950* (New York: Harry N. Abrams, 1983), 47–89.

17. Kenneth Frampton, "Louis Kahn and the French Connection," *Oppositions*, no. 22 (Fall 1980), reprinted in Latour, *Kahn*, 249.

18. Scully, interview with Latour, 147.

19. Among several accounts of Tyng's association with Kahn is Anne Griswold Tyng, "Architecture Is My Touchstone," *Radcliffe Quarterly* 70 (September 1984): 5–7.

20. Tyng, interview with Alessandra Latour, in Latour, *Kahn*, 51.

21. Kahn, notebook (K12.22), ca. 1955, Kahn Collection.

22. Letter, Kahn to John D. Entenza (director, Graham Foundation), March 2, 1965, "Letters of Recommendation, 1964," Box LIK 55, Kahn Collection.

23. Anne G. Tyng, "Louis I. Kahn's 'Order' in the Creative Process," in Latour, *Kahn*, 285. Fuller recalled speaking with Kahn during train trips between Philadelphia and New Haven; telegram, Fuller to Esther Kahn, March 20, 1974, in Latour, *Kahn*, 179.

24. Letter, Fuller to Entenza, April 5, 1965, "Fuller, R. Buckminster Correspondence, 1965," Box LIK 55, Kahn Collection.

25. Kahn began work on the project in May 1954; summary of expenses, "A.F. of L. Health Center (Melamed) Architects Fee," Box LIK 83, Kahn Collection. The building dedication in February 1957 is reported in "AFL-CIO Center Dedicated Here," *Philadelphia Inquirer*, February 17, 1957. The demolition was reported in "Kahn Finds Lesson in Ruins of His Work," *Philadelphia Inquirer*, August 27, 1973. At that time he reasserted his dislike of the penthouse projection, confirming David Wisdom's account of Kahn's initial reaction when the building was built; Wisdom, interview with David B. Brownlee, Peter S. Reed, and David G. De Long, July 5, 1990. I am grateful to Peter S. Reed for his research report on this project.

26. Tyng, interview with Latour, 43.

27. Letter, Fruchter to Kahn, September 10, 1951; time sheets, April 25–June 13, 1952; and letter, Kahn to Fruchter, January 30, 1953; "Fruchter," Box LIK 34,

Kahn Collection. I am grateful to Peter S. Reed for his research report on this project.

28. Emil Kaufmann, "Three Revolutionary Architects, Boullée, Ledoux, and Lequeu," *Transactions of the American Philosophical Society* 42 (October 1952): 510, fig. 135. Kenneth Frampton notes the similarity between the Ledoux plan and later designs by Kahn; Frampton, "Kahn and the French Connection," 240–41.

29. Kahn received the program and a retainer in June 1954; letter, Benjamin F. Weiss (chairman, building committee) to Kahn, June 29, 1954, "Synagogue & School Bldg . . . Adath Jeshurun," Box LIK 60, Kahn Collection. I am grateful to Peter S. Reed for his research report on this project.

30. Handwritten draft of a letter, Kahn to Gropius, n.d., responding to letter from Gropius to Kahn, March 16, 1953, "Louis I. Kahn (Personal) 1953," Box LIK 66, Kahn Collection.

31. Kahn had completed preliminary sketches by July 1954; letter, Edward C. Arn (American Seating Company) to Kahn, July 19, 1954, "Synagogue & School Bldg . . . Adath Jeshurun," Box LIK 60, Kahn Collection. Preliminary schemes were submitted in August; letter, Kahn to building committee, August 16, 1954, ibid. His design was rejected as "out of spirit with the type of building wanted by the Board" in April 1955; letter, Weiss to Kahn, April 29, 1955, "LIK Miscellaneous 1954–56," Box LIK 65, Kahn Collection.

32. "Frank Lloyd Wright Plans Synagogue Here," *Sunday Bulletin*, May 23, 1954; filed in "Personal," Box LIK 66, Kahn Collection. The design was also published in "Frank Lloyd Wright Has Designed His First Synagogue . . . ," *Architectural Record* 66 (July 1954): 20.

33. Published in "First Study of the City Hall Building," *Perspecta*, no. 2 (1953): 27. I am grateful to Peter S. Reed for his research report on this project.

34. Letter, Le Ricolais to Kahn, April 3, 1953, "Louis I. Kahn (personal)—1953," Box LIK 60, Kahn Collection. In the first paper, "Structural Approach in Hexagonal Design" (February 1953), it was claimed that hexagonal planning could also be applied to city traffic patterns; "Le Ricolais," Box LIK 56, Kahn Collection. Le Ricolais was later invited to Penn, where, beginning in 1955, he and Kahn taught together.

35. Kahn, "Toward a Plan for Midtown Philadelphia," *Perspecta*, no. 2 (1953): 23.

36. Kahn, quoted in Henry S. F. Cooper, "Dedication Issue: The New Art Gallery and Design Center," *Yale Daily News*, November 6, 1953.

37. Letter, Kahn to A. Whitney Griswold, July 30, 1958, "Yale Univ., Correspondence," Box LIK 60, Kahn Collection.

38. Kahn, "Architecture is the Thoughtful Making of Spaces," *Perspecta*, no. 4 (1957): 2–3.

39. Kahn, "Talk at the Conclusion of the Otterlo Congress," in *New Frontiers in Architecture: CIAM '59 in Otterlo*, ed. Oscar Newman (New York: Universe Books, 1961), 213.

40. Kahn had been retained to design the house by June 1954; letter, Mrs. Adler to Kahn, June 14, 1954, "Adler," Box LIK 32, Kahn Collection. Time sheets document work from August to February 1955, most intensely in September; time sheets, ibid. I am grateful to David Roxburgh for his research report on this project.

41. Kahn, quoted in "Louis Kahn Places Design as a Circumstance of Order," *Architecture and the University* (proceedings of a conference, Princeton University, December 11–12, 1953; Princeton, N.J.: School of Architecture, 1954), 29–30.

42. Letters, Mrs. Adler to Kahn, December 3 and 4, 1953, "Louis I. Kahn (personal)—1953," Box LIK 60, Kahn Collection.

43. Kahn, quoted in "How to Develop New Methods of Construction," *Architectural Forum* 101 (November 1954): 157. Kahn's remarks had been made at a conference on architectural illumination at the School of Design, North Carolina State College.

44. Letter, Constance H. Dallas (City Council) to Francis Adler, February 18, 1955, "Adler," Box LIK 32, Kahn Collection. Later, during the summer of 1955, Kahn undertook to remodel a kitchen in their existing house; letter, Kahn to Francis Adler, October 24, 1955, ibid.

45. Scully cites the beginning date as 1954; Scully, *Kahn*, 47. There are no records yet discovered in the Kahn Collection that confirm this. Drawings carry dates only from February 3 to 8, 1955. I am grateful to David Roxburgh for his research report on this project.

46. Kahn, quoted in Susan Braudy, "The Architectural Metaphysic of Louis Kahn," *New York Times Magazine*, November 15, 1970, 86.

47. Kahn, notebook (K12.22), 1955–ca. 1962, Kahn Collection.

48. Kahn, notebook, 1955–ca. 1962.

49. Rudolf Wittkower, *Architectural Principles in the Age of Humanism* (London: Alec Tiranti, 1952); Tyng, interview with David G. De Long, October 11, 1990.

50. Kahn, notebook, 1955–ca. 1962.

51. Kahn had been retained to design the Morris house by July 1955; letter, Lawrence Morris to Kahn, July 8, 1955, "Morris House," Box LIK 80, Kahn Collection. There are no time reports or dated records of any sort in the archive for 1956.

52. Letter, Rowe to Kahn, February 7, 1956, "Correspondence from Colleges and Universities," Box LIK 65, Kahn Collection.

53. Ibid. Two articles including a brief discussion of Kahn in the context of the 1950s that Rowe wrote in 1956–57 were published under the title "Neoclassicism and Modern Architecture," *Oppositions*, no. 1 (September 1973): 1–26.

54. Wittkower, *Architectural Principles*, 61.

55. Ibid., 30.

56. Letter, Tyng to Entenza, February 28, 1965, "Letters of Recommendation 1964," Box LIK 55, Kahn Collection. Tyng was applying for a grant to complete a book, *Anatomy of Form*.

57. D'Arcy Wentworth Thompson, *On Growth and Form*, abridged and edited by John Tyler Bonner (Cambridge: Cambridge University Press, 1943; 1961), 119–20, describing fig. 14.

58. "The Dream Builders," *Time*, October 17, 1960, 86.

Kahn confirmed Tyng's collaboration on the design in a letter to G. Holmes Perkins, June 21, 1968, "Perkins, Dean G. Holmes, Correspondence," Box LIK 57, Kahn Collection.

59. Tyng, interview with De Long, January 24, 1991.

60. Letter, William Mitchell (vice president, styling staff, General Motors Corporation) to Kahn, December 5, 1960, "General Motors—Contract," Box LIK 32, Kahn Collection. Kahn was expected to finish by late December; the last date carried on the drawings is February 17, 1961. I am grateful to David Roxburgh for his research report on this project.

61. Tyng remained associated with the office until Kahn's death, her position evolving from that of employee to consultant, and she continued, in 1991, to practice independently and teach at the University of Pennsylvania; Tyng, interview with De Long, February 15, 1991.

62. Kahn, "Space Form Use—A Library," *Pennsylvania Triangle* 43 (December 1956): 43.

63. Kahn, quoted in "On Philosophical Horizons" (panel discussion), *AIA Journal* 33 (June 1960): 100.

64. Kahn, "Louis I. Kahn: Talks With Students," *Architecture at Rice*, no. 26 (1969): 26–27.

65. Denise Scott Brown, "A Worm's Eye View of Recent Architectural History," *Architectural Record* 172 (February 1984): 73.

66. For example, letters, Kahn to the Philadelphia Art Alliance, June 23, 1961, "Master File, June 1, 1961 through July 31, 1961," Box LIK 9, Kahn Collection; Kahn to National Council of Architectural Registration Boards, May 20, 1963, "Venturi, Bob," Box LIK 59, Kahn Collection; Kahn to Gordon Bunshaft, February 17, 1971, "Master File, 1 Jan 1971 thru 30 August 71," Box LIK 10, Kahn Collection.

67. For example, in interviews with Alessandra Latour, in Latour, *Kahn*: Sue Ann Kahn, 35; Anne Tyng, 41–49; and Marshall D. Meyers, 77.

68. Memorandum, Paul Schweikher (chairman, department of architecture) to Messrs. Hansen, Kahn, Nalle, and Wu, April 14, 1955, "Yale University—LIK Classes," Box LIK 63, Kahn Collection.

69. Kahn, "1973: Brooklyn, New York" (lecture, Pratt Institute, Fall 1973), *Perspecta*, no. 19 (1982): 94.

70. For the Lawrence Hall of Science, a limited competition in which Kahn had participated and which he gave as a class problem in September 1962, while I was in the studio.

71. For example, Wilder Green, "Louis I. Kahn, Architect Alfred Newton Richards Medical Research Building," *Museum of Modern Art Bulletin* 28 (1961). An exhibition on the Richards Building was held at the Museum of Modern Art from June 6 to July 16, 1961.

72. "Kahn on Beaux-Arts Training," ed. William Jordy, *Architectural Review* 155 (June 1974): 332.

73. Kahn, "Architecture is the Thoughtful Making of Spaces," 2.

74. Kahn, "Form and Design," *Architectural Design* 31 (April 1961): 151. Kahn had first used these terms of description at the CIAM conference in Otterlo in September 1959.

75. August E. Komendant, *18 Years With Architect Louis I. Kahn* (Englewood, N.J.: Aloray, 1975).

76. Letter, Kahn to Eero Saarinen, March 23, 1959, "Master File, September 8, 1958–March 31, 1959," Box LIK 9, Kahn Collection.

77. August Komendant, "Architect-Engineer Relationship," in Latour, *Kahn*, 317.

78. For example, in Scully, *Kahn*, 28; and Scott Brown, "A Worm's Eye View of History," 71.

79. Scully, *Kahn*, 30.

80. Klumb (born Heinrich Klumb) later practiced in Puerto Rico; his work is mentioned in Henry-Russell Hitchcock, *Architecture, Nineteenth and Twentieth Centuries*, 3d rev. ed. (Baltimore and Harmondsworth: Penguin Books, 1968), 422, 465; and Edgar Tafel, *Apprentice to Genius: Years With Frank Lloyd Wright* (New York: McGraw-Hill, 1979), 37–38, 94.

81. "1952 A.I.A. Convention," *Architectural Record* 112 (August 1952): 204.

82. Letter, Kahn to Joseph Hazen, n.d., in response to a request from *Architectural Forum* for a testimonial; and telegram, April 10, 1959, Hazen to Kahn, "Architectural Forum—Louis I. Kahn," Box LIK 61, Kahn Collection.

83. Scully, *Kahn*, 30–31.

84. Kahn, quoted in "On the Responsibility of the Architect" (panel discussion), *Perspecta*, no. 2 (1953): 47.

85. The resumption of work is noted in a letter, Morris to Kahn, June 17, 1957, "Morris House, Mount Kisco, New York," Box LIK 32, Kahn Collection. Early design drawings in the Kahn archive are dated August 6, 1957. Time sheets record design activity from February to October 1958, with the greatest intensity of effort between April and July; "Morris House," Box LIK 80, Kahn Collection. Kahn's final bill is dated October 1, 1958; letter, Kahn to Morris, October 2, 1958, ibid. I am grateful to David Roxburgh for his research report on this project.

86. Vincent Scully, Introduction to *The Louis I. Kahn Archive: Personal Drawings*, 7 vols. (New York: Garland Publishing, 1987), lxviii.

87. Kahn, "Remarks" (lecture, Yale University, October 30, 1963), *Perspecta*, no. 9/10 (1965): 305.

88. Scott Brown, "A Worm's Eye View of History," 73.

89. The building was commissioned by Mrs. Robert B. Herbert, whose nephew, William Huff, had been a student of Kahn's at Yale. Huff was working in Kahn's office when the building was commissioned and became chief assistant for the design. Kahn visited the site in August 1958 and signed a contract for design services on September 8; "Greensburg Tribune-Review Publishing Company," Box LIK 35, Kahn Collection. Drawings dated November 7, 1958, show its compact form. I am grateful to P. Bradford Westwood for his research report on this project.

90. Construction began in November 1959; letter, David W. Mark to William Huff, November 11, 1959, "Greensburg Tribune-Review Publishing Company," Box LIK 35, Kahn Collection. It was completed by December 1960, but later additions have altered its appearance.

91. A survey of Fleisher's property was requested in March 1959; letter, Kahn to George Mebus, Inc., March 19, 1959, "Robert H. Fleischer Residence," Box LIK 34, Kahn

Collection. Fleisher asked Kahn to stop work in May; letter, Fleisher to Kahn, May 16, 1959, ibid. I am grateful to David Roxburgh for his research report on this project.

92. Kahn signed a design agreement with Goldenberg on January 12, 1959; time sheets record design activity beginning in February; contract documents were complete by late June; "Goldenberg House," Box LIK 80, Kahn Collection. Because of excessive bids the client terminated the contract in August; letter, Goldenberg to Kahn, August 18, 1959, ibid. I am grateful to Peter S. Reed for his research report on this project.

93. Kahn, quoted in "Kahn" (transcribed discussion in Kahn's office, February 1961), *Perspecta*, no. 7 (1961): 13.

94. Kahn, quoted in Heinz Ronner and Sharad Jhaveri, *Louis I. Kahn: Complete Work, 1935–1974*, 2d ed. (Basel and Boston: Birkhäuser, 1987), 98.

95. Wittkower, *Architectural Principles*, 7.

96. Kahn, "Kahn," 15.

97. Funerary basilicas are discussed in Richard Krautheimer, *Early Christian and Byzantine Architecture* (Baltimore and Harmondsworth: Penguin Books, 1960), esp. 30–32.

98. Kahn signed a design agreement on October 1, 1959; "Margaret Esherick Finance File," Box LIK 80, Kahn Collection. I am grateful to David Roxburgh for his research report on this project.

99. Its design was discussed in November; letter, Kahn to C. Woodard, November 12, 1959, "Master File November 2, 1959," Box LIK 9, Kahn Collection. Revised plans had been sent by March 1960; letter, Margaret Esherick to Kahn, March 16, 1960, "Miss Margaret Esherick's House, Correspondence," Box LIK 34, Kahn Collection. Construction began in November 1960; agreement with Thomas Regan for Rofis and Co., Contractors, November 2, 1960, "Esherick House, Philadelphia, Pennsylvania," Box LIK 139, Kahn Collection. Construction was essentially complete by the following November; letter, Kahn to Ross and Co., November 22, 1961, "Esherick Miscellaneous," Box LIK 31, Kahn Collection.

100. Kahn, "Kahn," 16–17.

101. Letter, Kahn to Richard Demarco (Richard Demarco Gall Ltd., Edinburgh), August 28, 1973, "Master File 1 July 1973 to 31 October 1973," Box LIK 10, Kahn Collection.

102. For example, Brown, *Roman Architecture*, 33. Kahn's conversations with Brown at the American Academy would have provided opportunities to exchange views.

103. The U.S. Department of State program for building embassies and consulates during the 1950s is discussed in Jane C. Loeffler, "The Architecture of Diplomacy: Heyday of the United States Embassy Building Program, 1954–1960," *Journal of the Society of Architectural Historians* 49 (September 1990): 251–78.

104. Kahn described his ideas for the building at a meeting on June 24, 1960. The perspective illustrated was apparently one of the sketches resulting from that meeting, and was probably one of those being criticized. Letter, William P. Hughes (director, Office of Foreign

Buildings, U.S. State Department) to Kahn, August 26, 1960, "Communications and Correspondence," Box LIK 34, Kahn Collection.

105. Letters and memoranda, including letters, R. Stanley Sweeley (supervising architect for residences, Office of Foreign Buildings, U.S State Department) to Kahn, August 30 and October 19, 1960, and D. Merle Walker (acting director, Office of Foreign Buildings, U.S. State Department) to Kahn, August 4, 1961, "Communications and Correspondence," Box LIK 34, Kahn Collection; memorandum of meeting with a Mr. Chappellier, September 20, 1960, "Program, Luanda, Angola," Box LIK 34, Kahn Collection. I am grateful to David Roxburgh for his research report on this project.

106. The construction of a model is documented by a card, August 26/27, 1961, "Luanda, Africa," Box LIK 80, Kahn Collection. Later drawings are described in a letter, Kahn to Walker, August 30, 1961, "Program, Luanda Angola," Box LIK 34, Kahn Collection. Kahn's final bill is included in a letter, Kahn to Earnest J. Warlow (assistant director for architecture and engineering, Office of Foreign Buildings, U.S. State Department), December 19, 1962, "Luanda, Africa," Box LIK 80, Kahn Collection.

107. Kahn, "Kahn," 9.

108. Anne Tyng has indicated what she believes are roots of this motif in Kahn's earlier work to which she contributed; Tyng, interview with Latour, 55.

109. Wittkower, *Architectural Principles*, 13.

110. Jan C. Rowan, "Wanting to Be: The Philadelphia School," *Progressive Architecture* 42 (April 1961): 141.

111. Kahn, typed transcript of a November 14, 1961, talk to the Board of Standards and Planning for the Living Theater, "Board of Standards & Planning—N.Y. Chapter—ANTA," Box LIK 57, Kahn Collection.

112. Neutra later praised Kahn's nearly completed laboratories at Salk; letter, Neutra to Kahn, May 12, 1965, "Neutra, Richard," Box LIK 57, Kahn Collection. For a discussion of Kahn's theories in relation to the modernism of his day, see Romaldo Giurgola and Jaimini Mehta, *Louis I. Kahn: Architect* (Zurich: Verlag für Architektur, 1975; English ed., Boulder, Colo.: Westview Press, 1975), 216–23.

113. Letter, Sibyl Moholy-Nagy to Kahn, January 22, 1964, "Sibyl Moholy-Nagy Correspondence, 1964," Box LIK 55, Kahn Collection.

114. Kahn's quotes that follow in the text are from the version "Form and Design," *Architectural Design* 31 (April 1961): 145–54.

115. Letter, Tim Vreeland to Monica Pidgeon (editor, *Architectural Design*) January 11, 1961, "Master File, November 1 through December 30, 1960," Box LIK 9, Kahn Collection.

116. Kahn, "Form and Design," 115, 148.

117. Ibid., 148.

118. Kahn, "Talk at the Otterlo Congress," 213.

119. Ibid.

120. For example, in Joseph Burton, "Notes from Volume Zero: Louis Kahn and the Language of God," *Perspecta*, no. 20 (1983): 69–90.

121. Kahn, "Form and Design," 148–49.

122. Ibid., 151–52.

123. For a discussion of these examples, see Vincent Scully, *American Architecture and Urbanism* (New York and Washington: Praeger, 1969), 190–212.

124. Kahn, "Form and Design," 148. The chapel had been identified by name in the 1959 version.

125. Kahn, quoted in "The Sixties; A P/A Symposium on the State of Architecture," *Progressive Architecture* 42 (March 1961): 123; and "The New Art of Urban Design-Are We Equipped?" *Architectural Forum* 114 (June 1961): 88.

126. Rowan, "Wanting to Be," 131.

127. Kahn, quoted in the minutes, "Summary of Preliminary Meeting of Committee on Arts and Architecture for the Kennedy Library," n.d., "Mrs. John F. Kennedy Correspondence," Box LIK 56, Kahn Collection. Kahn was invited to serve on the Arts and Architecture Committee for the Kennedy Library in February 1961; letter, Jacqueline Kennedy to Kahn, February 4, 1964, ibid. The selection of I.M. Pei as architect was announced in December 1964; letter, Jacqueline Kennedy to Kahn, December 8, 1964, ibid.

128. Kahn, notebook (K12.22), 1955–ca. 1962, Kahn Collection.

129. Kahn, "Form and Design," 148.

130. Kahn, "Law and Rule in Architecture" (annual discourse, Royal Institute of British Architects, March 14, 1962), typed transcript, "LIK Lectures 1969," Box LIK 53, Kahn Collection.

131. Among his own commissions that he gave his Penn studio as problems, two in the 1962–63 academic year reflect these types: St. Andrew's Priory (1961–67) and Sher-e-Bangla Nagar, the assembly complex at Dhaka (1962–83). The ideals of St. Gall and the Pantheon were much discussed in that year's studio.

132. Letter, Kahn to Stephen S. Gardner (chairman, Bicentennial Site Committee), January 16, 1972, "1972 Bicentennial Corporation Correspondence," Box LIK 50, Kahn Collection.

133. The Turkish architect Gönül Aslanoglu Evyapan, a former student who was in regular touch with Kahn at the time, recalled Kahn telling her that never had he felt more sympathetic to a commission and never had he wanted one more. I often saw Ms. Evyapan after her meetings with Kahn in 1964 and 1965, when her impressions were particularly strong.

134. Kahn, quoted in Patricia Cummings Loud, *The Art Museums of Louis I. Kahn* (Durham, N.C., and London: Duke University Press, 1989), 258.

135. The talk was given when he was inducted into the American Academy of Arts and Letters. Kahn's notes are undated but are filed with the letter informing Kahn of his election; letter, Aaron Copland to Kahn, November 23, 1973, "The American Academy of Arts & Letters (1972)," Box LIK 44, Kahn Collection.

Chapter 3
Assembly . . . a Place of Transcendence

1. Kahn, "A Synagogue," *Perspecta*, no. 3 (1955): 62.

2. Kahn, "Places of Worship" (review of *Synagogue Architecture in the U.S.*, by Rachel Wischnitzer), *Jewish Review and Observer*, clipping stamped February 17,

1956, Louis I. Kahn Collection, University of Pennsylvania Historical and Museum Commission (hereafter cited as Kahn Collection). Kahn had written the review before December 2, 1955.

3. Kahn, "Architecture: Silence and Light" (lecture, Solomon R. Guggenheim Museum, December 3, 1968), in Guggenheim Museum, *On the Future of Art* (New York: Viking Press, 1970), 25.

4. Letter, Kahn to Balkrishna V. Doshi, May 26, 1961, "Master File 3/1/61 thru 5/31/61," Box LIK 9, Kahn Collection.

5. Kahn, "Law and Rule in Architecture" (lecture, Princeton University, November 29, 1961), typed transcript, "LIK Lectures 1969," Box LIK 53, Kahn Collection.

6. Kahn, "Law and Rule in Architecture" (annual discourse, Royal Institute of British Architects, March 14, 1962), typed transcript, "LIK Lectures 1969," Box LIK 53, Kahn Collection.

7. Kahn, lecture at the International Design Conference, Aspen, Colorado, June 1962, typed transcript, "Aspen Conference—June 1962," Box LIK 59, Kahn Collection.

8. Kahn, "Louis Kahn: Statements on Architecture" (lecture, Politecnico di Milano, January 1967), *Zodiac*, no. 17 (1967): 55.

9. Peter Murray, *The Architecture of the Italian Renaissance* (New York: Schocken Books, 1963), 42–44.

10. For example, Kahn, "Remarks" (lecture, Yale University, October 30, 1963), *Perspecta*, no. 9/10 (1965): 320.

11. This parallel was identified by J. Kieffer, *Louis I. Kahn and the Rituals of Architecture* (privately published, 1981), later cited by Joseph Burton, "Notes from Volume Zero: Louis Kahn and the Language of God," *Perspecta*, no. 20 (1983): 80–83, among others.

12. Kahn, "Louis I. Kahn: Talks with Students" (lecture and discussion, Rice University, ca. 1969), *Architecture at Rice*, no. 26 (1969): 44.

13. Pattison, interview with David B. Brownlee, December 20, 1990.

14. Pattison, interview with David G. De Long, January 29, 1991.

15. Kahn, "Architecture and Human Agreement" (lecture, University of Virginia, April 18, 1972), *Modulus*, no. 11 (1975): n.p.

16. I was a student in Kahn's studio at the University of Pennsylvania during the 1962–63 academic year. According to my class notebook, Kahn's first meeting with our class after his return from Dhaka was February 11, 1963. His words then, which he further embroidered in later meetings, corresponded closely to his later talk at Yale in the fall of 1963. This talk, from which the quotations are taken, was subsequently published: "The Development by Louis I. Kahn of the Design for the Second Capital of Pakistan at Dacca," *Student Publication of the School of Design, North Carolina State College, Raleigh* 14 (May 1964): n.p.

17. Ibid.

18. According to my class notebook, Kahn assigned the Dhaka problem on February 25.

19. These remarks by Kahn on April 1, 1963, I had enclosed in quotation marks as I took notes of his discussion of Dhaka.

20. Kahn, lecture at Princeton University, March 3, 1968 quoted in Bruno J. Hubert, "Kahn's Epilogue," *Progressive Architecture* 65 (December 1984): 61.

21. Kahn, "Talks with Students," 28–29.

22. The drawings identified as dating from 1962 in Heinz Ronner and Sharad Jhaveri, *Louis I. Kahn: Complete Work, 1935–1974*, 2d ed. (Basel and Boston: Birkhäuser, 1987), 234–35, SNC.3–6, seem instead to have followed his first trip to Dhaka in 1963. There is no evidence of any design activity before that trip, when he first received information on the site and the program. The model that Ronner illustrates as first in the sequence (234, SNC.1) seems to predate the model presented in March 1963, but it could have been a study model done after Kahn's return and before his next presentation model was begun.

23. Kahn, quoted in "The Development of Dacca," n.p.

24. Kahn was in Chandigarh on November 11, 1962; hotel receipt, Oberoi Mount View, "National Institute of Design Incidentals," Box LIK 113, Kahn Collection.

25. Kahn, "Form and Design," *Architectural Design* 31 (April 1961): 152.

26. Ignacio de Sola-Morales i Rubio, "A Lecture in San Sebastian" (1982), reprinted in *Louis I. Kahn: L'uomo, il maestro*, ed. Alessandra Latour (Rome: Edizioni Kappa, 1986), 219. This thesis was earlier developed in Emil Kaufmann, "Three Revolutionary Architects, Boullée, Ledoux, and Lequeu," *Transactions of the American Philosophical Society* 42 (October 1952).

27. Kahn, "Law and Rule" (Princeton).

28. Kahn, "Law and Rule" (RIBA). Also recounted in "The Architect and the Building," *Bryn Mawr Alumnae Bulletin* 43 (Summer 1962): 2–3.

29. Kahn, address to the Boston Society of Architects, April 5, 1966, typed transcript, "Boston Society of Architects," Box LIK 57, Kahn Collection. It was later published: "Address by Louis I. Kahn," *Boston Society of Architects Journal*, no. 1 (1967): 5–20.

30. Kahn, quoted in "The Development of Dacca" n.p. In the fall of 1963 Kahn added similar "hollow columns" to the school component of Mikveh Israel, later relating them to Dhaka; Kahn, "Remarks," 320.

31. Kahn, lecture in Aspen, 1962; Kahn, "Law and Rule" (Princeton).

32. As recounted in August Komendant, "Architect-Engineer Relationship," in Latour, *Kahn*, 319.

33. Roy Vollmer, an architect in Kahn's office assigned to Dhaka, designed a portion of the housing; reference is made in a letter quoting Kahn, Louise Badgley (Kahn's secretary) to James K. Merrick (Philadelphia Art Alliance), May 23, 1968, "April 1968 Master File, May & June 1968 & July 1968," Box LIK 10, Kahn Collection.

34. "The Observatories of the Maharajah Sawai Jai Singh II," *Perspecta*, no. 6 (1960): 68–77.

35. Marco Frascari (associate professor of architecture, University of Pennsylvania), interview with David G. De Long, November 15, 1989.

36. For example, William J. R. Curtis, "Authenticity, Abstraction and the Ancient Sense: Le Corbusier's and Louis Kahn's Ideas of Parliament," *Perspecta*, no. 20 (1983): 191.

37. Darah Diba, "Return to Dacca," *L'architecture d'aujourd'hui*, no. 267 (February 1990): 11.

38. Kahn, "Remarks," 313.

39. For example, Michael Graves, revised interview with Kazumi Kawasaki (1983), reprinted in Latour, *Kahn*, 167.

40. Monthly bulletin, Doxiadis Associates, "The Administrative Sector of Islamabad," May 1, 1961, "President's Estate, West Pakistan Gen. Correspondence," Box LIK 82, Kahn Collection. Among articles recounting the early history of Islamabad are B. S. Saini, "Islamabad: Pakistan's New Capital," *Design* 9 (May 1964): 83–89; C. A. Doxiadis, "Islamabad: The Creation of a New Capital," *Ekistics* 20 (November 1965): 301–5; Maurice Lee, "Islamabad The Image," *Architectural Design* 37 (January 1967): 47–50; and Leo Jamoud, "Islamabad The Visionary Capital," *Ekistics* 25 (May 1968): 329–35.

41. Kahn's selection as architect is confirmed in a letter, Masoodur Rouf (Capital Development Authority) to Robert Matthew (coordinating architect for the Administrative Sector, Islamabad), July 26, 1963, "Prespak Capital Development Authority Correspondence," Box LIK 82, Kahn Collection. The basic components of the complex are contained in the document "Revised Space Requirements in Respect to the President's Estate . . . April 1963," "President's Estate, Islamabad, Program," Box LIK 82, Kahn Collection. I am grateful to David Roxburgh for his research report on this project.

42. Kahn had been expected to present his preliminary designs in June 1964; letter, Sarfraz Khan (deputy director of planning, Capital Development Authority) to Kahn, July 13, 1964, "President's Estate, Islamabad, Corres. Cap. Dev. Auth," Box LIK 82, Kahn Collection. Kahn promised something by September; letter, Matthew to Zahir ud-Deen (director of planning, Capital Development Authority), August 13, 1964, "President's Estate . . . Correspondence, Sir Robert Matthew," Box LIK 82, Kahn Collection.

43. Letter, Kahn to Matthew, January 8, 1965. "Master File—January 1965—February," Box LIK 10, Kahn Collection.

44. Ajaz A. Khan, *Progress Report on Islamabad (1960–1970)* (Islamabad: Capital Development Authority, 1970), 26.

45. Letter, Matthew to Kahn, March 3, 1965, "President's Estate . . . Correspondence, Sir Robert Matthew," Box LIK 82, Kahn Collection.

46. Kahn, notebook (K12.22), ca. 1963, Kahn Collection. Following these notes are sketches for the final version of the assembly building in Islamabad.

47. Auguste Choisy, *Histoire de l'architecture* (Paris: Edouard Rouveyre, [1899]), 1:529, fig. 15.

48. Among several documents emphasizing this are a letter, N. Faruqi (newly appointed chairman, Capital Development Authority) to Matthew, Kahn, and Ponti, May 11, 1965, "Prespak, Capital Development Authority

Correspondence," Box LIK 82, Kahn Collection.

49. Letter, Kahn to Matthew, August 27, 1965, "Master File, June 1965 July . . . October," Box LIK 10, Kahn Collection.

50. Cable, Kahn to his Philadelphia office, January 11, 1966, "Cablegrams—Pak. Estate," Box LIK 82, Kahn Collection.

51. Letters, S. Budd Simon (chair, architect selection committee) to Kahn, July 15, 1966, and David Wisdom (Kahn's office) to Morton Rosenthal (first chair, building committee), March 20, 1967, "Temple Beth El Correspondence Client," Box LIK 38, Kahn Collection. I am grateful to Marcia Fae Feuerstein for her research report on this project.

52. Letter, Simon to Kahn, May 29, 1966, ibid.

53. Construction report, Guzzi Bros. & Singer, Inc., August 31, 1970, "I Temple Beth El Cuzzi Bros. & Singer, Inc. All Corres.," Box LIK 38, Kahn Collection; invitation to dedication, May 5, 1972, "Temple Beth El Correspondence Client," Box LIK 38, Kahn Collection.

54. Letter, Yacoov Salomon (holder of the synagogue property lease) to Kahn, October 9, 1967, "Hurva Synagogue," Box LIK 39, Kahn Collection. An original synagogue, built in 1700 by an Ashkenazic sect, had been destroyed in 1720; a second synagogue on the site, built in 1857, had been destroyed in 1948. Nahman Avigad, *Discovering Jerusalem* (New York: Nelson Publishers, 1980), 18; Pierre Loti, *Jerusalem* (Philadelphia: David McKay, 1974), 20.

55. Telegram, Kahn to Salomon, July 8, 1968, "Hurva Synagogue," Box LIK 39, Kahn Collection. The feverish work on the first proposal was described by Marvin Verman in an unpublished interview with Maria Isabel G. Beas in the fall of 1989; Verman, Kahn's employee at the time, had been in charge of the first presentation. I am grateful to Maria Beas for her research on this project.

56. Letter, Kahn to Yehuda Tamir (prime minister's office), March 28, 1969, "Hurva Synagogue," Box LIK 39, Kahn Collection.

57. Letter, Kahn to Harriet Pattison, September 15, 1964, published in Alexandra Tyng, *Beginnings: Louis I. Kahn's Philosophy of Architecture* (New York: John Wiley & Sons, 1984), 166.

58. Kollek, quoted in J. Robert Moskin, "Jewish Mayor of the New Jerusalem," *Look*, October 1, 1968, 71. Controversy surrounding Kahn's first presentation is noted in a letter, Kollek to Kahn, August 29, 1968, "Hurva Synagogue," Box LIK 39, Kahn Collection.

59. For instance, Robert Coombs, "Light and Silence: The Religious Architecture of Louis Kahn," *Architectural Association Quarterly* 13 (October 1981): 32, 34.

60. Letter, Kahn to Mrs. Serata (librarian, Jewish Theological Seminary), July 2, 1968, "Hurva Synagogue," Box LIK 39, Kahn Collection. The article was Louis Finkelstein, "The Origin of the Synagogue," *Proceedings of the American Academy for Jewish Research* 1 (1928–30): 49–59.

61. Rudolf Wittkower, *Architectural Principles in the Age of Humanism* (London: Alec Tiranti, 1952), 91.

62. Letter, Kollek to Kahn, June 6, 1969, "Jerusalem Committee," Box LIK 39, Kahn Collection. This version

is sometimes identified as the third rather than the second, but dated drawings show otherwise.

63. Letter, Kollek to Kahn, April 23, 1972, ibid.

64. Letter, Kollek to Kahn, December 28, 1973, "Hurva Garden," Box LIK 39, Kahn Collection.

65. Kahn, "Silence and Light" (lecture, School of Architecture, ETH Zurich, February 12, 1969), in Ronner and Jhaveri, *Complete Work*, 8.

66. Kahn, lecture at the Sala dello Scoutinio, Venice, January 30, 1969, typed transcript, "Venezia," Box LIK 55, Kahn Collection.

67. Neslihan Dostoglu, Marco Frascari, and Enrique Vivoni, "Louis Kahn and Venice: Ornament and Decoration in the Interpretation of Architecture," in Latour, *Kahn*, 307.

68. Pattison, interview with De Long, January 29, 1991.

69. Dostoglu, Frascari, and Vivoni, "Kahn and Venice," 307.

70. Kahn, lecture in Venice, 1969.

71. In addition to the simple dimensions of the related buildings, drawings in the archive of the Canadian Centre for Architecture repeatedly contain simple numerical notations, such as 40, 60, 100 (CCA DR 1982.0006); 20, 40, 80 (CCA DR 1982.0007); and 15, 30, 120 (CCA DR 1982.0009).

Chapter 4
The Houses of the Inspirations

1. Kahn, "Remarks" (lecture, Yale University, October 30, 1963), *Perspecta*, no. 9/10 (1965): 310. A second often-cited inspiration was "to meet," and he sometimes added a third, variously called "to express" and "well-being"; e.g. Kahn, interview with Karl Linn, May 14, 1965, typed transcript, "Linn, Karl," Box LIK 58, Louis I. Kahn Collection, University of Pennsylvania and Pennsylvania Historical and Museum Commission, Philadelphia (hereafter cited as Kahn Collection); Kahn, *Architecture: The John Lawrence Memorial Lectures* (New Orleans: Tulane University School of Architecture, 1972), n.p.

2. Kahn, quoted in University of Pennsylvania, School of Medicine, *Report of the Proceedings, Sixth Annual Conference on Graduate Medical Education: Medicine in the Year 2000.* Philadelphia, Pennsylvania, December 1964 (Philadelphia: University of Pennsylvania 1965), 149.

3. Kahn, quoted in "Kahn" (interview, February 1961), *Perspecta* no. 7 (1961): 10.

4. Kahn, "Our Changing Environment" (panel discussion, June 18, 1964), in American Craftsmen's Council, *First World Congress of Craftsmen, June 8 through June 19, 1964. Columbia University, New York* (New York: American Craftsmen's Council, [1965]), 120.

5. Kahn, lecture recorded November 19, 1960, and broadcast November 21, 1960; published as *Structure and Form*, Forum Architecture Series no. 6 (Washington, D.C.: Voice of America, [1961]), 2. The tree metaphor was introduced at least as early as 1955; see Kahn, review of *Synagogue Architecture in the U.S.*, by Rachel Wischnitzer, MS, ca. November 1955, "Descriptions of Buildings," Box LIK 54, Kahn Collection.

6. Kahn, "Space and the Inspirations" (lecture, New England Conservatory of Music, Boston, November 14, 1967), *L'architecture d'aujourd'hui*, 40 (February–March 1969): 15.

7. Kahn, "Remarks," 305.

8. Ibid., 332.

9. C. P. Snow, *The Two Cultures and the Scientific Revolution*, The Rede Lecture 1959 (Cambridge: Cambridge University Press, 1959).

10. Salk, interview with David B. Brownlee and David G. De Long, May 24, 1990.

11. Salk, interview with David B. Brownlee et al., April 18, 1983.

12. Kahn, "Law and Rule in Architecture" (lecture, Princeton University, November 29, 1961), typed transcript, "LIK Lectures 1969," Box LIK 53, Kahn Collection.

13. Letter, Monica Bromley (RIBA) to Kahn, February 21, 1962, "Discourse for R.I.B.A. 1962 Correspondence," Box LIK 55, Kahn Collection; Kahn, "Louis I. Kahn: Talks with Students" (lecture and discussion, Rice University, ca. 1969), *Architecture at Rice*, no. 26 (1969): 13.

14. Esther McCoy, "Dr. Salk Talks about His Institute," *Architectural Forum* 127 (December 1967): 31–32.

15. Kahn, *Medicine in the Year 2000*, 150.

16. Kahn, "Law and Rule" (Princeton).

17. Kahn, *Medicine in the Year 2000*, 153.

18. Kahn, "Kahn," 11. The project under discussion was the consulate in Luanda.

19. Kahn, "Law and Rule in Architecture" (annual discourse, Royal Institute of British Architects, March 14, 1962), typed transcript, "LIK lectures 1969," Box LIK 53, Kahn Collection.

20. Kahn, "Talks with Students," 13–14.

21. Vincent J. Scully, *Louis I. Kahn* (New York: George F. Braziller, 1982), 37.

22. Kahn, "Remarks," 330.

23. Salk, interview with Brownlee and De Long.

24. Kahn, *Medicine in the Year 2000*, 151.

25. Kahn, "Remarks," 332.

26. Kahn, "I Love Beginnings" (lecture, International Design Conference, "The Invisible City," Aspen, Colorado, June 19, 1972), *Architecture + Urbanism*, special issue "Louis I. Kahn," 1975, 282.

27. Kahn, "Silence," *Via 1* (1968): 89.

28. Kahn, "Remarks," 305.

29. Kahn, interview with Linn.

30. Kahn, "The Architect and the Building," *Bryn Mawr Alumnae Bulletin* 43 (Summer 1962): 2.

31. Kahn, unidentified discussion, International Design Conference, "The Invisible City," Aspen, Colorado, June 1972, quoted in *What Will Be Has Always Been: The Words of Louis I. Kahn*, ed. Richard Saul Wurman (New York: Access Press and Rizzoli, 1986), 170.

32. Kahn, "Law and Rule" (RIBA).

33. Kahn, "Kahn," 12–13.

34. Kahn, "Architect and Building" 5.

35. Ibid., 3.

36. Kahn, "Law and Rule" (RIBA). Peter S. Reed sug-
gests that the book was probably William Douglas Simpson, *Castles from the Air* (London: Country Life; New York: Charles Scribner's Sons, 1949). Alexandra Tyng notes that in 1962 he was given Stewart Cruden, *The Scottish Castle* (Edinburgh: Spurbooks, 1962); Tyng, *Beginnings: Louis I. Kahn's Philosophy of Architecture* (New York: John Wiley & Sons, 1984), 19.

37. Susan Braudy, "The Architectural Metaphysic of Louis Kahn: 'Is the Center of a Column Filled with Hope?' 'What Is a Wall?' 'What Does This Space Want To Be?' " *New York Times Magazine*, November 15, 1970, 80. Comlongan Castle, Dumphriesshire, is illustrated in Scully, *Kahn*, fig. 116. and Kahn, "Remarks," figs. 42–45. Both were published with Kahn's consultation.

38. Kahn, "Space and the Inspirations," 16; for another version, see Kahn, "Address by Louis I. Kahn, April 5, 1966," *Boston Society of Architects Journal*. no. 1 (1967): 8.

39. Kahn, *Medicine in the Year 2000*, 151.

40. Research assistance for the Chemistry Building, University of Virginia, was provided by Peter S. Reed.

41. Letter, Edgar F. Shannon to Kahn, November 19, 1962, "UVA—University Correspondence," Box LIK 33, Kahn Collection.

42. Research assistance for Shapero Hall, Wayne State University, was provided by Peter S. Reed.

43. Memo, Douglas R. Sherman (president, Wayne State University) to Arthur Neef (vice president and provost, WSU), Stephen Wilson (dean, College of Pharmacy, WSU), and Mark Beach, February 5, 1962, "Wayne University Correspondence," Box LIK 33, Kahn Collection.

44. Research assistance for Lawrence Memorial Hall, University of California, Berkeley, was provided by Peter S. Reed.

45. Kahn, "Talk at the Conclusion of the Otterlo Congress," in *New Frontiers in Architecture: CIAM '59 in Otterlo*, ed. Oscar Newman (New York: Universe Books, 1961), 212.

46. Balkrishna V. Doshi, "Louis Kahn in India," *Architecture + Urbanism*, special issue "Louis I. Kahn," 1975, 313.

47. Kahn, "Remarks," 324.

48. Ibid., 327.

49. Kahn, "1973: Brooklyn, New York" (lecture, Pratt Institute, Fall 1973), *Perspecta*, no. 19 (1982): 92; another version: Kahn, "I Love Beginnings," 281.

50. Kahn, quoted in James Bailey, "Louis Kahn in India: An Old Order at a New Scale," *Architectural Forum* 125 (July–August 1966): 40.

51. Doshi, "Louis Kahn in India," 312.

52. Ibid., 311.

53. Kahn, "Architecture and Human Agreement" (lecture, University of Virginia. April 18, 1972), *Modulus*, no. 11 (1975): n.p.

54. Kahn, *Structure and Form*, 3

55. Kahn, "Talks with Students," 40.

56. Kahn, "Address," 17.

57. Kahn, "Remarks," 322.

58. Kahn, quoted in Doshi, "Louis Kahn in India," 311.

59. Kahn, "Remarks," 305.

60. Research assistance for St. Andrew's Priory was provided by Peter S. Reed.

61. Shari Wigle, "The World, the Arts, and Father Raphael," *Los Angeles Times West Magazine*, September 18, 1966, 32–33, 46–51.

62. Kahn, "Law and Rule" (RIBA).

63. Letter, Kahn to Father Vincent Martin, September 25, 1961, "Master File-August 1–61 through 9/28/61," Box LIK 9, Kahn Collection. The architect was Foster Rhodes Jackson.

64. Letter, Kahn to Father Philip Verhaegen (prior, St. Andrews Priory), November 26, 1965, "St. Andrew's Priory Valyermo, California," Box LIK 81, Kahn Collection; letter, John Duncan (priory's attorney) to Father de Morchoven, April 26, 1966, ibid.

65. Wigle, "Father Raphael," 32.

66. Kahn, "Architecture and Human Agreement," n.p.

67. Kahn, "Talks with Students," 7–8.

68. Ibid., 8.

69. Kahn, *Architecture*, n.p .

70. Kahn, "Address," 13.

71. Letter, Mother Emmanuel to Kahn, December 16, 1966, "Mother Mary Emmanuel Motherhouse—Media," Box LIK 32, Kahn Collection.

72. Research assistance for the Maryland Institute College of Art was provided by Peter S. Reed.

73. Letter, Leake to David Wisdom, March 30, 1967, "Maryland Institute College of Art Correspondence," Box LIK 33, Kahn Collection.

74. Letter, Wisdom to Leake, April 6, 1967, ibid.

75. Letter, Leake to Kahn, April 9, 1969, ibid.

76. Research assistance for the Art Center, Rice University, was provided by Peter S. Reed.

77. Kahn, "Talks with Students," 39–40.

Chapter 5
The Forum of the Availabilities

1. Kahn, "Architecture and Human Agreement" (lecture, University of Virginia, April 18, 1972), *Modulus*, no. 11 (1975): n.p.

2. Kahn, "1973: Brooklyn, New York" (lecture, Pratt Institute, Fall 1973), *Perspecta*, no. 19 (1982): 100.

3. Kahn, "The Room, the Street and Human Agreement" (AIA Gold Medal acceptance speech, Detroit, June 24, 1971), *AIA Journal* 56 (September 1971): 33.

4. Kahn, "1973: Brooklyn," 100.

5. Kahn, "Harmony Between Man and Architecture" (lecture, Paris, May 11, 1973), *Design* 18 (Bombay, March 1974): 25.

6. Kahn, interview with Karl Linn, May 14, 1965, typed transcript, "Linn, Karl," Box LIK 58, Louis I. Kahn Collection, University of Pennsylvania and Pennsylvania Historical and Museum Commission, Philadelphia (hereafter cited as Kahn Collection).

7. Kahn, "The Room, the Street and Human Agreement," 33–34.

8. Kahn, "Architecture and Human Agreement," n.p.

9. Ibid.

10. Kahn, address to the Boston Society of Architects, April 5, 1966, typed transcript, "Boston Society of Architects," Box LIK 57, Kahn Collection. It was later published: "Address by Louis I. Kahn," *Boston Society of Architects Journal*, no. 1 (1967): 5–20.

11. Kahn, interview with Linn. At this point he referred to the "inspiration to live," later redefined as the "inspiration to express"; explained in "Architecture and Human Agreement."

12. Kahn, "Louis I. Kahn: Talks With Students," *Architecture At Rice*, no. 26 (1969): 40.

13. Kahn, lecture for the Board of Standards and Planning for the Living Theatre, New York, November 14, 1961, transcript, "Board of Standards and Planning, N.Y. Chapter ANTA," Box LIK 57, Kahn Collection.

14. "Group Abandons Levy Memorial," *New York Times*, October 7, 1966. I am grateful to David Strauss for his research report on this project.

15. Letter, Noguchi to Kahn, August 2, 1961, "Levy Memorial Playground," Box LIK 33, Kahn Collection.

16. Letter, David Wisdom (Kahn's office) to Noguchi, January 10, 1963, ibid.

17. "Model Play Area for Park Shown," *New York Times*, February 5, 1964.

18. A model conforming to this "final version" was photographed by George Pohl on January 21, 1965; Pohl records, Kahn Collection.

19. Letter, Noguchi to Arthur W. Jones, Jr. (Kahn's office), December 3, 1964, "Levy Memorial Playground," Box LIK 33, Kahn Collection.

20. Kahn, interview with Linn.

21. "Court Battles and Confusion Over Playground," *New York Herald Tribune*, February 27, 1965; "Fight Over Park Nearing Climax," *New York Times*, February 13, 1966; "Group Abandons Levy Memorial."

22. Kahn, quoted in "Kahn Designs a 'Non-College,'" *Philadelphia Inquirer*, March 29, 1966.

23. Ibid.

24. Lines of responsibility are not always made clear in surviving correspondence, and later at least one other developer—Leonard G. Styche and Associates, Incorporated—was also involved; letter, Leonard G. Styche to Kahn, September 1, 1966, "Broadway Church," Box LIK 33, Kahn Collection. I am grateful to Peter S. Reed for his research report on this project.

25. Notes, June 30, 1966, "Broadway Church," Box LIK 33, Kahn Collection; letter, William J. Conklin to Kahn, July 13, 1966, "Broadway United Church of Christ," Box LIK 85, Kahn Collection. Conklin, a noted New York architect who with James Rossant had designed the new town of Reston, Virginia, was then president of the board of trustees for the church.

26. A gray chipboard model of this version was presented but evidently no longer exists; I saw the model when William Conklin brought it back to his office (where I was working at the time) after Kahn had presented it to the board.

27. Kahn, "Talk at the Conclusion of the Otterlo Congress," in *New Frontiers in Architecture: CIAM '59 in Otterlo*, ed. Oscar Newman (New York: Universe Books, 1961), 214.

28. Letter, Conklin to Kahn, September 19, 1966, "Broadway United Church of Christ," Box LIK 85, Kahn

Collection; letter, Stych to Kahn, September 1, 1966, "Broadway Church," Box LIK 33, Kahn Collection.

29. Letters, James A. Austrian (James D. Landauer Assoc., Inc., Real Estate Consultants) to Kahn, March 13, 1970; Kahn to Austrian, April 23, 1970; Austrian to Kahn, June 22, 1970; and John R. White (Landauer Assoc.) to Kahn, September 10, 1970; "Saint Peter's Lutheran Church," Box LIK 13, Kahn Collection. Again the church was supportive of Kahn's involvement as architect, but the First National City Bank engaged another architect instead.

30. Letter, Altman to Kahn, July 11, 1966, "Kansas City Office Building Client Correspondence I," Box LIK 39, Kahn Collection. I am grateful to Arnold Garfinkel for discussing this commission with me on several occasions, especially on May 23, 1990, when David B. Brownlee and I interviewed him in his Kansas City office.

31. Meeting notes, January 5, 1967, and letter, Altman to David Polk (Kahn's office), May 8, 1967, "Kansas City Office Building Correspondence," Box LIK 39, Kahn Collection. I am grateful to Peter S. Reed for his research report on this project.

32. Polk, revised interview with Kazumi Kawasaki (1983), reprinted in *Louis I. Kahn: L'uomo, il maestro*, ed. Alessandra Latour (Rome: Edizioni Kappa, 1986), 95.

33. Minutes of a meeting in the office of Emery Roth, September 19, 1967, "Broadway Church; Komendant's Information; Late Meeting Notes," Box LIK 33, Kahn Collection.

34. A variation of this scheme showed the tower as L-shaped, with additional columns straddling the outer corner of the church; Heinz Ronner and Sharad Jhaveri, *Louis I. Kahn: Complete Work, 1935–1974* 2d. ed. (Basel and Boston: Birkhäuser, 1987), 316–17, BCA.9 and BCA.10.

35. As first claimed by Polk, interview with Kawasaki, 95.

36. Kahn submitted his final invoice the following year; letter, E. J. Sharpe (Kahn's accountant) to Conklin, July 17, 1968, "Broadway United Church of Christ," Box LIK 85, Kahn Collection.

37. The possibility of a new site was discussed in several letters during spring and summer of 1970, including Richard Altman to Carles Vallhonrat (Kahn's office), July 9, 1970, "Kansas City Office Building Client Correspondence I," Box LIK 39, Kahn Collection. The original site, on property partly held by Altman, was bounded by Walnut, Grand, and 11th Streets; the new site was bounded by Main, Baltimore, 11th, and 12th Streets.

38. Komendant's scheme is identified as being by Kahn in Ronner and Jhaveri, *Complete Work*, 321, AOT.24 and AOT.25. Kahn's final invoice was submitted in December 1973; letter, Wisdom to Garfinkel, December 21, 1973, "Master File," Box LIK 20, Kahn Collection.

39. The six-and-a-half-acre site was located south of Pratt and Light Streets, and the developer was the Hammerman Organization; memorandum, Abba Tor (structural engineer) to file, February 18, 1971, "Engineer's Resumes," Box LIK 12, Kahn Collection; letter Kahn to I. H. Hammerman/S.L., June 14, 1971, and

contract for architectural services, June 18, 1971, "Miscellaneous," Box LIK 11, Kahn Collection. By late 1972 the Ballinger Company, Architects and Engineers, was also engaged to collaborate with Kahn; letter, Louis deMoll (vice president, Ballinger) to Thomas Karsten president, Thomas L. Karsten Associates), November 6, 1972 "BIHP 1/Ballinger," Box LIK 12, Kahn Collection. I am grateful to Joan Brierton for her research report on this project.

40. Kahn, quoted in Ronner and Jhaveri, *Complete Work*, 393.

41. Abba Tor, "A Memoir," in Latour, *Kahn*, 127.

42. Letter, I. H. Hammerman II to Kahn, March 13, 1973, "Hammerman Correspondence," Box LIK 12, Kahn Collection.

43. Kahn, "Harmony Between Man and Architecture," 23.

44. Kahn was contacted in October 1973; in addition to Tange, the Teheran architect Nader Ardalan was to coordinate local efforts. John Reyward was named as developer. Letter, Kahn to Aaron, October 9, 1973, and undated note, "Prospective, Tehran," Box LIK 106, Kahn Collection. I am grateful to David Roxburgh for his research report on this project.

45. Letter, Kahn to Farah Pahlavi Shahbanan, November 13, 1973, ibid.

46. As suggested by David Roxburgh. These and other images are contained in "Teheran Studies," Box LIK 106, Kahn Collection.

47. From my class notes, January 1963, master's studio, the University of Pennsylvania.

48. The Fisher House was commissioned in August 1960; agreement, August 23, 1960, "Fisher Residence . . . ," Box LIK 83, Kahn Collection. A preliminary, H-shaped scheme, developed between January and April 1961, was left undeveloped; drawings and time sheets, January 5 to April 30, 1962, ibid. Construction of the final scheme, designed between June and December 1963, began in October 1964 and was completed in June 1967; drawings and time sheets, June 4 to December 10, 1963, and contract for construction, October 24, 1964, ibid.; final certificate of payment, June 26, 1967, "Dr. and Mrs. N.J. Fisher Res Certificates of Payment," Box LIK 83, Kahn Collection. Minor additions were made later, including a bridge over the backyard stream in 1969; transmittal, Vincent Rivera (Kahn's office) to Fisher, April 25, 1969, "Dr. Norman Fisher Corres. 1968–1969," Box LIK 69, Kahn Collection. I am grateful to Peter S. Reed, who completed the research report begun by Elizabeth D. Greene Wiley.

49. Oscar Stonorov and Louis I. Kahn, *You and Your Neighborhood; A Primer for Neighborhood Planning* (New York: Revere Copper and Brass, 1944), n.p.

50. The house was commissioned before May 10, 1971, when plot plans were sent to Kahn together with the Kormans' program; letter, Steven H. Korman to Kahn, May 10, 1971, "Korman Res. Client Correspondence," Box LIK 36, Kahn Collection. I am grateful to Stephen G. Harrison for his research report on this project.

51. Construction began in October 1972 and was nearly completed by November 1973; agreement between

owner and builder, October 18, 1972, and site inspection reports, September 28, 1973, "Korman Residence," Box LIK 36, Kahn Collection.

52. Letter, Herbert Fineman (chairman, Architects/Engineers Committee, General State Authority) to Kahn, November 30, 1972, "Pocono Arts Center Appointment Letter," Box LIK 121, Kahn Collection. Kahn's first drawings carry the date of July 1972. I am grateful to David Roxburgh for his research report on this project.

53. Kahn, quoted in Gerard J. McCullough, "Foes in Legislature Gird to Fight Shapp's Pocono Arts Center Plan," *Sunday Bulletin*, December 16, 1973, section 5, 3.

54. This complex was fully revealed only as a result of the Second World War, when modern buildings above it were destroyed. Published sources include Frank E. Brown, *Roman Architecture* (New York: George Braziller, 1961), fig. 18.

55. Letter, Leslie M. Pockell (articles editor, *Avant Garde*) to Kahn, November 18, 1968, "Avant Garde," Box LIK 69, Kahn Collection.

56. Kahn, undated manuscript prepared in response to November 18, 1968, request, "Avant Garde," Box LIK 69, Kahn Collection.

57. Pattison, interview with David G. De Long, January 29, 1991.

58. Kahn, "1973: Brooklyn," 89.

Chapter 6
Light, the Giver of All Presences

1. Kahn, "Space and the Inspirations" (lecture, New England Conservatory of Music, Boston, November 14, 1967), *L'architecture d'aujourd'hui* 40 (February–March 1969): 16.

2. Kahn, "Architecture is the Thoughtful Making of Spaces," *Perspecta*, no. 4 (1957): 2.

3. Kahn, "The Room, the Street and Human Agreement" (AIA Gold Medal acceptance speech, Detroit, June 24, 1971), *AIA Journal* 56 (September 1971): 33.

4. Kahn, *Architecture: The John Lawrence Memorial Lectures* (New Orleans: Tulane University School of Architecture, 1972), n.p.

5. Kahn, unidentified discussion, International Design Conference, "The Invisible City," Aspen, Colorado, June 1972, in *What Will Be Has Always Been: The Words of Louis I. Kahn*, ed. Richard Saul Wurman (New York: Access Press and Rizzoli, 1986), 159.

6. Kahn, "Remarks" (lecture, Yale University, October 30, 1963), *Perspecta*, no. 9/10 (1965): 330.

7. Scully, interview with Alessandra Latour, September 15, 1982, in *Louis I. Kahn: L'uomo, il maestro*, ed. Latour (Rome: Edizioni Kappa 1986), 149.

8. Prown, interview with Alessandra Latour, June 23, 1982, in Latour, *Kahn*, 137.

9. Meyers, quoted in "Louis I. Kahn, Yale Center for British Art, Yale University, New Haven, Connecticut," in Hayden Gallery, Massachusetts Institute of Technology, *Processes in Architecture: A Documentation of Six Examples*, published as *Plan*, no. 10 (Spring 1979): 34.

10. Kahn, "Law and Rule in Architecture" (lecture,

Princeton University, November 29, 1961), typed transcript, "LIK Lectures 1969," Box LIK 53, Louis I. Kahn Collection, University of Pennsylvania and Pennsylvania Historical and Museum Commission, Philadelphia (hereafter cited as Kahn Collection).

11. Kahn, "Remarks," 304.

12. Kahn, "Space and the Inspirations," 14.

13. Kahn, ibid., 13–14.

14. Kahn, "Architecture: Silence and Light" (lecture, Solomon R. Guggenheim Museum, December 3, 1968), in Guggenheim Museum, *On the Future of Art* (New York: Viking Press, 1970), 21.

15. Kahn, "Talk at the Conclusion of the Otterlo Congress," in *New Frontiers in Architecture: C.I.A.M. '59 in Otterlo*, ed. Oscar Newman (New York: Universe Books, 1961), 210.

16. Kahn, quoted in *The Notebooks and Drawings of Louis I. Kahn*, ed. Richard S. Wurman and Eugene Feldman (Philadelphia: Falcon Press, 1962), n.p.

17. Patricia McLaughlin, "'How'm I Doing, Corbusier?' An Interview with Louis Kahn," *Pennsylvania Gazette* 71 (December 1972): 23.

18. Kahn, "I Love Beginnings" (lecture, International Design Conference, "The Invisible City," Aspen, Colorado, June 19, 1972), *Architecture + Urbanism*, special issue "Louis I. Kahn," 1975, 283–84.

19. Peter Kohane, "Louis I. Kahn and the Library: Genesis and Expression of 'Form,'" *Via* 10 (1990): 119–29.

20. Quoted in Rodney Armstrong, "New Look Library at Phillips Exeter Academy," *Library Scene* 2 (Summer 1973): 23.

21. Robert Hughes, "Building with Spent Light," *Time* 101 (January 15, 1973): 65.

22. Kahn, quoted in "The Mind of Louis Kahn," *Architectural Forum* 137 (July–August 1972): 77.

23. Kahn, "The Continual Renewal of Architecture Comes from Changing Concepts of Space," *Perspecta*, no. 4 (1957): 3.

24. Kahn, "Architecture and Human Agreement" (lecture, University of Virginia, April 18, 1972), *Modulus*, no. 11 (1975): n.p.

25. Kahn, quoted in Israel Shenker, "Kahn Defines Aim of Exeter Design," *New York Times*, October 23, 1972, L40.

26. Kahn, quoted in Ada Louise Huxtable, "New Exeter Library: Stunning Paean to Books," *New York Times*, October 23, 1972, L33.

27. Kahn, "Comments on the Library, Phillips Exeter Academy, Exeter, New Hampshire, 1972" (from unidentified source at Phillips Exeter Academy), in Wurman, *What Will Be Has Always Been*, 178.

28. Kahn, quoted in William Jordy, "The Span of Kahn: Criticism, Kimbell Art Museum, Fort Worth, Texas; Library, Philips [sic] Exeter Academy, Exeter, New Hampshire," *Architectural Review* 155 (June 1974): 334.

29. Patricia Cummings Loud, *The Art Museums of Louis I. Kahn* (Durham, N.C., and London: Duke University Press, 1989), 103.

30. Ibid., 105–6.

31. Kahn, "Talk at the Otterlo Congress," 213.

32. Kahn, unidentified discussion, International Design Conference, 159.

33. "Kahn's Museum: An Interview with Richard F. Brown," *Art in America* 60 (September–October 1972): 48.

34. Kahn, interview with Jaimini Mehta, October 22, 1973, in Wurman, *What Will Be Has Always Been*, 230.

35. Kahn, quoted in Latryl L. Ohendalski, "Kimbell Museum To Be Friendly Home, Says Kahn," *Fort Worth Press*, May 4, 1969, as quoted in Loud, *The Art Museums*, 264.

36. Kahn, unidentified discussion, International Design Conference, 159.

37. Kahn, quoted in "Mind of Kahn," 57.

38. Kahn, quoted in "Louis Kahn," *Conversations with Architects*, ed. John W. Cook and Heinrich Klotz (New York: Praeger, 1973), 212.

39. Kahn, interview with William Marlin, June 24, 1972, typed transcript, Kimbell Art Museum Files, quoted in Loud, *The Art Museums*, 156; Kahn, quoted in "Mind of Kahn," 59.

40. Kahn, "I Love Beginnings," 285.

41. Kahn, "The Room," 33. The misquotation is apparently from Wallace Stevens, "Architecture," in Stevens, *Opus Posthumous*, rev., enl., and corrected ed., ed. Milton J. Bates (New York: Alfred A. Knopf, 1989), 37–39. Alan Filreis brought this poem to my attention. Pattison, interview with David B. Brownlee and Peter S. Reed, December 20, 1990.

42. Kahn, "Space and the Inspirations," 16.

43. Kahn, quoted in Shenker, "Kahn Defines," L40.

44. Ibid.

45. Esther Kahn, remarks at a symposium sponsored by the Architectural League of New York, January 22, 1990.

46. Kahn, quoted in Heinz Ronner and Sharad Jhaveri, *Louis I. Kahn: Complete Work, 1935–1974*, 2d ed. (Basel and Boston: Birkhäuser, 1987), 322.

47. Ibid., 323.

48. Prown, interview with Latour, 141.

49. Kahn, quoted in Susan Braudy, "The Architectural Metaphysic of Louis Kahn: 'Is the Center of a Column Filled with Hope?' 'What is a Wall?' 'What Does This Space Want To Be?'" *New York Times Magazine*, November 15, 1970, 96.

50. Kahn, "Louis I. Kahn: Talks with Students" (lecture and discussion, Rice University, ca. 1969), *Architecture at Rice*, no. 26 (1969): 14.

51. Prown, interview with Latour, 137, 141.

52. Kahn, quoted in Jules David Prown, *The Architecture of the Yale Center for British Art*, 2d ed. (New Haven: Yale University, 1982), 43.

53. Scully, interview with Latour, 151.

54. Kahn, "Lecture, Drexel (University) Architectural Society, Philadelphia, PA, 5 November 1968," in Wurman, *What Will Be Has Always Been*, 27.

55. Ibid., 29.

56. Kahn, quoted in "Memorials: Lest We Forget," *Architectural Forum* 129 (December 1968): 89.

57. Kahn, "Space and the Inspirations," 15.

58. Kahn, "Monumentality," in *New Architecture and City Planning*, ed. Paul Zucker (New York: Philosophical Library, 1944), 577.

59. Research assistance for the Roosevelt Memorial, Washington, D.C., was provided by Peter S. Reed. Hélène Lipstadt, "Transforming the Tradition: American Architectural Competitions, 1960 to the Present," in *The Experimental Tradition: Essays on Competitions in Architecture*, ed. Lipstadt (New York and Princeton: Architectural League of New York and Princeton Architectural Press, 1989), 97–98, 158–59.

60. Research assistance for the Roosevelt Memorial, New York City, was provided by David Roxburgh.

61. Liebman, quoted in Paul Goldberger, "Design by Kahn Picked for Roosevelt Memorial Here," *New York Times*, April 25, 1974, L45.

62. Kahn, "1973: Brooklyn, New York" (lecture, Pratt Institute, Fall 1973), *Perspecta*, no. 19 (1982): 90.

63. Invoice, October 25, 1973, "Roosevelt Island Xerox Copies of Billing," Box LIK 121, Kahn Collection; schematic plans estimate, May 4, 1973, "Master File 1 May 1973 to 30 June 1973," Box LIK 10, Kahn Collection.

64. Laurie Johnston, "Plans for Memorial at Roosevelt Island Announced During Dedication Ceremony at Site," *New York Times*, September 25, 1973, L25.

65. Kahn, quoted in Wolf Von Eckardt, "Famed Architect Louis Kahn Dies," *Washington Post*, March 21, 1974, C13.

66. Esther Kahn, unidentified interview, in Wurman, *What Will Be Has Always Been*, 283.

67. Steven and Toby Korman, interview with David B. Brownlee, Julia Moore Converse, and David G. De Long, August 1, 1990.

68. The details of Kahn's itinerary are from a log of the events of March 18 and 19, 1974, maintained by Kathleen Condé, his secretary; Kahn Collection.

69. Tigerman, unidentified interview, in Wurman, *What Will Be Has Always Been*, 299.

70. Jim Mann, "Police Here Failed to Notify Wife of Kahn's Death," *Philadelphia Inquirer*, March 21, 1974, 1.

71. Jonas Salk, "An Homage to Louis I. Kahn," *L'architecture d'aujourd'hui* 45 (May–June 1974): vi.

72. Shepheard, eulogy quoted in Wurman, *What Will Be Has Always Been*, 304.

73. Vincent J. Scully, "Education and Inspiration," *L'architecture d'aujourd'hui* 45 (May–June 1974): vi.

Buildings and Projects, 1925–74

Sesquicentennial International Exposition. Packer Avenue, 10th Street, Pattison Avenue, 11th Street, Government Avenue, and 12th Street, Philadelphia, Pennsylvania; Chief of design for all buildings for the Exhibition Association; 1925–26; built, demolished

Model Slum Rehabilitation Project. South Philadelphia, Pennsylvania; Architectural Research Group (Kahn, organizer and designer); 1933; unbuilt

Northeast Philadelphia Housing Corporation Housing Project. Algon Avenue, Faunce Street, Elgin Avenue, Frontenac Street, and Cottman Avenue, Philadelphia, Pennsylvania; Architectural Research Group (Kahn, organizer and designer), associated with Louis Magaziner and Victor Eberhard; 1933; unbuilt

M. Buten Paint Store (alterations). 6711 Germantown Avenue, Philadelphia, Pennsylvania; Kahn and Hyman Cunin; 1934; built, demolished

St. Katherine's Village Housing Project. Between Frankford Avenue and Pennsylvania Railroad right-of-way at Liddonfield Station, Philadelphia, Pennsylvania; Magaziner and Eberhard, and Kahn; 1935; unbuilt

Ahavath Israel Synagogue (now Grace Temple). 6735 North 16th Street, Philadelphia, Pennsylvania; 1935–37; built

Jersey Homesteads (now Roosevelt Borough housing, factory, school, stores, pumping station, and sewage plant). Near Hightstown, New Jersey; Kahn, assistant principal architect and co-designer with Alfred Kastner, as employees of the Resettlement Administration; 1935–37 (Kahn's employment); houses and factory built; sewage plant and school built to Kastner's designs

Unidentified Housing Project. Magaziner and Eberhard, and Kahn; 1936; unbuilt

Unidentified House. Magaziner and Eberhard, and Kahn; ca. 1936; unbuilt

Dr. David K. Waldman Dental Office (alterations). 5203 Chester Avenue, Philadelphia, Pennsylvania; 1937; built

Prefabricated House Studies (sponsored by Samuel Fels). Magaziner, Kahn, and Henry Klumb; 1937–38; unbuilt

Horace Berk Memorial Hospital (now Philadelphia Psychiatric Hospital; alterations). 1218–48 North 54th Street, Philadelphia, Pennsylvania; 1937–38; unbuilt

Old Swedes' (or Southwark) Housing Project (housing and community building). Catherine Street, Swanson Street, Washington Avenue, 2nd Street, Christian Street, and Front Street, Philadelphia, Pennsylvania; Kahn and Kenneth Day; 1938–40; unbuilt

Pennsylvania Hospital (or Kirkbride's) Housing Project (housing and community building). Site bordered by Haverford Avenue, 42nd Street, Market Street, and 46th Street, Philadelphia, Pennsylvania; 1939–40; unbuilt

Illustrations for United States Housing Authority Booklets: Housing Subsidies: How Much and Why? Tax Exemption of Public Housing; The Housing Shortage; Public Housing and the Negro; Housing and Juvenile Delinquency; 1939; published

"Housing in the Rational City Plan" (panels for "Houses and Housing" exhibition, organized by the United States Housing Authority). Museum of Modern Art, New York; 1939; executed

Philadelphia Psychiatric Hospital. Ford Road and Monument Avenue, Philadelphia, Pennsylvania; 1939; unbuilt; commission reassigned to Thalheimer and Weitz

A. Abraham Apartment and Dental Office (alterations).

5105 Wayne Avenue, Philadelphia, Pennsylvania; 1940; built

Van Pelt Court Apartments (for E.T. Pontz; alterations). 231 South Van Pelt Street, Philadelphia, Pennsylvania; 1940; unbuilt

Battery Workers Union, Local 113 (now Commandment Keepers of the House of God; alterations). 1903 West Allegheny Avenue, Philadelphia, Pennsylvania; 1940; built

Mr. and Mrs. Jesse Oser House. 628 Stetson Road, Elkins Park, Pennsylvania; 1940–42; built

Pine Ford Acres (housing, community building, and maintenance building). Middletown, Pennsylvania; Howe and Kahn; 1941–43; built, housing demolished

Pennypack Woods (housing, community building, and stores). Philadelphia, Pennsylvania; Howe, Stonorov, and Kahn; 1941–43; built

Mr. and Mrs. Louis Broudo House. Juniper Park Development, Elkins Park, Pennsylvania; 1941–42; unbuilt

Carver Court (or Foundry Street Housing; housing and community building). Caln Township (near Coatesville), Pennsylvania; Howe, Stonorov, and Kahn; 1941–43; built

M. Shapiro and Sons Prefabricated Houses. Newport News, Virginia Stonorov and Kahn (Stonorov in charge);1941–42; unbuilt

Stanton Road Dwellings (housing and community building). Bruce Place, Stanton Road, Alabama Avenue, and 15th Street, S.E., Washington, D.C.; Howe and Kahn; 1942–47; unbuilt

Willow Run (or Bomber City), Neighborhood III (housing and school). Washtenaw County (near Ypsilanti), Michigan; Stonorov and Kahn; 1942–43; unbuilt

Lincoln Highway Defense Housing (housing and community building). Caln Road and Lincoln Highway, Caln Township (near Coatesville), Pennsylvania; Stonorov, Howe, and Kahn; 1942–44; built

House for 194X (sponsored by *Architectural Forum*). Stonorov and Kahn; 1942; not submitted, unbuilt

Lily Ponds Houses (housing and community building). Anacostia, Eastern, and Kenilworth Avenues, N.E., Washington, D.C.; Stonorov and Kahn; 1942–43; built, housing demolished

Hotel for 194X (sponsored by *Architectural Forum*). Stonorov and Kahn; 1943; published, unbuilt

International Ladies Garment Workers Union Health Care Center (now law offices; alterations). 2136 South 22nd Street, Philadelphia, Pennsylvania; Stonorov and Kahn; 1943–45; built

Model Neighborhood Rehabilitation Project for *Why City Planning is Your Responsibility.* (New York: Revere Copper and Brass, 1943) Morris, 20th, McKean, and 22nd Streets, Philadelphia, Pennsylvania; Stonorov and Kahn (Stonorov in charge); 1943; published, unbuilt

"Design for Postwar Living" House (competition sponsored by California Arts and Architecture). Stonorov and Kahn; 1943; submitted, unbuilt

Model Neighborhood Rehabilitation Project (sponsored by Architects' Workshop on City Planning, Philadelphia Housing Association, and Citizens' Council on City Planning). Moore Street, Howard Street, Water Street, Snyder Avenue, and Moyamensing Avenue, Philadelphia, Pennsylvania; Stonorov and Kahn; 1943; model built and published in *You and Your Neighborhood: A Primer for Neighborhood Planning* (New York: Revere Copper and Brass, 1944).

Industrial Union of Marine and Shipbuilding Workers of America, Local 1 (alterations). 2332–34 Broadway, Camden, New Jersey; Stonorov and Kahn (Stonorov in charge); 1943–45; built

Phoenix Corporation Houses. Bridge Street, Phoenixville, Pennsylvania; Stonorov and Kahn (Stonorov in charge); 1943–44; unbuilt

Philadelphia Moving Picture Operators' Union. Vine and 13th Streets, Philadelphia, Pennsylvania; Stonorov and Kahn; 1944; unbuilt

Parasol Houses (for Knoll Associates Planning Unit). Stonorov and Kahn; 1944; unbuilt

Model Men's Shoe Store and Furniture Store (for Pittsburgh Plate Glass). Stonorov and Kahn; 1944; published, unbuilt

Dimitri Petrov House (alterations and addition). 713 North 25th Street, Philadelphia, Pennsylvania; Stonorov and Kahn; 1944–48; unbuilt

National Jewish Welfare Board. (clubhouse furnishings). Washington, D.C.; Stonorov and Kahn (Stonorov in charge); 1944; built

Paul W. Darrow House (adaptation of old power plant). Vare Estate, Fort Washington, Pennsylvania; Stonorov and Kahn; 1944–46; unbuilt

Philadelphia Psychiatric Hospital (new wing). Philadelphia, Pennsylvania; Stonorov and Kahn; Isadore Rosenfield, hospital consultant; 1944–46; unbuilt

Borough Hall (alterations). Phoenixville, Pennsylvania; Stonorov and Kahn (Stonorov in charge); 1944; unbuilt

Dr. and Mrs. Alexander Moskalik House (alterations). 2018 Spruce Street, Philadelphia, Pennsylvania; Stonorov and Kahn; 1944–45; built

Radbill Oil Company (renovation of offices). 1722–24 Chestnut Street (second floor), Philadelphia, Pennsylvania; Stonorov and Kahn; 1944–47; built

Westminster Play Lot. Markoe Street, Westminster Avenue, and June Street, Philadelphia, Pennsylvania; Stonorov and Kahn; ca. 1945; unbuilt

Unidentified House. Stonorov and Kahn; ca. 1945; unbuilt

Mr. and Mrs. Edward Gallob House (alterations). 2035 Rittenhouse Square Street, Philadelphia, Pennsylvania; 1945–47; unbuilt

Gimbels Department Store (interior alterations). 8th and Market Streets, Philadelphia, Pennsylvania; Stonorov and Kahn (Stonorov in charge); 1945–46; built, demolished

"House for Cheerful Living" (composition sponsored by Pittsburgh Plate Glass and Pencil Points). Stonorov and Kahn; 1945; submitted, unbuilt

Business Neighborhood in 194X (advertisement for Barrett Division, Allied Chemical and Dye Corporation). Stonorov and Kahn; 1945; published, unbuilt

B. A. Bernard House (addition). 195 Hare's Hill Road at Camp Council Road, Kimberton, Pennsylvania; Stonorov and Kahn; 1945; built

Department of Neurology, Jefferson Medical College (alterations). 1025 Walnut Street, Philadelphia, Pennsylvania; Stonorov and Kahn; 1945–46; built

Mr. and Mrs. Samuel Radbill Residence (alterations). 224 Bowman Avenue, Merion, Pennsylvania; Stonorov and Kahn; 1945–46; partially built

William H. Harman Corporation Prefabricated Houses. 420 Pickering Road, Charlestown, Chester

County, Pennsylvania; Rosedale Avenue and New Street, West Chester, Pennsylvania; Stonorov and Kahn (Stonorov in charge); 1945–47; built, some demolition

Drs. Lea and Arthur Finkelstein House (addition); 645 Overhill Road, Ardmore, Pennsylvania; Stonorov and Kahn; 1945–48; unbuilt

Pennsylvania Solar House. (for Libbey-Owens–Ford Glass Company); Stonorov and Kahn; 1945–47; published, unbuilt

"Action for Cities" (panel for "American Housing" exhibition). France; 1945–46; executed

Thom McAn Shoe Store (alterations). 72 South 69th Street, Upper Darby, Pennsylvania; Stonorov and Kahn; 1945–46; unbuilt

Two Dormitories, Camp Hofnung. Pipersville, Bucks County, Pennsylvania; Stonorov and Kahn; 1945–47; built

Philadelphia Building, International Ladies Garment Workers Union. Unity House, Forest Park, Pike County, Pennsylvania; Stonorov and Kahn; 1945–47; built

Mr. and Mrs. Arthur V. Hooper House (addition). 5820 Pimlico Road, Baltimore, Maryland; Stonorov and Kahn; 1946; unbuilt

Container Corporation of America (cafeteria, offices, and depot). Nixon and Fountain Streets, Manayunk, Philadelphia, Pennsylvania; Stonorov and Kahn; 1946; unbuilt

Memorial Playground, Western Home for Children. 715 Christian Street, Philadelphia, Pennsylvania; Stonorov and Kahn; 1946–47; built, demolished

Triangle Redevelopment Project. Benjamin Franklin Parkway, Market Street, and Shuylkill River, Philadelphia, Pennsylvania; Associated City Planners (Kahn, Oscar Stonorov, Robert Wheelwright, Markley Stevenson, and C. Harry Johnson); 1946–48; unbuilt

Tana Hoban Studio (alterations). 2018 Rittenhouse Square Street, Philadelphia, Pennsylvania; Stonorov and Kahn; 1947; unbuilt

Coward Shoe Store (now Lerner Woman). 1118 Chestnut Street, Philadelphia, Pennsylvania; Stonorov and Kahn (Stonorov in charge); 1947–49; built, altered

Dr. and Mrs. Philip Q. Roche House. 2101 Harts Lane, Conshohocken, Pennsylvania; Stonorov and Kahn; 1947–49; built

X-ray Department, Graduate Hospital, University of Pennsylvania (alteration). Lombard and 19th Streets, Philadelphia, Pennsylvania; 1947–48; built

Mr. and Mrs. Harry A. Ehle House Mulberry Lane, Haverford, Pennsylvania; Kahn and Abel Sorensen; 1947–48; unbuilt

Jefferson National Expansion Memorial (competition, first stage). St. Louis, Missouri; 1947; submitted, unbuilt

Mr. and Mrs. Morton Weiss House. 2935 Whitehall Road, East Norriton Township, Pennsylvania; 1947–50; built

Dr. and Mrs. Winslow T. Tompkins House. Lot 18, Apologen Road, Philadelphia, Pennsylvania; 1947–49; unbuilt

M. Buten Paint Store (alterations). Kaighns and Haddon Avenues, Camden, New Jersey; Kahn and George Von Uffel, Jr.; 1947–48; built, demolished

Mr. and Mrs. Harry Kitnick House. 2935 Whitehall Road, East Norriton Township, Pennsylvania; 1948–49; unbuilt

Mr. and Mrs. Joseph Rossman House (alteration). 1714 Rittenhouse Square Street, Philadelphia, Pennsylvania; 1948–49; unbuilt

Jewish Community Center. 1186 Chapel Street, New Haven, Connecticut; Kahn, consultant architect; associated with Jacob Weinstein and Charles Abramowitz, Architects; 1948–54; built, altered

Bernard S. Pincus Building and Samuel Radbill Building, Philadelphia Psychiatric Hospital. Kahn; Isadore Rosenfield, hospital consultant; 1948–54; built, altered

Mr. and Mrs. Samuel Genel House. 201 Indian Creek Road, Wynnewood, Pennsylvania; 1948–51; built

Jewish Agency for Palestine Emergency Housing. Israel; 1949; unbuilt

Dr. and Mrs. Jacob Sherman House (alterations). 414 Sycamore Avenue, Merion, Pennsylvania; 1949–51; unbuilt

Mr. and Mrs. Nelson J. Leidner House (addition to former Oser House). 626 Stetson Road, Elkins Park, Pennsylvania; 1950–51; built, addition demolished

Ashton Best Corporation Garden Apartments. 200 Montgomery Avenue, Ardmore, Pennsylvania; 1950; unbuilt

American Federation of Labor Health Center, St. Luke's Hospital (now Girard Medical Center; alterations). Franklin and Thompson Streets, Philadelphia, Pennsylvania; 1950–51; built, demolished

Southwest Temple Public Housing. Philadelphia, Pennsylvania; Kahn, consultant architect; Architects Associated (1951–52): Kenneth Day, Louis E. McAllister, Sr., George Braik, Anne Tyng; 1950–52; unbuilt

East Poplar Public Housing. Philadelphia, Pennsylvania; Architects Associated: Kahn, Day, McAllister, Braik; 1950–52; unbuilt

University of Pennsylvania Study (for Philadelphia City Planning Commission). Philadelphia, Pennsylvania; Architects Associated: Kahn, Day, McAllister, Braik, Tyng; 1951; unbuilt

Row Houses Studies (for Philadelphia City Planning Commission). Philadelphia, Pennsylvania; Architects Associated: Kahn, Day, McAllister, Braik, Tyng); 1951–53; unbuilt

Traffic Studies. Philadelphia, Pennsylvania; 1951–53; unbuilt Yale University Art Gallery; 1111 Chapel Street, New Haven, Connecticut; Kahn and Douglas Orr, associated architects; 1951–53; built

Mr. and Mrs. H. Leonard Fruchter House. 51st Street and City Line Avenue, Philadelphia, Pennsylvania; 1951–54; unbuilt

Penn Center Studies. Philadelphia, Pennsylvania; 1951–58; unbuilt

Mill Creek Project (first-phase housing). 46th and Aspen Streets, Philadelphia, Pennsylvania; Kahn, Day, Braik, McAllister; 1951–56; built

Cinberg House (alterations). 5112 North Broad Street, Philadelphia, Pennsylvania; 1952; unbuilt

Zoob and Matz Offices (alterations). 1600 Western Saving Fund Building, Philadelphia, Pennsylvania; 1952; built

Apartment Redevelopment Project. New Haven, Connecticut; Published in *Perspecta*, 1953

Riverview Competition. State Road at Rhawn Street, Philadelphia, Pennsylvania; Kahn and Tyng, associated architects; 1953; unbuilt

City Tower Project. Philadelphia, Pennsylvania; Kahn and Tyng, associated architects; 1952–57; unbuilt

Ralph Roberts House. Schoolhouse Lane, Germantown,

Philadelphia, Pennsylvania; 1953; unbuilt

Adath Jeshurun Synagogue and School Building. 6730 Old York Road, Philadelphia, Pennsylvania; 1954–55; unbuilt

Dr. and Mrs. Francis H. Adler House. Davidson Road, Philadelphia, Pennsylvania; 1954–55; unbuilt

Mr. and Mrs. Weber DeVore House. Montgomery Avenue, Springfield Township, Pennsylvania; 1954–ca. 1955; unbuilt

American Federation of Labor Medical Services Building. 1326–34 Vine Street, Philadelphia, Pennsylvania; 1954–57; built, demolished

Jewish Community Center (bathhouse, day camp, and community building). 999 Lower Ferry Road, Ewing Township (near Trenton), New Jersey; Kahn, architect; John M. Hirsh and Stanley R. Dube, supervising architects; Louis Kaplan, associated architect; 1954–59; bathhouse and day camp built

Dr. and Mrs. Francis H. Adler House (kitchen remodeling). 7630 Huron Avenue, Philadelphia, Pennsylvania; 1955; built

Wharton Esherick Workshop (addition). Horseshoe Trail, Paoli, Pennsylvania; 1955–56; built

Mr. and Mrs. Lawrence Morris House. Mt. Kisco, New York; 1955–58; unbuilt

Washington University Library Competition. St. Louis, Missouri; 1956; submitted, unbuilt

Enrico Fermi Memorial. Fort Dearborn, Chicago, Illinois; 1956–57; unbuilt

Civic Center Studies. Philadelphia, Pennsylvania; 1956–57; unbuilt

Research Institute for Advanced Science. Near Baltimore, Maryland; 1956–58; unbuilt

Mill Creek Project (second-phase housing and community center). 46th Street and Fairmount Avenue, Philadelphia, Pennsylvania; 1956–63; built

Mr. and Mrs. Irving L. Shaw House (additions and alterations). 2129 Cypress Street, Philadelphia, Pennsylvania; 1956–59; built

Dr. and Mrs. Bernard Shapiro House. 417 Hidden River Road, Narbeth, Pennsylvania; 1956–62; built (addition by Kahn and Tyng, associated architects; completed by Tyng, 1975)

Mr. and Mrs. Eugene Lewis House. 2018 Rittenhouse Square Street, Philadelphia, Pennsylvania; 1957; unbuilt

American Federation of Labor Medical Center (Red Cross Building; remodeling of hospital and office building). 253 North Broad Street, Philadelphia, Pennsylvania; 1957–59; unbuilt

Fred E. and Elaine Cox Clever House. 417 Sherry Way, Cherry Hill, New Jersey; 1957–62; built

Alfred Newton Richards Medical Research Building and Biology Building (now David Goddard Laboratories), University of Pennsylvania. 3700 Hamilton Walk, Philadelphia, Pennsylvania; 1957–65; built

Mount St. Joseph Academy and Chestnut Hill College. Chestnut Hill, Philadelphia, Pennsylvania; 1958; unbuilt

Zoob and Matz Offices (alterations). Western Saving Fund Building (14th floor), Philadelphia, Pennsylvania; 1958; built

Tribune Review Publishing Company Building. Cabin Hill Drive, Greensburg, Pennsylvania; 1958–62; built

Mr. and Mrs. M. Morton Goldenberg House. Frazier Road, Rydal, Pennsylvania; 1959; unbuilt

Robert H. Fleisher House. 8363 Fisher Road, Elkins Park, Pennsylvania; 1959; unbuilt

Space Environment Studies (for General Electric Co., Missile and Space Vehicle Department). Philadelphia, Pennsylvania; Kahn, consultant architect; 1959; unexecuted

Awbury Arboretum Housing Development (for International Ladies Garment Workers Union). Walnut Lane, Ardleigh Street, and Tulpehocken Street, Philadelphia, Pennsylvania; 1959–60; unbuilt

Margaret Esherick House. 204 Sunrise Lane, Chestnut Hill, Philadelphia, Pennsylvania; 1959–61; built

U.S. Consulate and Residence. Luanda, Angola; 1959–62; unbuilt

Salk Institute for Biological Studies (laboratory, meeting house, and housing). 10010 North Torrey Pines Road, La Jolla, California; 1959–65; laboratory built

First Unitarian Church and School. 220 South Winton Road, Rochester, New York; 1959–69; built

Fine Arts Center, School, and Performing Arts Theater (now Performing Arts Center). 303 East Main Street, Fort Wayne, Indiana; Kahn, architect; T. Richard Shoaff, supervising architect; 1959–73; theater and offices built

Bristol Township Municipal Building. 2501 Oxford Valley Road, Levittown, Pennsylvania; 1960–61; unbuilt

General Motors Exhibit, 1964 World's Fair. Grand Central Parkway and Long Island Expressway, New York, New York; 1960–61; unbuilt

Barge for the American Wind Symphony Orchestra. River Thames, England; 1960–61; built

Market Street East Studies. Philadelphia, Pennsylvania; 1960–63; unbuilt

University of Virginia Chemistry Building. Charlottesville, Virginia; Kahn, architect for design; Stainback and Scribner, architects; 1960–63; unbuilt

Eleanor Donnelly Erdman Hall, Bryn Mawr College. Morris and Gulph Roads, Bryn Mawr, Pennsylvania; 1960–65; built

Philadelphia College of Art (now University of the Arts). Broad and Pine Streets, Philadelphia, Pennsylvania; 1960–66; unbuilt

Franklin Delano Roosevelt Memorial Competition. West Potomac Park, Washington, D.C.; 1960; unbuilt

Dr. and Mrs. Norman Fisher House. 197 East Miller Road, Hatboro, Pennsylvania; 1960–67; built

Carborundum Company Warehouses and Offices. Chicago, Illinois; Mountain View, California; and Niagara Falls, New York; 1961; built

Plymouth Swim Club. Gallagher Road, Montgomery County, Pennsylvania; 1961; unbuilt

Shapero Hall of Pharmacy, Wayne State University. Detroit, Michigan; 1961–62; unbuilt

Carborundum Company Warehouses and Offices. Atlanta, Georgia; 1961–62; unbuilt

Gandhinagar, Capital of Gujarat State, India. 1961–66; unbuilt

Levy Memorial Playground. Between 102nd and 105th Streets in Riverside Park, New York, New York; Isamu Noguchi, sculptor; Louis I. Kahn, architect; 1961–66; unbuilt

Mikveh Israel Synagogue. Commerce Street between 4th and 5th Streets, Philadelphia, Pennsylvania; 1961–72; unbuilt

Lawrence Memorial Hall of Science, University of California Competition. Berkeley, California; 1962; unbuilt

Mrs. C. Parker House (addition to former Esherick House). 204 Sunrise Lane, Chestnut Hill, Philadelphia, Pennsylvania; 1962–64; unbuilt

Delaware Valley Mental Health Foundation, Family and Patient Dwelling. 833 Butler Avenue, Doylestown, Pennsylvania; 1962–71; unbuilt

Indian Institute of Management. Vikram Sarabhai Road, Ahmedabad, India; 1962–74; built

Sher-e-Bangla Nagar, Capital of Bangladesh. Dhaka, Bangladesh; 1962–83; built (design and construction completed after Kahn's death by David Wisdom and Associates)

Peabody Museum, Hall of Ocean Life, Yale University. New Haven, Connecticut; 1963–65; unbuilt

President's Estate, First Capital of Pakistan. Islamabad, Pakistan; 1963–66; unbuilt

Barge for the American Wind Symphony Orchestra. Pittsburgh, Pennsylvania; 1964–67; built

Interama Community B. Miami, Florida; Kahn, architect; Watson, Deutschman & Kruse, associate architects; 1963–69; unbuilt

St. Andrew's Priory. Hidden Valley Road, Valyermo, California; 1961–67; unbuilt

Maryland Institute College of Art. Site bordered by Park Avenue, Howard Street, and Dolphin Street, Baltimore, Maryland; 1965–69; unbuilt

The Dominican Motherhouse of St. Catherine de Ricci. Providence Road, Media, Pennsylvania; 1965–69; unbuilt

Library and Dining Hall, Phillips Exeter Academy. Exeter, New Hampshire; 1965–72; built

Broadway United Church of Christ and Office Building. Broadway and Seventh Avenue between 56th and 57th Streets, New York; 1966–68; unbuilt

Mr. and Mrs. Max L. Raab House. Waverly, Addison, and 21st Streets, Philadelphia, Pennsylvania; 1966–68; unbuilt

Olivetti-Underwood Factory. Valley View Road and Township Line, Harrisburg, Pennsylvania; 1966–70; built

Mr. and Mrs. Philip M. Stern House. 2710 Chain Bridge Road, Washington, D.C.; 1966–70; unbuilt

Kimbell Art Museum. 3333 Camp Bowie Boulevard, Fort Worth, Texas; Kahn, architect; Preston Geren, associate architect; 1966–72; built

Memorial to the Six Million Jewish Martyrs. Battery Park, New York, New York; 1966–72; unbuilt

Temple Beth-El Synagogue. 220 South Bedford Road, Chappaqua, New York; 1966–72; built

Kansas City Office Building. Walnut, 11th, and Grand Streets (site 1); Main, Baltimore, 11th, and 12th Streets (site 2); Kansas City, Missouri; 1966–73; unbuilt

Rittenhouse Square Housing. Philadelphia, Pennsylvania; 1967; unbuilt

Hurva Synagogue. Jerusalem, Israel; 1967–74; unbuilt

Hill Renewal and Redevelopment Project (housing and school). New Haven, Connecticut; 1967–74; unbuilt

Albie Booth Boys Club. 1968; unbuilt

Palazzo dei Congressi. Giardini Pubblici (site 1); Arsenale (site 2) Venice, Italy; 1968–74; unbuilt

Wolfson Center for Mechanical and Transportation Engineering (mechanical and electrical buildings). Tel Aviv, Israel; Kahn, architect; J. Mochly-I. Eldar, Ltd., resident architect; 1968–74; mechanical building built, 1976–77, after Kahn's design, by J. Mochly-I. Eldar, Ltd.

Raab Dual Movie Theater. 2021–23 Sansom Street, Philadelphia, Pennsylvania; 1969–70; unbuilt

Rice University Art Center. Houston, Texas; 1969–70; unbuilt

Inner Harbor; Pratt and Light Streets, Baltimore, Maryland. Kahn, architect; Ballinger Company, associate architects; 1969–73; unbuilt

Yale Center for British Art. 1080 Chapel Street, New Haven, Connecticut; 1969–74; built (design and construction completed after Kahn's death by Pellecchia and Myers, Architects)

John F. Kennedy Hospital (addition). Philadelphia, Pennsylvania; 1970–71; unbuilt

President's House, University of Pennsylvania (alterations and additions). 2216 Spruce Street, Philadelphia, Pennsylvania; 1970–71; built

Family Planning Center and Maternal Health Center. Ram Sam Path, Kathmandu, Nepal; 1970–75; partially built

Treehouse, Eagleville Hospital and Rehabilitation Center. Eagleville, Pennsylvania; 1971; unbuilt

Washington Square East Unit 2 Redevelopment. Philadelphia, Pennsylvania; ca. 1971; unbuilt

Bicentennial Exposition. Eastwick, Southwest Philadelphia, Pennsylvania; Kahn with a team of architects; 1971–73; unbuilt

Mr. and Mrs. Steven Korman House. 6019 Sheaf Lane, Fort Washington, Pennsylvania; 1971–73; built

Mr. and Mrs. Harold A. Honickman House. Sheaf Lane, Fort Washington, Pennsylvania; 1971–74; unbuilt

Government House Hill Development. Jerusalem, Israel; 1971–73; unbuilt

Graduate Theological Union Library. Ridge Road and Scenic Avenue, Berkeley, California; Schematic design by Kahn; 1971–74; designed and built after Kahn's death by Esherick Homsey Dodge and Davis, and Peters Clayberg & Caulfield

De Menil Foundation (now Menil Collection). Yupon, Sul Ross, Mulberry, and Branard Streets, Houston, Texas; 1972–74; unbuilt

Independence Mall Area Redevelopment (in conjunction with Bicentennial). Philadelphia, Pennsylvania; 1972–74; unbuilt

Pocono Arts Center. Luzerne County, Pennsylvania; 1972–74; unbuilt

Rabat Project (cultural and commercial complex). Bou-Regreg zone on the River Oued, Rabat, Morocco; 1973–74; unbuilt

Franklin Delano Roosevelt Memorial. Roosevelt Island, New York; 1973–74; unbuilt

Abbasabad Development (financial, commercial, and residential areas). Tehran, Iran; Kahn and Kenzo Tange; 1973–74; unbuilt

Bishop Field Estate. Lenox, Massachusetts; 1973–74; designed and built after Kahn's death based on Kahn's site plan

Index

Numbers in *italic*
indicate pages bearing
illustrations. The letter
"n" indicates the num-
bered reference note